Off to a Good Start

A Baby Boomer's Memoir

Thomas Rundall

Off To A Good Start: A Baby Boomer's Memoir

Copyright © 2020 Thomas Rundall

ISBN: 978-1-61170-296-5

All rights reserved. No part of this publication may be reproduced, stored in a retrieval system or transmitted in any form or by any means, electronic, mechanical, photocopies, recording or otherwise, without the prior written consent of the publisher, except in the case of brief quotations embodied in critical reviews.

The photo of Malott Hall on page 139 is reproduced with the permission of Edward Tremel.

All other photos come from Thomas Rundall's personal collection.

Published by:

Robertson Publishing™
www.RobertsonPublishing.com

Printed in the USA and UK on acid-free paper.

Dedication

I dedicate this book to Jane, Owen, Mananya, and Genevieve, four of the biggest reasons I am off to a good start.

Contents

Preface i

1. My Ancestors, Difficult Lives for Both Families in the 1940s, Moving to a Warm, Dry Place 1

2. A Decade in Yuma 19

3. Life in the 1960s 37

4. Stanford, the Vietnam War, and Becoming a Conscientious Objector 55

5. Two Years as a VISTA Volunteer 73

6. Returning to Stanford 97

7. Meeting and Marrying Jane Tiemann 109

8. My First Academic Job: Cornell University 1976-1980 123

9. A U.C. Berkeley Professor's Life: Three Decades of Family, Work, Friends, and Community 145

10. Owen, Mananya, and Genevieve 193

11. It's Not Retirement, It's My Next Phase 213

Appendix 1. Genealogy of the Rundall and Serbousek Families in America 237

Appendix 2. My Curriculum Vitae 249

Preface

In the 71 years that have passed since my birth I have experienced what I call getting off to a good start on life, one in which I "leaned in" to many challenges and opportunities, and achieved success in my professional life and happiness in my personal life beyond what any reasonable person has a right to expect. I wrote this memoir to capture my memories of the people, places, and experiences that have made my journey memorable and fulfilling, and created opportunities for me to pursue in my "next phase" of life.

I was born in 1948, during the early part of the Baby Boom generation, the demographic cohort born between 1946 and 1964. It was called a "boom" because of the marked rise in the population's birth rate during those years. In part, this was due to millions of men and women in the armed services returning home from World War II and starting families. Baby Boomers have more in common than the calendar period of their births. We share memories of growing up in post-World War II America. Our collective identity is complex, shaped by the greatest social changes in history during the 1960s and 1970s. But there are several patterns in the behaviors of Baby Boomers that form our generational identity. For example, compared to previous generations, more Boomers pursued higher education or relocated away from family for careers or educational opportunities. My memoir is filled with stories of how these and other Baby Boomer traits shaped my life.

To set the stage for this memoir, Chapter 1 includes a brief genealogy of the branches of my dad's Rundall and my mom's Serbousek families, beginning with the arrival in America of the Puritan William Rundle, Sr., from England in about 1665, and Ignac and Jozefa Serbousek from Bohemia in the Czech Republic in about 1848.

Much more information is available about the genealogy of the Rundall family. This is due to a lifetime of research on the Rundall genealogy by my first cousin once removed, George Ardel (Bud) Rundall. He and several other relatives who helped with the research published a book summarizing what they learned. Acknowledging the many different spellings of our last name used by our ancestors, the book is entitled, *The Rundle, Rundel, Randle, Randol, Randall, Rundall, Rundell, Runnell Ancestry of Long Island and Greenwich, 1667-1992*. In Appendix 1, I present a more detailed, annotated genealogy of my branch of the Rundall family in America, building on Bud's excellent work. I also present an annotated genealogy of the Serbousek family, based on family records and my own research.

I want those interested in the history of the Rundalls and Serbouseks to understand the challenges my ancestors overcame and the sacrifices they made to make my life, and those of my son, granddaughter, and other family members possible. Chapter 1 (with additional detail provided in Appendix 1) tells the stories of the arrivals of the first generation of Rundalls and Serbouseks in America, and provides a brief history of these families in South Dakota and Iowa beginning in the 20th century.

In many ways, the stories of the lives of the Rundall and Serbousek immigrants and their descendants are interwoven with important stories of America's birth and growth: the early settlement of the new land by Puritans seeking religious freedom; the Revolutionary War; the founding of the United States of America; the westward expansion; large scale emigration of people from Europe to the United States; the practice of homesteading to acquire free land; creation of farms and ranches to provide food to a growing country; the struggle to survive during the Great Depression and two World Wars; and the political, social, and economic changes that emerged in the United States after World War II. Rundalls and Serbouseks were very much a part of that history, and their lives captured much of what is sometimes called the American experience over the past 350 years.

In addition to being a genealogy and history of two families, this book is, of course, also my memoir. In eleven chapters, I have described what I think are noteworthy stories of my life from my birth in Cedar Rapids, Iowa, in 1948 through my first ten years as an emeritus professor at the University of California, Berkeley, concluding in 2020. Appendix 2 is my curriculum vitae, which presents the details of my professional life as a university professor. The book chapters tell the story of why and how I became a university professor and place my academic life in the context of my family life, friendships, and community activities. I describe many positive and exciting events and tell stories of my successes and the joyful changes in my life. Along the way I describe my connections to some famous athletes, an Emmy awardee, a Hawaiian Queen, the luckiest man on earth, an excommunicated priest, two Nobel Prize winners, a United States Senator, students who make me proud of the next generation, and a group of amazing VISTA volunteers who set out to make the world a better place, and did. I also explain why I became a conscientious objector to the Vietnam War, and share the story of how I surprisingly became a Talking Chief for a Samoan clan. An honest memoir must also recount the difficult times in one's life and the emotional toll they took. I have shared the pain of many of those moments as well. The hardest part of writing this memoir was telling the sad stories of the deaths of family members and friends, many of whom died much too soon.

My life has been a remarkable journey, one that has enabled me to surpass the ambitious goals I set for myself when I was a teenager. Aristotle once said, "The unexamined life is not worth living." I certainly agree with the sentiment implied by that strong statement. I have tried to be conscious of what I was learning from the experiences I was going through, especially my efforts to seize opportunities to grow professionally and personally, establish strong ties with family and friends, and provide leadership in organizations to which I was connected. In the last few pages of this memoir, I share some of the most important things I've learned so far. I look forward to seeing what the future brings.

Thomas Rundall
Orinda, California
2020

1

My Ancestors, Difficult Lives for Both Families in the 1940s, Moving to a Warm, Dry Place

I am a baby boomer, one of those 76 million Americans born between 1946 and 1964. Like many people in my generation, I have a strong work ethic, a good deal of self-confidence, a drive to try and make the world a better place, and I am generally optimistic about the future. I was imbued with these traits by the complex experiences of family and social life while growing up in the United States. Some of the experiences that influenced me occurred when I was so young I now have only faint memories of them. Other experiences later in life I remember more vividly. With some effort I believe I have been able to recall the important events and activities over the past 71 years that caused the path I was taking to bend one way or another and to present unexpected opportunities and challenges. Here is my story, beginning with a little family genealogy and history, and the Rundall family's move out of Iowa.

I was born on September 13, 1948 at 6:15 am in Mercy Hospital in Cedar Rapids, Iowa. I weighed six pounds and three and a quarter ounces and was nineteen inches in length: a little on the small side, but eager. My mother, Georgiena Alice Serbousek (born February 17, 1922; died March 28, 2006), and father, Richard Earl Rundall (born, June 21, 1918; died December 22, 1986), grew up in Cedar Rapids with their parents and near many relatives.

My Serbousek Ancestors

Cedar Rapids had a large Czech community, most of whom were farmers or small shopkeepers. The Serbousek family was one of them: many still speaking the Czech language; practicing their Catholic faith; and maintaining Czech customs, food, and family ties.

Off To A Good Start

My maternal great great grandparents, Ignac Enos Serbousek (born in 1816 in Bohemia) and his wife, Jozefa (Josephine) Kopetska Serbousek (born in 1819 in Bohemia), were my first Serbousek relatives to immigrate to America. They came from Javornice, a village in Bohemia (now the Czech Republic), which is about 100 miles south of Prague. Javornice was, and still is, a small village. In 2011, there were only 933 people living there. Based on their birth years and the birth year of one of their seven children, my great grandfather William Michael Serbousek (born 1860, died 1939) who was born in Johnson County, Iowa, it is likely that Ignac and Jozefa immigrated to the United States between 1835 and 1858. The free uncultivated land in America attracted immigrants throughout the nineteenth century, and many immigrants were farmers and settled in midwestern states. The primary emigration of Czechs out of Bohemia came in 1848 when the Czech "Forty Eighters" fled to the United States to escape political persecution by the Austrian Habsburgs. Many Czechs settled in and around Cedar Rapids. There is a festival celebrating Czech culture and cuisine held each June at St. Ludmila Catholic Church in Cedar Rapids.

My maternal great grandparents were Jozefa and Ignac's son, William Michael Serbousek (1860-1939), and Anna Skala Serbousek (1868-1941), who had nine children, including my grandfather Josef Serbousek. Josef was born May 27, 1891 and died at age 51 on May 15, 1943. Josef married my grandmother, Alice Blanche Housar, born November 16, 1895 and died at age 47 on July 14, 1943.

The Housar and Serbousek families were friendly with one another. I have two very large panoramic photographs taken at the 50th (1923) and 60th (1933) wedding anniversaries of Alice's parents, my Housar great-grandparents Josef Housar and Magdaline Jindrich Housar. The people in these photos are members of the Housar (some spelled their name Houser) and Serbousek families and close friends of the Housars, all dressed in their Sunday best clothes and presenting the serious, semi-sad expressions common in photos of people in that era. There are many children. Large families with four or five children or more were common back then. In the 1923 photo, the names of all the people are listed on the back of the photo. In the second row from the top, Grandmother Alice is holding my one-year old mother who alone among all these people is laughing and excited. This is the Czech family and social world into which I was born.

My Rundall Ancestors

William Rundle, Sr. was a Puritan who emigrated from England to America around 1665-1667. He settled in an area near Greenwich, Connecticut. My granddaughter, Genevieve Araya Rundall, is the 11th generation of the Rundall family in America. Previous generations include Reuben Rundle, who fought in the Revolutionary War; John Rundall, Sr., who was the first in our family to spell his last name Rundall; and George Washington Rundall, who married Catherine (Kate) Sherwood in 1874. Wash and Kate are my great grandparents. They had three sons, including my grandfather, Earl Sherwood (born January 18, 1886; died January 21, 1971). The family worked their farm in Linn County, Iowa. Kate died in 1897.

In 1909, Earl joined his father and two brothers in selling their farm and moving to land near Philip, South Dakota. They were homesteaders. Earl met Edna Minnie Hoag (born April 17, 1890; died November 10, 1958) in South Dakota, and they married in 1912. Earl and Edna had three children: Wilma (born February 28, 1915; died August 30, 1976), my father Richard (born, June 21, 1918; died December 22, 1986), and Wayne (born June 15, 1920; died November 13, 1942). Their property was near the Rosebud Indian Reservation, and the first playmates of the Rundall children were children from the Sioux Tribe. Wash died in 1915. In 1928, Earl and Edna sold their land in South Dakota and moved to Cedar Rapids. The Rundall house in Cedar Rapids was located at 1626 N Street, S.W., and is still standing today.

Mom and Dad's Wedding

Mom and Dad met in Cedar Rapids, but I am not sure how they met. Mom's father, Josef Serbousek, worked at a company called Penick and Ford, a plant that made molasses and other food products. After graduating from high school Dad also worked at that plant. Dad may have met Mom through Josef. They may also have met at Wilson High School before Mom dropped out of school to care for her sick mother. However they met, they started a relationship

Off To A Good Start

that would last nearly fifty years. They were married on Saturday, January 18, 1941 at 8:30 am in St. Ludmilla Church. The Reverend Francis Hruby performed the ceremony. Dad's sister, Wilma Rundall, and my mom's cousin, Stanley Holub, "stood up" for Dad and Mom at the wedding. Mom wore a satin gown and a fingertip length veil. She carried a white prayer book, a gift from my dad. Dad was 22, and Mom was only 18 years old! Mom and Dad moved into a cottage located at the back of Earl and Edna's property.

Difficult Lives for Both Families in the 1940s

The Serbouseks

My maternal grandparents, Alice and Joe Serbousek, had a difficult life. Sometime during the 1920s they moved from their farm to Cedar Rapids. Their first house was 1221 K St., S.W. Joe and Alice had four daughters: Agnes, Rose Mary, Georgiena, and LaVerne. Alice made sure all of them were raised in the faith of the Catholic Church. The four sisters remained devout Catholics all their lives. The Serbousek family endured very difficult circumstances during the Great Depression. In the 1930s, Joe worked at Penick and Ford. My dad and granddad Earl also worked at the plant, and I believe they knew Joe. But, as the depression worsened Joe lost that job and could not find steady work. His family lived in near poverty. To help support the family, Mom had to leave high school and work. Although at fifteen years of age Mom's picture should appear in Dad's 1937 yearbook from Wilson High School, it is not there. Several times, when their rent was raised, the family had to move to a different house. The last house in which they all lived together was 1406 M St., S.W. In 1939 Alice was diagnosed with colon cancer. She had surgery performed by a recent medical graduate, the son of her long-time doctor, who apparently did a remarkably good job. Alice lived four years longer than anyone expected. The four sisters cared for their mother at home. My mom worked at odd jobs to earn money for the family. Life was very hard for all of them.

On May 15, 1943, suffering from stress and depression brought on by their financial struggles and Alice's illness, Joe committed suicide by hanging himself from a rafter in his bedroom. His daughters had to cut him down. Alice died only two months later on July 14,

1943. Joe and Alice are buried at the Czech National Cemetery in Cedar Rapids. Looking back, I think these difficult years, and the deaths of both her parents over a short period of time, left deep scars on my mom. She rarely talked about her childhood. I learned the circumstances of her parents' deaths only by asking direct questions when I started to wonder about them. I have a picture of Joe and Alice in middle age, standing outdoors on a pleasant day, not imagining what awful times were yet to come. It is very special.

The Rundalls

Pearl Harbor was attacked on December 7, 1941. Uncle Wayne joined the Navy less than a month later. In November of 1942, my Dad got drafted and decided to join the Navy as well. Dad left Cedar Rapids to begin his military service on Thanksgiving Day, November 26, 1942. At the time Dad left, I don't think he or his family knew that Wayne had already died in battle just 13 days earlier. Apparently, the official notification of Wayne's death was given to the family in December. Dad was given emergency leave from December 23 through December 28, to return to Cedar Rapids. What an awful Christmas that was for the Rundall family.

Uncle Wayne attended Wilson High School, where he was a member of the debate team. He graduated from Wilson High in 1939. There is a picture of him as a sophomore in Dad's 1937 (senior year) Wilson High yearbook. Prior to enlisting in the Navy, Wayne worked for the Coca Cola Bottling Company of Cedar Rapids. After just three weeks of training, Wayne was assigned to the USS Laffey (DD-459), a destroyer that saw a lot of action in the Pacific. On November 13, 1942 at the beginning of the Naval Battle of Guadalcanal in the Solomon Islands, the Laffey encountered a Japanese fleet of two battleships, one light cruiser, and 14 destroyers. The Laffey fought the Japanese ships at point blank range. A 14-inch shell hit her. Then a torpedo in her fantail put Laffey out of action. As the order to abandon ship was passed, a huge explosion ripped the Laffey apart and she sank immediately. Of the 247 crewmembers aboard, 59 were killed, including Fireman 1st Class Wayne C. Rundall.

Note on the USS Laffey: soon after the loss of the Laffey, the Navy set about building another destroyer, which they also named the USS Laffey (DD-724). Bartlet Laffey was a civil war hero for the Union forces, who was awarded the Medal of Honor for his stand against Confederate forces on March 5, 1864. The Navy was determined that his name should continue to be honored in this way. The second USS Laffey would be built and commissioned in time to serve in the war, and it provided artillery cover for the allied forces landing in Normandy on D-Day, June 6, 1944. The second Laffey is now part of the Patriots Point Naval & Maritime Museum in Charleston Harbor, South Carolina.

For most of 1943, while Dad's training and stateside service schedule permitted, Mom followed Dad, first to the naval training facility in Norman, Oklahoma. Mom and Dad must have known by then that she was pregnant with their first child and was expected to deliver their baby in July 1944. Eventually Dad was assigned to the Kadashan Bay (CVE-76), an escort aircraft carrier being built by the Kaiser Shipbuilding Company in Vancouver, Washington. The Kadashan Bay was launched in December 1943, and commissioned in January 1944. Dad and Mom went to Vancouver for his further training. I remember her stories of working as a housemaid in the homes of wealthy families in Seattle and Vancouver to earn extra money. She and Dad also spent time in San Francisco and then San Diego, for the Kadashan Bay's shakedown cruise. As July approached, I'm sure they were both hoping their baby would be born, and Dad would be able to hold their child before his ship sailed. That was not to be. On July 10, 1944, Dad shipped out aboard the Kadashan Bay for Tulagi in the Pacific.

Their parting must have been heartbreaking for Mom and Dad. Mom was 22 years old, due to deliver her baby any day, and didn't know when or if she would see Dad again. Somehow, presumably by bus or train, Mom found her way back to Cedar Rapids. She moved in with her in-laws, Earl and Edna Rundall at 1626 N St., S.W. I have a picture of Jane and me standing in front of that house on our 1985 visit to Cedar Rapids. Mom gave birth to her daughter, whom she named Jovette Sherwood, on July 23, 1944. Because of the color of Jovette's hair, Grandfather Earl called her Sandy, and family and friends knew her by that name ever after.

Throughout 1944, the Kadashan Bay served in support of the Mariana and Palau Islands campaign, the Battle off Samar, and the Invasion of Lingayen Gulf. On January 8, 1945, The Kadashan Bay was attacked off the coast of Luzon Island in the Philippines. In the battle that ensued, a Kamikaze plane hit the carrier below the bridge at the water line. The Kadashan Bay nearly sank. The crew managed to keep her afloat, but the damage required her to retire from operations. The ship returned to San Diego for repairs. The Kadashan Bay was sailing back to Pearl Harbor when on August 15, 1945 Japanese Emperor Hirohito announced their unconditional surrender. Dad was going home to his family.

My father's war experiences and the death of his younger brother had a strong psychological effect on him. Everyone that knew him liked Dad. He had a terrific sense of humor. In high school he got the nickname "Huck," after Mark Twain's fictional character Huckleberry Finn. He loved telling stories and being happy with family and friends. Yet, he never talked about his war experiences. Later in life, when I lived in Hawaii for a while, I urged my mom and dad to visit me. I thought we could see some of the sights Dad remembered from his wartime visits to Pearl Harbor. He had no interest in doing that. The war made those memories painful and he wanted no part of Hawaii or any other place in the Pacific Ocean.

Some things cannot be explained. The USS Laffey Uncle Wayne served on was built by Bethlehem Shipbuilding Company in San Francisco and launched in October of 1941. It is special and mysterious to me that all of Uncle Wayne's immediate relatives eventually ended up living in or near San Francisco, including his father; his brother Richard and his family; and his sister, Wilma Rundall Zavoral. My parents named my brother Wayne in memory of him.

Life After the War

Dad was discharged on October 9, 1945. He returned to Cedar Rapids. I can imagine the joyous celebration in the Rundall household for his safe return. Mom, Dad, and Sandy lived with Dad's parents. Dad returned to his job at the Penick and Ford plant. Over time, our family grew, eventually becoming a rather large clan, very large by today's standards. Carol Anne was born August 26, 1946.

Off To A Good Start

By the time I was born on September 13, 1948, the five of us were living at 1002 2nd St., S.W. I also have a picture of Jane and me standing in front of that house. Three more children were yet to be born after we left Cedar Rapids: Catherine Sarah, born in Yuma on March 27, 1954; Susanne Marie, born in Yuma on May 5, 1956; and Wayne Michael, born in San Jose, California on April 25, 1962.

By 1948, the world was emerging from the violence and chaos of World War II, with many political and military forces attempting to seize dominance. In 1948:

- Mahatma Gandhi was assassinated in India

- Communists supported by the Soviet Union seized power in Czechoslovakia (to the dismay I'm sure of many of my family members in Cedar Rapids)

- The U.S. Congress approved the Marshall Plan providing $17 billion in aid to help rebuild Europe after the war

- The State of Israel was created, and admitted over 200,000 war refugees

- The Soviet Union sealed off land routes to Berlin, and the U.S. responded with an airlift of provisions

- President Harry S. Truman was re-elected in an upset victory over Thomas E. Dewey

But in day-to-day life, millions of Americans from the armed services and civilians working in war-related industries were attempting to return to normal life: starting new jobs, having babies, buying homes, and planning their futures. They were fortunate relative to people who lived in other countries. The United States had the only functioning, intact economy in the world. The US Congress and President Truman were approving a great deal of legislation to make it easy for industries to grow, add employees, build new houses, and for men and women who were leaving the armed services to find jobs, buy homes and start their civilian lives.

Moving to a Warm, Dry Place

My dad's lungs were susceptible to pneumonia. During successive winters, Dad caught pneumonia and was hospitalized more than once. During the 1948 winter he was hospitalized, and his doctor told him that he needed to move to a warm, dry place in order to avoid the continuing life-threatening problems with his lungs. My health was a concern, too. During my first few months I had serious ear infections that caused me to cry until eventually exhaustion allowed me to fall asleep, only to wake up later and cry some more. During my first six months a lump formed on my neck that remained until I was a teenager, then gradually went away. In fact, each of the Rundall family members wanted to move out of Iowa. They developed a plan to move to Yuma, Arizona together. I like to say that in looking for a warm, dry place to live, they over-achieved.

Off To A Good Start

Here are my paternal grandparents, Edna and Earl Rundall, probably in South Dakota, circa 1925

These are my maternal grandparents, Alice and Josef Serbousek, near Cedar Rapids, circa 1938

Off To A Good Start

Grandfather Earl Rundall's Homestead in South Dakota

Jane and I standing in front of 1626 N St SW,
Earl and Edna Rundall's house in Cedar Rapids

Aunts Rose Mary and Agnes in 1985 standing in front of one of the Serbousek family's homes in Cedar Rapids, IA

Jane and I standing in front of 1002 2nd St SW, Dad and Mom's 1948 family home in Cedar Rapids

Wayne, Wilma, and Dad, in Cedar Rapids, 1940

My mom, Georgiena Serbousek Rundall

Mom, Rose Mary, and Agnes Serbousek

Off To A Good Start

Mom's confirmation picture

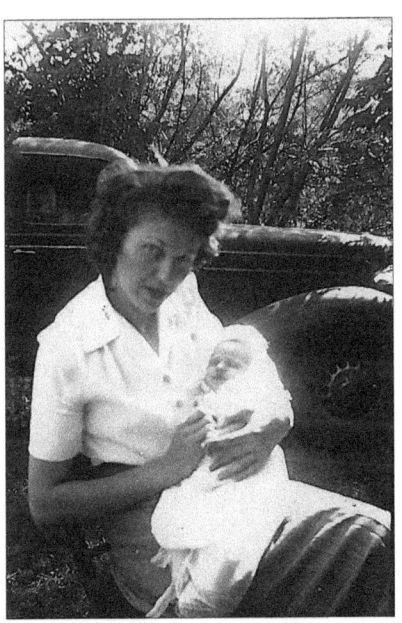
Mom with Sandy
on her Christening Day

Dad, Sandy, and Mom
in Cedar Rapids, circa 1946

Carol with her tricycle in Cedar Rapids, circa 1948

Off To A Good Start

2

A Decade in Yuma

With headwaters in the Rocky Mountains, the Colorado River is 1,450 miles long, very wide in many stretches, and courses through deep canyons including the Grand Canyon. For nearly all of its length, the river was virtually impassible until modern bridges were built in the 20th century. But in the southwest corner of Arizona, the river narrows to a thousand feet across. This spot is the easiest place to cross the river, and it became a strategic, if isolated, part of Arizona. Everyone who wanted to cross the river did so at this place. It was an ideal location for a town. Native Americans have lived in this area for hundreds of years. Their descendants now occupy the CoCopah and Quechan reservations. In the mid-1800s a small settlement of European Americans was established. The settlement had various names in its early years, but in 1873 it took the name Yuma, a variation of a Cocopah Tribal term Yuum. The Yuma Crossing became famous, particularly during and after the California Gold Rush when tens of thousands of prospectors and others traveled to California in seek of fortune, or at least a better life. In 1949, about 9,000 people called Yuma home.

In the late 1940s, all of the Rundall family made plans to move to Yuma. I do not know the details of this, but the desire to live in a warm dry place and family connections were involved. On June 14, 1943, my Aunt Wilma married Lee Victor Zavoral in Cedar Rapids. Lee was a linotypist. A few years after their marriage, Lee and Wilma moved to Yuma, where Lee took a job at the Yuma Sun newspaper. He became manager and part owner of Southwest Printers when it was formed early in 1949. Next, in early winter 1949 my grandparents moved to Yuma. They bought a house on property that contained a small walnut orchard. My parents moved us to Yuma in the late winter of 1949, and my dad was hired by Uncle Lee to be trained as a linotypist and work at Southwest Printers. My parents rented a house and we started to settle into our new lives. In 1950, my mom's sister, LaVerne, came to visit us. Laverne liked living in Yuma so much she decided to stay, taking a room at Clymer's Boarding House and getting a job at the local hardware store.

A canal ran behind our house. The canals were created to deliver water to the watermelon, cantaloupe, and lettuce farms throughout the region. Access to the canals was unprotected. There were no fences or barriers of any kind along their banks, and the sides of the canals were so steep, if someone fell in they could not get out. Once in a while a child would fall into a canal and drown. My parents were always worried that one of their children would wander off and fall into the canal behind our house. My earliest memory is from when I was about three years old and I did wander off to visit neighbor friends and ride on the swing under the shade of their backyard tree. For about 20 minutes my parents did not know where I was. They were frantically looking everywhere in the neighborhood, and trying not to believe their son had fallen into the canal. I vividly remember leaving my neighbor's house, casually walking up the street, and seeing my mom running to me and wrapping her arms around me in relief. My parents immediately decided they could no longer live in that neighborhood. Only a few days later, the whole family drove in our car to look at a house that my parents eventually rented: 307 17th Place. This house was located on the outskirts of town on a dirt road, and far from any canals. It was a small two-bedroom one-bath house with a fireplace, eating table in the kitchen, and a screened back porch. It had a detached garage that no one went into because it was filled with various types of equipment belonging to our landlord and spiders. The yard had a couple of shade trees; bushes, including a beautiful bougainvillea that covered the fence across the front yard; a picnic table and patches of grass in the back yard. The backyard had no fence and opened up to another dirt road. It was a small, inexpensive, cute family house. We lived in this house from 1952 until we left Yuma in the summer of 1959.

Yuma is hot. In June, July, August, and September, the average daily high temperature is over 100 degrees (F). It has more days of sunshine per year than any other metropolitan area in the United States. The warm, sunny weather did wonders for my dad's health. He never suffered from pneumonia or any other lung problems for the ten years we lived in Yuma. The move to Yuma probably saved his life.

The Rundall kids were able to handle the heat well. Only on the hottest days did Sandy, Carol, and I have to stay in the shade or cool off by running through the spray of the lawn sprinkler. I grew up walking and riding my bike on desert trails, hunting lizards with a bow and arrow, playing in the sand dunes, riding my bike to the Carnegie Library, occasionally taking a swim in the local motel's swimming pool, and exploring Yuma. Of course, I had Sandy and Carol to play with, and there were several kids in the neighborhood about our ages. We played many common children's games, like hide-and-seek. But not surprisingly, many of our play times were devoted to western themes: being cowboys, cowgirls, and Indians (as everybody called Native Americans at that time); galloping on make-believe horses; using ropes; and pretending to shoot rifles at any target we thought might be a bad guy.

The old west was all around us. There were many old buildings from the 19th and early 20th centuries, such as abandoned ranch houses that were falling to pieces, with horse corrals now missing most of the posts and rails. One of the most memorable places tied to Yuma's early days is the Yuma Territorial Prison. It was a must field trip every year for my school class. The prison was opened in 1876 when Arizona was still a territory. Many of the early cells were carved out of the rock escarpment that overlooks the Colorado River. It is a beautiful, beguiling view that held the promise of freedom for the 3,069 prisoners, including 29 women, who were imprisoned there. I saw signs of prisoners, probably driven mad by the heat and confinement, trying to claw their way through the rock walls. It scared me to think of being locked behind bars in such a place. The prison was closed in 1909, and it was eventually repurposed as the Yuma Territorial Prison Park.

In the early 20th century, the Yuma Union High School burned down. The high school occupied the prison buildings from 1910-1914. When the school's football team played against Phoenix and unexpectedly won, the Phoenix team called the Yuma team "criminals." Yuma High adopted the nickname with pride. On one return visit to Yuma over forty years after my family moved to California, Jane and I went to the high school and overlooking the football field we saw a large cut out figure of the school's symbol: the face of a hardened criminal in his prison garb. The school's student merchandise shop is called the Cell Block. What a place!

Right next to the prison was the Yuma Crossing Historic Park, now known as the Yuma Quartermaster Depot State Historic Park, which more aptly describes its role in the 1870s of storing goods and supplies that were to be shipped to the southwestern territories. After our school trips to the prison, we walked to the park and had lunch while thinking about the people who were imprisoned and died at what was otherwise a beautiful spot on the Colorado River.

Not far from the prison is downtown Yuma, a charming town with many old-west style buildings. Main Street is the heart of Yuma. In 1849, more than 60,000 California-bound-gold-seekers walked or road horses down Main Street to the rope ferry across the Colorado. In 1916, a flood washed away most of the town's adobe buildings. So the downtown buildings now date from the 1920s. I recall walking Main Street and the cross streets downtown with my mother as she did shopping. Colonnades covered the sidewalks to block the sun. It was a small town, easy to walk everywhere. There were many small shops, the Kress department store, and two movie theaters: the Lyric, which had two spectacular murals of Native American pueblo life over the ticket window, and the Yuma Theater with its beautiful art deco murals of mermaids on the interior walls. There was also the Imperial Hardware store, where my Aunt LaVerne worked. She met her future husband, Chester Leonard, when he came into the store to buy some supplies. Uncle Chet was a civil engineer who was working on putting a huge water pipe under an existing freeway, a very difficult thing to do. Southwest Printers was located just a block off Main St. at 30 W. 3rd St. My Uncle Lee Zavoral managed this print shop, which printed a local agricultural newspaper and any print jobs that came their way. Uncle Lee stayed with Southwest Printers for a few years, then he and Wilma moved to San Francisco, where he took a job as assistant manager of a large printing company.

A linotype machine is an amazing invention. It combines the casting, setting, and distributing of type in one machine, in one operation, by one operator. The name of the machine refers to the fact that it produces an entire line of metal type one at a time. Using a complicated keyboard, an operator types out letters that he wants the machine to cast. The machine lines up the type matrices (small pieces of brass that have letters and other characters indented on their edges) for each letter. Pressing a lever sends the group of matrices further into the machine where molten lead is poured onto the casting parts. Then, the finished line of type is sent out of the machine to cool, where it can be checked for accuracy. The words on each line of type are produced backwards, which produces properly oriented words when ink is applied and paper is pressed to the tray of type. There is a great deal of mechanical know how required to operate a linotype machine, plus the skill to type on the complicated keyboard, and the intelligence to understand how the whole process works and to fix problems when something breaks down. Before we moved to Yuma, I believe Dad had never seen a linotype machine in his life. But he was smart, a good machinist, and he had a mentor in Uncle Lee. Dad joined the International Typographical Union when he started working for Southwest Printers. I have a picture that was taken in 1954 of the entire staff of Southwest Printers and their families. Dad is standing in the back row. Mom is sitting at the end of the middle row. She is pregnant with Cathy. Sandy, Carol, and I are sitting on the floor. The general manager at that time, a man named Meryl, is standing in the middle of the group. I remember vividly sitting for this picture. It was a fun photo shoot.

Dad worked as a linotype operator his entire life. He excelled at his work and earned the reputation of being a master printer. He was among the last generation of linotype operators. In the 1960s, modern offset printing (a type of lithography) and later computer word processing and printing replaced virtually all linotype machines. Linotype machines are considered mechanical works of art. You can see many of them exhibited in the Smithsonian Institution's National Museum of American History in Washington, D.C.

Given the heat and desolate surroundings, Yuma was a difficult place to live. Also, with three, eventually five, children at home money was always a worry. I knew that we lived on the edge of poverty. But my mom and dad made the best of our circumstances. We found small ways to find more food to eat and supplement our income. Dad loved the outdoor life, and we frequently went to one of the canals around Yuma for recreational fishing. Mom and Dad caught catfish and carp, which we took home for dinner. Every December Mom and I (before I started to attend school) walked the neighborhoods around where we lived selling boxes of Christmas cards to make some extra money. Very near our house was a fenced lot where cantaloupe trucks were parked for a day or so after being loaded up in the fields. There were hundreds of cantaloupes on each truck. When Mom saw one of the trucks drive by our house she would give me a large sack and tell me to run over to the men tending the trucks and ask if we could have a few cantaloupes. It was a little humiliating to do this. But the truck drivers, all Mexican-Americans, shared an important bond with me. We all knew how difficult it was to feed a large family without much money. They always gave me five or six cantaloupes. But we never seriously suffered. We always had food, although sometimes it was a fried egg sandwich or some other inexpensive meal. I do not recall ever going to a restaurant. Gradually, as Dad's income grew our material life improved: a new car in 1954 (a two-tone, red and white Nash Rambler), a swamp cooler to air condition the house in about 1956, a television set in about 1957. Dad and Uncle Chet remodeled our screened porch, replacing the mesh screen with wood siding and turning one half of it into my bedroom. Until then, Sandy, Carol, and I shared a bedroom. I think everybody was happy when I moved to the "porch" bedroom.

I was glad that my grandparents, Aunt Wilma and Uncle Lee, and Aunt LaVerne and Uncle Chet lived in Yuma. Having family nearby was comforting, and we all enjoyed being with each other. I have several special memories of family members. Many times I walked the walnut orchard with my Grandfather Earl, opening and closing breaks in the irrigation ditch that fed water to the trees. He also took me with him when he delivered the agricultural newspaper printed at my Dad's shop to farmers in the region. I have a faint memory of Aunt LaVerne and Uncle Chet's wedding day, April 6, 1951. They were married at 8:00 pm in the Immaculate Conception Church in Yuma. Reverend George F. Sturm performed the marriage ceremony. Aunt LaVerne and Uncle Chet made their home at 599 Orange Ave. in Yuma. In 1952, LaVerne and Chet took me on a car ride around town. We stopped in a shoe store, and they bought me a pair of cowboy boots. I have a picture taken by Chet of me sitting on a chair showing off those new boots. We enjoyed going with Aunt Wilma and Uncle Lee to the reservations to buy jewelry. Wilma bought a beautiful silver squash blossom necklace that years later she willed to Jane.

In time our relatives moved away from Yuma. In 1953, Chet and LaVerne moved to Riverside, California where Chet took a job working for a civil engineering company. In 1954, Aunt Wilma and Uncle Lee moved to San Francisco, where Lee accepted a job as assistant manager of a large printing plant. About 1956, Grandparents Earl and Edna moved to Anaheim, California, probably to get out of the Yuma heat. I was sorry when each of them moved.

Other relatives visited us on their vacations. Mom's sister Teta Rose Mary (Aunt Rose Mary in Czech) and her husband Elmer Smith, who lived in Waterloo, Iowa, visited us during several vacations. Aunt Agnes and Uncle Roy Crosby, Mom's oldest sister and her husband, also visited. In winter, Yuma was a popular destination for my Iowa family members. I liked that they came to visit us.

I attended two schools in Yuma. For first and second grade (there was no kindergarten) I attended O.C. Johnson. Then C.W. McGraw School was built closer to us, and I went there for third through fifth grade. Sandy, Carol and I walked to school together. We didn't think much about these walks to school, though in each case the walk was over a mile: a long way to carry books (no backpacks in those days). The students in our classes came from military families assigned to the military air base, civilian employees working at the base (the largest employer in town), and white and Mexican-American families working in blue-collar jobs. School was fun and the classrooms were air-conditioned. The teachers were quite devoted to their students, and teachers got to know their students' parents. When Sandy and Carol wanted to tease me, they sometimes would tell me that I was adopted. One day in second grade, the teacher asked if anyone in class was adopted (presumably to qualify for some benefit). I raised my hand. The teacher laughed and said, "Tom, you look exactly like your father."

As I played with neighborhood kids and attended classes at school I became aware that I was a very good student and enjoyed learning things. I also learned that I was a good athlete, playing football and baseball at a level a grade or two higher than I was. I loved sports and spent as much time as possible playing catch, hitting baseballs, and pretending to be the latest hot football or baseball star. One highlight was serving as the batboy for the Chicago Cubs one spring when some of the team (none of the big stars) practiced and played at the old Yuma baseball stadium. My better-than-average ability in sports was made most apparent during a1957 vacation that my family took to visit Aunt LaVerne and Uncle Chet, now living in Riverside, California. My cousins, Geoff and Tiger invited me to join them at their school, which was having a sports festival with lots of races and contests of various sorts. There were ribbons awarded for the best performances. I watched my cousins throw baseballs in the "longest throw" contest. The person in charge of this event handed me a ball. I said I didn't go to that school, so I couldn't participate. He said, "Don't worry about that. We want all the kids here to participate." I threw the ball farther than anyone else and was awarded a gold ribbon. In fact, I returned to the house that day with three ribbons, two gold and one silver. My cousins were not happy with me. But that didn't last. We laughed about it later.

My sister Catherine Sarah (Cathy) was born in 1954, and Susanne Marie (Sue) came along in 1956. When they were old enough, they joined Sandy and Carol in the "girls'" bedroom. We were a family of five children in a small house where money was scarce and the heat made life generally stressful. All of this took its toll on Mom. In the mid-fifties, she developed heart problems, what I think would now be called tachycardia. Her heart would beat faster than normal while she was at rest. I recall anxiously observing two house calls by doctors who examined Mom while she lay in her bed. At that time there were no approved pharmaceuticals for this type of heart problem. So the doctors gave her a type of medication that had proven useful for heart problems for many years: whiskey. Each time it seemed to work. In a few hours, Mom's heart converted to a normal rhythm. Maybe it was coincidence. I don't know.

The heart problem was not indicative of any general weakness in Mom. She was a strong, resilient woman. On a family vacation in 1953, we set out for the Grand Canyon, planning to take a week to travel there and back. On the afternoon of the first day of the trip, Dad pulled the car over to take a break. We kids got out of the car. There was a bit of a slope away from the car with gravel on the surface. As Mom got out of the car, she slipped and landed very hard on her butt. She was in obvious pain, and Dad said we should go to a hospital. But Mom would not hear of that. Going to a hospital would ruin her family's vacation. She eased herself back into the front seat of the car, and we continued our trip. She moved very gently for the next few days, not walking at all if possible. We saw the Grand Canyon and headed home a little sooner than expected. Once back in her house, Mom went to bed and stayed there as much as possible for several weeks. Many years later when Mom had some pelvic x-rays, the doctor told her that she had suffered a broken pelvis. She simply said, "I thought that was what happened." Throughout her life, Mom withstood physical pain and emotional turmoil better than anyone I knew. She had a pioneer woman's "let's get on with it" attitude. Mom was an amazing woman. She never complained about anything. Regardless of what circumstances befell us, she made sure we were fed and clothed, did our homework, attended Mass every Sunday at St. Francis of Assisi Catholic Church, and always felt we were loved.

The years in Yuma rolled along. Of course there were some crises. One afternoon, while she was playing in the street that ran across the back of our house, a car hit Sue and broke her leg. She was carried into our house by an elderly woman neighbor who was blinded by the low sun and didn't see Sue playing in the street. Sue looked dead, but was only unconscious. She wore a cast for several weeks, and eventually her leg healed completely. One night, the house next door to us owned by a wonderful Mexican-American woman named Amelia Norton (who every Christmas gifted us the best enchiladas and tamales) suffered heavy damage from a fire. Mom discovered the fire and called the fire department. Dad and Uncle Elmer Smith who, with Aunt Rose Mary, was vacationing with us, tried to enter the house but were beat back by the flames. The fire department rescued one of Mrs. Norton's relatives who was unconscious in the kitchen. The sirens, the hustle and bustle of saving a man's life and putting out the fire, and the conversation among the fire fighters during the coffee service my mom prepared after the fire was extinguished all happened between 11:30 pm and 5:00 am. I slept through the whole thing. But over these years there was little drama in the family. That was about to change.

Teta Rose Mary and Uncle Elmer lived In Waterloo, Iowa, but loved Arizona and liked to visit us. In January of 1958 they came to visit for a week. Little did I know that their visit would alter my life.

Off To A Good Start

During Rose Mary and Elmer's visit we took them for a drive in the desert. During the drive Elmer told my parents they would love to have one of us kids return with them to Waterloo and spend the rest of the school year with them. I was stunned at the thought. But Dad and Mom said something like "That's an interesting idea." The next day, I was asked if I would like to go to Waterloo with Rose Mary and Elmer. I got a bit of a sell job from Elmer, and Mom and Dad encouraged me to do it. To this day I do not know why all this happened, though, I know that back in those days it was not unusual for related families to have a child stay with the other family for a while. But staying with my aunt and uncle's family 1,700 miles away seemed pretty extreme to me. But the more I thought about it, the more excited I got at the chance to live in a totally different environment, see snow, and learn about Iowa. I liked Teta Rose and Uncle Elmer. They were fun to be around. It would be a six-month adventure. I said yes.

We drove several days and arrived at their Waterloo home around midnight. Snow had recently fallen, and I jumped out of the car to touch snow for the first time. The next morning I met Rose Mary and Elmer's children who were still living at home: Patty (a senior in high school), Carl (a year older), and Kelly (a year younger). Another daughter, Marcia, had already graduated from high school and was living in her own place (two other daughters, twins Sarita and Sue, would join the family a few years later). When school re-started after Christmas break, I was enrolled in Sacred Heart Catholic School and joined the fourth grade class. I fit in well there. Since my mom took us to church every Sunday, I knew what Catholicism was about. But this was an intense religious lifestyle. We had religious service every day at school, and I went to Mass on Sundays with the Smiths. For a while I served as an alter boy. Our teachers were nuns, and yes they occasionally rapped someone's hand with a ruler. But I have fond memories of Sacred Heart. I made friends easily, having some star status for being from exotic Yuma. I could read at an advanced level, so my teacher liked me. I enjoyed playing in the gymnasium and small outdoor playground. The window near my classroom seat gave me a chance to watch, for the first time, a change of season. Patty was like a second mother. She was kind and fun to be around, but also tried to keep us from causing too much trouble. Carl, Kelly, and I became friends, although sometimes our snowball wars and other games got too intense and we were temporarily mad at each other. As the weather grew warmer, we explored the meadows and shallow creeks near their home. We also had chores to do every day. Mine was to weed the garden.

At the end of the school year in June, Rose Mary suggested that we three boys spend two weeks on her sister's farm. Aunt Ag (Agnes) and Uncle Roy Crosby operated a farm in Coggon, Iowa. They had no children of their own and loved having nieces and nephews stay with them. So off we went to be farmers. It was one of the greatest experiences of my life. I enjoyed learning about growing corn; raising pigs, cows, and sheep; and keeping an eye on the weather. You haven't lived until you've been chased out of the sheep yard by the boss black-faced sheep. I rode on a tractor while Uncle Roy plowed a cornfield. I learned some things about the life of a farm family, and the continuous hard work required of successful farmers. We ate huge volumes of food prepared by Aunt Ag for each meal; then we burned it off doing chores. I grew very fond of Aunt Ag and Uncle Roy. I have thought of them many times over the years and deeply appreciated the time I spent with them on the farm. I learned so much about what it meant to be a farmer. Everyone should live on a farm for two weeks.

With the end of my two weeks on the farm, it was time for me to go home to Yuma. How was I to get there? The solution was for me to travel from Waterloo to Yuma by train. Uncle Elmer worked for the railroad. He got me an inexpensive (maybe free) ticket. Miraculously, there was a train route I could take from Iowa to Yuma that did not require me to change trains. Teta Rose put together a suitcase full of peanut butter and jelly sandwiches, apples, and other things to eat. At the train station we said our good-byes. I promised not to get off the train until it arrived in Yuma. Elmer gave the conductor a twenty-dollar bill and asked him to look out for me, and away I went. A wonderful middle-aged woman sitting near me for most of the trip took me under her wing and made sure nothing bad happened to me. I don't remember all the towns and cities the train stopped at. I believe we passed through Kansas City, Wichita, and Amarillo. When we pulled into El Paso, I knew we were getting close to Arizona, and a day later at 6:00 a.m. the train pulled into

Yuma. From my window on the train I could see my parents with our family dog, Smokey, standing on the ramp leading from the parking lot to the platform. I was thrilled to see them. I'm sure they breathed a huge sigh of relief when they saw me walk off the train. We ran to each other and hugged for a long time. A nine-year-old boy traveled from Waterloo to Yuma on a train by himself. No one would think of allowing such a thing today. But that was life in the 1950s. It was possible to assume other people would be kind and helpful if necessary, and that children would be safe on a train.

My arrival back home marked the beginning of my last year in Yuma. In the fall of 1958 Mom and Dad told us kids that they were thinking of moving to California. No specific moving date was mentioned, and the topic was not talked about much. In September I entered the fifth grade and picked up with friends pretty much where I left off the previous year. I loved playing football and baseball at school and was doing well academically, notably winning a hard fought spelling-bee among the fifth graders. But as summer approached, the talk about moving increased. I think my mom decided she could not go through another hot summer in Yuma. Also, by then all of our relatives had moved away, making Yuma a lot less appealing. Through his International Typographical Union, my dad got referred to a linotype operator job in northern California. In late July 1959 we packed our belongings into the Nash Rambler and a small rented trailer, and the seven of us drove away from Yuma. None of us was to return there until I did so forty years later.

Our first stop was our grandfather's house in Anaheim. Grandmother Edna had died the previous November of stomach cancer, and Grandfather Earl was living alone. We kids were asked to stay with Grandfather (Gramp) while Mom and Dad drove to check out the job opportunity in Roseville. Poor Gramp. We were five wild kids terrorizing a man who had grown accustomed to living alone. He was extremely patient and kind, although after the first day he did start eating his meals in a separate room. I have always felt badly about how hard that week was for him. But he never said a cross word to us about it then or later.

Mom and Dad drove to Roseville, which is located near Sacramento. They arrived in town during the afternoon, and it was over 100 degrees outside. Mom opened the car door and immediately said "This is no better than Yuma. We can't move here." So Dad contacted the union and asked if there were any other job openings in California. He was told that in Los Gatos, a town near San Jose, the local newspaper needed a linotype operator. Los Gatos is located in one of the most beautiful regions in California. It is a lovely town tucked up next to the Santa Cruz mountain range. The summer weather is warm, but not hot. Dad quickly accepted the position at the Los Gatos Times, and Mom and Dad drove back to Anaheim to pick us up. As we were packing, Gramp gave Dad a check for $2,000 to help pay the expenses of moving his family. A day later we moved to Campbell, a town next to Los Gatos. Dad was eligible for benefits from the GI Bill, passed by Congress in the 1940s to help men and women who served in the military in World War II return to civilian life. He used the reduced interest rate loan enabled by the GI Bill to buy our house at 565 Weston Drive. If one looks at the street view of the house on Google today, the small size of the house and property are apparent. The house had three bedrooms and one bath. Also very visible is a huge tree in the middle of the front yard that towers over the house. Dad and I planted that tree.

Off To A Good Start

Mom and Dad in Yuma, circa 1951

My grandparents, Edna and Earl Rundall, in Yuma, circa 1950

Dad and Mom in Yuma, 1958

Me at 1 ½ years old, taking a stroll in Yuma, 1950

Our home in Yuma, 307 17th Place, 1952 - 1959

Carol, Sue, Cathy, Sandy, and I in our yard at 307 17th Place, circa 1956

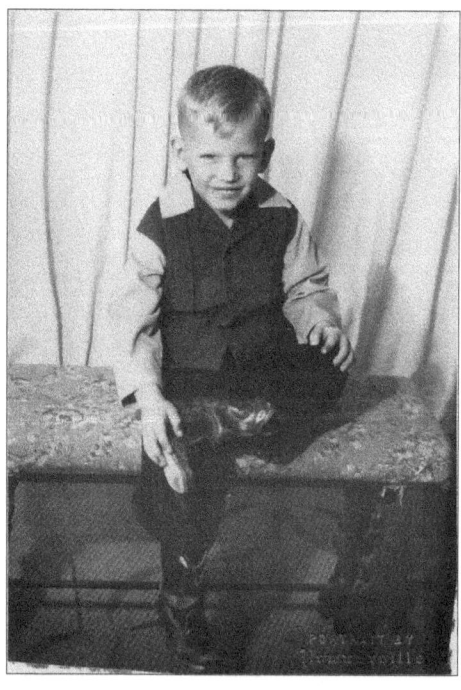

Cowboy boots Aunt LaVerne and Uncle Chet bought me, 1952

The site of Southwest Printers in the 1950s,
later the home of Cactus Press

Dad at his linotype machine with a lot of interested spectators

Southwest Printers, staff and families, 1954

Mom and Dad, Carol, Sandy, Sue, Cathy, and I
in our backyard with the red and white Nash Rambler, 1958

3

Life in the 1960s

Campbell is located in the Santa Clara Valley of California. The valley, named after the Spanish Mission Santa Clara, was for a time known as the Valley of Heart's Delight for its concentration of orchards and flowering trees and plants. Until the 1960s, it was the largest fruit producing and packing region in the world. When we moved into our house on Weston Dr. (originally named Komsthoeft Dr., but no one could spell that name so it was changed), it was a dead-end street that was completely surrounded by apricot and plum orchards. In fact, nearly everywhere we went there were orchards. Even today, the town of Campbell refers to itself as the Orchard City. For several years, my friends and I worked during the summer picking fruit and helping in the drying sheds. But Santa Clara Valley was experiencing rapid population growth. Gradually, the orchards gave way to houses and shopping centers, and over a ten-year period electronics, technology, manufacturing, and research firms and the consumer industries that provided goods and services to the growing population replaced agriculture as the economic base of the valley. Our dead-end street was extended into a new housing development. It was a dramatic change in a short period of time. Similar change was happening in many cities and towns in California.

During the decade of the 1960s, California's population surpassed that of New York, making California the most populous state in the U.S. At the same time as this growth was occurring, social change was unfolding rapidly. Long existing anger and resentment fueled militant action by farm workers, African-Americans, women, gay men and lesbian women, peace activists, and others. Cesar Chavez (who coincidentally was born in Yuma) organized the National Farm Workers Association in Delano, California in 1962, and led farm workers in picketing many farms and vineyards and a boycott of table grapes. The civil rights movement, which had been going on in some ways for decades, became more organized and strident in its efforts to end racial discrimination and gain equal rights under the law. Although the movement was mostly peaceful, major riots broke out in African-American communities in many cities, including Los Angeles. The women's rights movement sought equal rights and greater personal freedom for women. Homosexual men and women were increasingly coming out and organizing to achieve legal and social equality. As the United States' military involvement in South Vietnam increased, eventually leading to a war against the North Vietnamese, peace activists protested and, increasingly, "brought the war home" through violent actions. Advocates of these various causes demanded change by pressuring elected leaders; staging public meetings and rallies, marches, sit-ins, acts of civil disobedience; and at times defacing and damaging buildings. All of these social movements, and a more general rebellion by young people against the values of their parents' generation, were quickly unfolding during the 1960s in California. Bob Dylan's song "The Times They are a Changin'" was the anthem of social and political change and it captured a lot of what was going on. With national media coverage every day, it was impossible not to know of these social dynamics. The shrill advocates for change and equally shrill conservative voices for traditional family, social, and economic structures seemed to be everywhere. There was a lot of tension in life for everyone. Family members fought over how much relationships between parents and their children would change. Many kids insisted on more personal freedom. Drug use and premarital sex were increasing. This wasn't Yuma any more.

During the early 1960s in Campbell, I was not especially engaged with these issues. I was in elementary school, and I didn't feel part of the social struggles going on personally. But that would change, and by 1970 I was marching in the streets, too.

Elementary School Years

One of the good things about the 1960s and living in California was the quality of the state's educational system. California legislators invested heavily in education. Schools at every level received what we would call today generous funding. Elementary schools had music classes and musical instruments to loan to students.

There were after-school, Saturday, and summertime clubs, activities, and sports programs. Similarly, high schools had a wide array of required and elective classes, including college preparatory courses. There were well-supplied laboratories and other science facilities. The libraries were well stocked with reference and pleasure reading books. There were music and art classes, after-school clubs for special interests, many athletic teams for boys and girls, marching bands, school plays, and much more. The cost of students' class books, lab supplies, uniforms for athletic teams, instruments and uniforms for the marching band, and any other school activity was paid for by the school district. California had a master plan that identified the roles and relationships among its Community Colleges system (associate of arts degrees for practical training and preparation for four-year college), the California State College system (undergraduate degrees heavily oriented to the preparation of teachers), and the University of California system (research universities providing liberal arts and sciences undergraduate degrees and graduate degrees in academic and professional disciplines). The University of California nine-campus system was the envy of college faculty and administrators everywhere, and the campuses at Berkeley and Los Angeles were rated among the world's best universities. None of the state's public colleges and universities charged tuition. In addition, the state legislature created the California State Scholarship Program, which provided scholarships for high school graduates with outstanding academic performance and high Scholastic Aptitude Test (SAT) Scores. These scholarships paid full tuition cost at any public or private university in California. The public education system in California in the 1960s might have been the best educational system in history. We probably will not see anything like it again.

Soon after moving to Weston Dr. I started sixth grade classes at Bucknell Elementary School, which was about a half mile from our house. It was an easy walk. But when I foolishly attempted to learn to play the baritone, I lugged the instrument in its case onto the school bus that stopped near our house at the corner of Weston Dr. and McCoy Ave. For seventh and eight grades, I attended Elvira Castro Junior High School. Castro was a much bigger school, the biggest I had ever attended. It had the usual courses, but also a wood shop and a metal shop for teaching students, mostly boys as I recall, how to use tools and make things. Castro also had organized sports teams. I played flag football during the school year and little league baseball during the summer months. I got good grades in my classes. But during the fall semester of 1961, Mom decided it would be fun if we studied together. She would quiz me with prepared questions at the end of my textbook and ask me her own questions about the material I had read. I still remember how happy she was when at the end of that semester I brought home my report card with straight As. It was a team effort!

While I was attending Castro Junior High, our family went through big changes. I think we all were surprised to learn in 1961 that my Mom was pregnant. She was 39 years old and had a history of heart problems. Her doctor told her attempting to deliver the baby would put her at significant risk. He advised Mom to get an abortion. Being a devout Catholic, Mom refused. She gave birth to my brother Wayne Michael on April 25, 1962. In 1961 Sandy married Carl Richard (Dick) Davis, and of course she moved out of our house to live with her husband. In time, Sandy and Dick would have two daughters: Deborah Lynn and Julia Ann. In 1962 Carol married Richard Frederick Vasquez, and they later had two boys: Richard Earl and Ronald Edward. Having two young sisters leave our house, especially one leaving so soon after the first, was hard on all of us. We were trying to find our way as a family through the stress brought about by the social changes we were experiencing and the additional stress of my sisters going through their teenage years. Fortunately, our family ties were very strong, and all of us remained close to Sandy and Carol for the rest of their lives. By late 1962, Cathy, Sue, Wayne, and I were still living with Mom and Dad at 565 Weston Dr. I was 14 years older than Wayne, but I enjoyed spending time with him, and I was the go-to baby sitter whenever Mom and Dad went out. We developed a strong bond. When he got a little older, Wayne would sometimes come into my room late at night and sleep next to me often accompanied by our dog, Snooks.

High School Years

In the fall of 1962 I started my freshman year of high school at Campbell High. The high school is a beautiful Spanish mission revival style building. It was built in the 1930s as a Works Projects

Administration (WPA) construction project. In 1989 the school was added to the Register of Historic Places because it is the only example of a 1930s WPA construction built in the Spanish mission style. Due to declining enrollment, the school was closed in 1980 and eventually repurposed in 1985 as the Campbell Community Center.

I took the regular courses and enjoyed spending time with friends from Castro Junior High who were now also at Campbell High. I played second-string quarterback on the frosh-soph football team. In a game in the middle of the season, I was "sacked" and sprained my knee badly. I had to use crutches for several weeks and receive physical therapy. I thought the job of a physical therapist was interesting and might be a career path for me. In my freshman year I also played baseball. Campbell High had three baseball teams: the freshman, frosh-soph, and varsity teams, all taught by the great coach, John Oldham. I played centerfield on the freshman and frosh-soph teams. All three teams had undefeated seasons, a record that will never be broken. One of my friends on those teams was Don Hahn, who in previous years was my teammate on Little League teams. Don was a terrific athlete. He was a star baseball, basketball, and football player throughout his four years at Campbell High. Later, Don played professional baseball for several major league teams, including the New York Mets. In 1973, Don was a part-time centerfielder for the Mets, most often coming into a game in the late innings as a substitute for Willie Mays. The Mets won the National League Pennant that year, but lost the World Series to the Oakland Athletics in seven games. When Owen was a boy we often went to baseball card shows, He would buy various players' cards. I only looked for Don Hahn. I probably have the largest collection of Don Hahn cards outside of his family.

During my sophomore year I enjoyed my classes, especially algebra and geometry. I didn't play football. I badly strained my back earlier in the summer, and I could not play. I did play baseball in the spring, but my back was still a little painful. It was somewhat of a lost season.

The event that made all else completely trivial by comparison was the assassination of President John Kennedy on November 22, 1963 in Dallas, Texas. Our teachers were crying as they told us the terrible news. It was truly shocking. I did not believe such a thing could happen in the United States. Two days after Kennedy's assassination, the accused killer, Lee Harvey Oswald, was fatally shot by local nightclub owner Jack Ruby on live television in the basement of the Dallas Police Headquarters. My world was changed forever, and the same was true for nearly every American. Sadly, it was not the last such terrible tragedy in the 1960s. Martin Luther King, Jr., the great civil rights leader, was assassinated April 4, 1968 in Memphis, Tennessee. Only a few months later Presidential candidate Robert F. Kennedy, the slain President's brother, was assassinated on June 6, 1968 in Los Angeles.

On the positive side of things, the 1960s had the best music. The best of the best was the music written and performed by the Beatles. The members of the band, John Lennon, Paul McCartney, Ringo Starr, and George Harrison, were each immensely talented musicians. Together they were simply brilliant. The Beatles are the best-selling musical act in history, and they are generally regarded as the most influential band of all time. Of course, I didn't know all that in the 1960s. I just knew the Beatles played the best music I ever heard. "I Want to Hold Your Hand" was the first Beatles song to be ranked #1 on the pop charts in the United States on February 1, 1964. Over fifty years later the Beatles are still my favorite band. In 2019, Jane, Mananya, Owen, and I went to Paul McCartney's concert in San Jose. At the age of 77, Paul performed flawlessly for over three hours. It was the best concert ever. There are too many great songs to list them all, but listening to "Here Comes the Sun," "Yesterday," "Blackbird," "The Long and Winding Road," "A Hard Day's Night," "While My Guitar Gently Weeps," "Penny Lane," "Help!," "Back in the USSR," "I Feel Fine," "Something in the Way She Moves," and the brilliant "A Day in the Life" would make anyone a lifetime Beatles fan. But my favorite is not one of those. My favorite song, the one that most fully captures my feelings about the experiences I have had over the past fifty years, is "In My Life."

In the fall of 1964, a new high school was opened near my home, Westmont High School. I completed my junior and senior years there. I could easily walk to Westmont, crossing a new pedestrian bridge over a small creek that ran roughly parallel to McCoy Avenue. The two years at Westmont were happy times filled with interesting courses taught by great teachers and, of course, playing on the school's athletic teams.

For my junior year I played on what was called the "B" football team. This was the team for smaller guys. I was about 5'9" tall and weighed 140 pounds. So this was the right team for me. I shared quarterback duties with another student. When the coach wanted to have a series of running plays he put in the other quarterback. When he wanted to have a series of passing plays he put me in. I think the opposing teams figured this out. In any event, we had a successful season, winning five and losing four games. The varsity team had a terrible season, losing seven and tying two games they played. They didn't win a single game. It was an inauspicious start for the first year of a new school. Later that year, I also played on the "B" basketball team, and on the varsity baseball team. I had a strong baseball season, batting over .300, and I was a very good defensive outfielder. I was selected for the all-league team.

During the summer of 1965, I did some soul searching about my future. I was anxious about where my life was heading. Thinking through the reasons for my anxiety, I realized that most of it had to do with the realization that I had a great deal of ambition and I was not sure what to do about that. One day, I decided I had to have a plan, or at least the beginning of a plan for my future. The plan I developed had the following ideas: I wanted to pursue a career as a professional in some field that was interesting to me and also provided some social benefit; I wanted to be considered one of the top professionals in my field; I wanted a career that provided financial security; I wanted a career and lifestyle that would allow me to travel, not only around the United States but to other countries as well; finally, I wanted the branch of the family I started to follow in this path and to enjoy each other's success. Looking back it is stunning that at the age of sixteen I would think this way. But I did. Then, my anxiety shifted to worrying about what career would fit into my plan. I didn't talk about my anxiety to my parents. I was afraid they would think I was ungrateful or unappreciative of all the sacrifices they made and hard work they did to get my siblings and me to be able to live in the beautiful Santa Clara Valley and attend schools in the greatest educational system in the world. In fact, I didn't talk to anyone about my plan until I met Jane nine years later.

Her understanding of what I told her, and her unflinching commitment to help make my plan come true, were two of the many reasons I fell in love with her.

Having figured out what I wanted my future life to be like inspired me to work even harder in school at academics and sports, in effect preparing myself to take advantage of any appealing opportunities that came up. In my senior year I fell into a routine: attend classes all day, practice with my team after school, arrive home in time for dinner, and study at night until I fell asleep. I worked hard on all my classes, including English, Spanish, physics, and mathematics. But by far my favorite class was history, taught by my favorite teacher, David Cripe. Dave was a remarkable man: intelligent, a lover of sports and the outdoors, full of humor and good will, and able to inspire his students. We became friendly during my senior year. After I graduated we became good friends. I joined him on fishing and camping trips in the Sierra Nevada Mountains. He and his fiancé, Joanne Casey, invited me to their wedding. Jane and I invited Dave and Joanne to our wedding.

I stayed in touch with Dave through the years, especially after he was diagnosed with Lou Gehrig's disease, amyotrophic lateral sclerosis (ALS). During the last six years of his life, Dave was unable to walk. But, he never lost his wit, memory, or ability to laugh and make others laugh with him. Dave died on Christmas Day, 2017. Jane and I attended his memorial service at the former Campbell High School, which was the biggest gathering of friends I have ever seen at such a service. Dave was much loved.

By the fall of 1965 I had grown half an inch and put on a little weight. I stood at nearly 5'11" and weighed 150 pounds. I decided I would try out for the varsity football team. I not only made the team, but I was selected to be the starting quarterback. I was an excellent passer and we had good receivers and backs to run the ball. Most importantly, we had a strong, resilient defense that gave up very few points to any team. Our team went undefeated, winning all nine games we played. This was quite a turnaround from the previous year when the team, with mostly the same players, failed to win a single game. Our head coach, Don Stillwell, was asked by reporters many times, "what was the difference in this year's team?" I was more than flattered when he said it was my play at quarterback. I was selected as the team's most valuable player, and Dad and I were invited to join other players and their fathers from all the teams in our area at an awards banquet. Jim Plunkett, the quarterback for another undefeated team at James Lick High, was one of the other awardees. We sat at the same table. I knew all about Jim. I was in awe of him and never thought for a moment I was his equal. A few years later we were both undergraduates at Stanford. While I was studying hard, Jim was studying hard and leading his team to the Rose Bowl, where Stanford defeated Ohio State. Shortly after that game Jim was awarded the Heisman Trophy. In his pro career Jim went on to win two Super Bowls with the Oakland/Los Angeles Raiders.

Two of my teammates on that football team have remained friends for over fifty years. Richard Brandt was a mainstay on our defensive line. Richard and I were close friends throughout our senior year and after. When in 1971 Richard and Artis Finlay, also a Westmont graduate, decided to get married he asked me to be his best man. I was proud to do so, and spent hours preparing and memorizing a speech I gave at the wedding. We talk by phone or text message every few months and, without fail, on their anniversary. My other long-term friend from that team is John Beebe. John was the tight end and my favorite passing target. We were good friends, and our friendship grew even stronger when we both attended West Valley Community College and played on the school's football team. He also married a Westmont graduate, Joanne Quintel. John and Joanne are wonderful people and still good friends. Jane and I have enjoyed sharing birthdays and anniversaries with them, and our high school class fiftieth year reunion, which John and Joanne hosted at their home.

One afternoon in May 1966 during baseball practice my sister Cathy came running across the outfield grass toward me. She was sobbing and yelled to me that Dad had an accident at work. At first I thought she said he had caught his head in a press, which froze me in my tracks. One of the coaches saw what was happening and immediately offered to drive us home. When we saw my Mom, she clarified that Dad had caught his HAND in the rollers that passed a continuous feed of paper to the press. I was greatly relieved, but

Off To A Good Start

this was still terrible news. Dad's hand was made almost flat by the rollers. He would spend several months recuperating and receiving physical and occupational therapy. During this time, the Los Gatos newspaper decided to install an offset printing system (a type of lithographic printing) and to eliminate the linotype machines. Dad was out of a job. As his hand healed and he regained function, Dad applied for a job and was hired as a linotype operator at the Stanford University Press, the publishing house of Stanford University. The Stanford Press was founded in 1892, making it the first university press to be established on the West Coast. It was a highly respected printing and publishing organization. When he told the family this news we were all excited and proud of Dad. The only downside was that Dad would have to commute to Stanford every day. But he was going to work the late afternoon/night shift, so the traffic would not be a problem. Then he told us some of the employee benefits of working for Stanford. I was especially excited to hear about one of them. Children of Stanford employees who were granted admission to the University would have tuition waived. But employees had to work for Stanford for two years before their children were eligible for this benefit. Immediately, I sensed a shift in my world.

During the rest of my senior year, I served on the School's Student Council and played on the varsity basketball and baseball teams. I was co-captain of the football and baseball teams. At the end of the school year I was selected as Westmont High's outstanding athlete. My picture still hangs on the wall of the lobby of the basketball gymnasium with the pictures of the school's other athletes of the year. I loved high school and I think I got a lot out of my classes, sports teams, and other activities at Westmont. Importantly, I was dimly starting to see that I especially liked the social sciences and had an interest in understanding the causes and consequences of the social changes we were all experiencing in the United States.

Like all my friends in June of 1966, I was excited to graduate from high school. What would the future bring? I knew I wanted to go to college. I would be the first one in my immediate family or in my line of ancestors to attend college. This lack of family experience with college left me little knowledge of how college worked and how to assess the alternatives it presented. I didn't even know what an academic "unit" was. These "units" seemed to be attached to lots of things, including classes, major and minor requirements, and graduation requirements. It took me a while to figure out this and other equally unfamiliar things. I had little hope of going away to college. I knew my parents could not afford to pay tuition and room and board costs. It turned out the tuition problem was solved for me. I was awarded one of those prized California State Scholarships that would pay tuition at any public or private university in California. That was an enormous benefit. But I still did not have any funds to pay for room and board. On somewhat of a whim, I had applied to U.C. Santa Barbara, motivated more by its location than its academic strengths. I got accepted, but I declined admission. In the spring of 1966, a local recruiter interviewed me to talk about my interest in attending the Naval Academy in Annapolis, Maryland. I had several conversations with him. He said he wanted to recommend me to one of our U.S. Senators, who would then request my admission to the Academy. This was a big deal. I thought it would make may father, the former Navy seaman, proud. It would make possible at least some of my life plan. Near the end of our discussions, I asked the recruiter what was the academic major of most of the students at the Academy. He said most students were engineering majors. That was a problem for me. Although I did not know what the many different subfields of engineering were, I didn't think I wanted to be any kind of engineer. I knew my interest was in the social sciences. It was a difficult decision, but I turned down the Naval Academy. Time would show that this was the right decision, especially after I became so strongly opposed to our military involvement in Vietnam. In the end, I decided my only option was to attend West Valley Community College and continue to live at home.

West Valley College Years

West Valley College was the newest addition to the state's community college system. A permanent campus had not yet been built (the new campus would eventually be built in Saratoga). Somehow, permission was granted for the college to be housed in the no longer used Campbell Elementary School, located at the corner of Campbell Ave. and Winchester Blvd. Going to West Valley Community College was a little like returning to Campbell High. The schools were across Winchester Blvd. from one another, and the buildings looked very similar. The elementary school was also built in the Spanish mission style to match the look of the high school. Years later, the beautiful elementary school was torn down and apartments were put up in its place. Ugh!

My two years at West Valley College flew by quickly for me. This was partly because I was always busy. I was taking a full load of classes that would make me competitive for admission to a four-year college, serving on the student council, and I was active in sports. I was also working part time. I greatly appreciated living in my parent's home and not having to pay rent. They also allowed me to use their second car to drive to the college each day and to go to work. I didn't want to ask them also to pay for my college expenses, clothes, gasoline, social activities with friends, and other needs. So I worked at the Kinney Shoes store on Camden Ave. to earn money for those things and to build up a reserve for paying tuition at a four-year college.

In the fall of 1966, I decided not to play on West Valley's football team. I thought it was better for my "plan" to focus on my course work. I did go as a spectator to many of the games, and I discovered that I missed the fun of practicing and playing games, the camaraderie with teammates, and the competition. Halfway through the season I vowed to try out for the team the next year. In the spring I did play on the baseball team. I was the starting centerfielder. I had a decent batting average, around .280, but I really excelled in the outfield. I became well known among local baseball people for my defensive ability. In the fall of 1967 I did try out for the college's football team, and was picked to be the starting quarterback. I once again enjoyed all those things I missed by not playing the previous year. We had a winning season, with five wins and four losses. One of our best games was against Menlo College in Menlo Park. I threw five touchdown passes. John Beebe, my friend from Westmont High now also playing for West Valley, caught three of them. The headline of the article in the San Jose Mercury News that reported on the game read "Rundall Runs Wild." The next week John received our league's player of the week honor for his three touchdown catches. Go figure. My ego was salved a bit when at the end of the season I was selected as the team's most valuable player. However, the season was not as much fun for me as I had hoped, primarily because

I did not like our head coach He was the only coach I ever had that I did not like. He was manipulative and embarrassed me in front of the team by trying rather obviously to get me to date his daughter. I was not the least bit interested. I had a girlfriend, Jeannie Vierra, and everybody knew that. Geez coach!

In the spring of 1968, my last semester at West Valley, I played baseball and was having my best season ever. But it was cut short by an eye injury I suffered playing in a pick-up basketball game on a Saturday in the Westmont High gym. I got poked in the eye, and the eyeball filled with blood. It looked gruesome, and I couldn't see out of the eye. The doctor put a patch over my eye and told me to stay in my bedroom, preferably in bed, with the lights off for ten days. In fact my eye did mostly clear up after about ten days, but I could not return to playing baseball.

Throughout my second year at West Valley, I continued taking a full load of courses required at four-year colleges. My football and baseball teammates would in a teasing way yell at me for carrying my calculus, chemistry, biology, and sociology books into the locker room. But a little teasing was not a problem for me. I was doing well in my course work. I was especially attracted to sociology, which gave me insights into social change and the social forces that influence our attitudes and behaviors.

Earlier in the year I completed my application to Stanford University and, if accepted, to be enrolled as a third-year student. Such matriculated students were typically called "transfer students." The two years that had to pass before I was eligible for the tuition waiver that was a benefit of Dad's employment at the university would pass by the time I registered for classes. I had a lot of leadership experiences to include in the application, I had taken the courses that would be required of freshmen and sophomores at Stanford, I had high SAT scores, and I had two strong letters of recommendation from West Valley College instructors. Now, my acceptance heavily depended on my overall grade point average during my two years at West Valley. When the grades for my final semester were available, I didn't wait to be sent a transcript by mail. I rushed to each of my instructors and asked what grade I received in their class. I did very well. After including those grades with grades from the three previous semesters I ended up with a 3.7 overall grade point average. I was thrilled to think I had a realistic chance to be admitted to Stanford. Only one more hurdle remained. I had to be interviewed by Stanford's Dean of Admissions, Rixford Snyder.

I made an appointment for the interview. On the appointed day Dad and I drove to Stanford. He knew right where to go. Dean Snyder invited us into his office. He asked me questions about why I wanted to go to Stanford, what did I think were my strengths and weaknesses, what were my career aspirations, and similar things. I was well prepared and answered each question with confidence. He asked Dad what type of work he did at Stanford. He took notes on a piece of paper. After about thirty minutes the Dean thanked us for coming and we drove home. In a few days I received a letter from Stanford. It was a surrealistic feeling to hold in my hand the decision that would dramatically change my life one way or another. Taking a deep breadth, I opened the envelope and read the first sentence congratulating me for being accepted to Stanford University. I did it!

Me with Grandfather Earl, Dad, and Wayne, outside our home in Campbell, circa 1966

My grandfather in his San Francisco apartment, circa 1969

Me in Campbell, in probably the sixth grade, circa 1960

My sister Cathy in Campbell
at age 14

My sister Carol in Campbell,
circa 1960

My sister Sue in Campbell
at age 8

My sister Sandy in Campbell,
circa 1960

Sandy with her husband Dick Davis and their two children, Debbie and Julie, 1967

Sister Carol, with her husband Richard, and their two children, Ron and Rick, 1967

Off To A Good Start

Dad after all the Christmas presents have been opened, circa 1969

Mom looking beautiful at Grandfather Earl and Aunt Wilma's apartment in San Francisco, July 1969

4

Stanford, the Vietnam War, and Becoming a Conscientious Objector

During the summer of 1968 I was hired by the City of Santa Clara Recreation Department to be a recreation leader at one of their elementary schools. The city offered recreation programs for kids every weekday during the summer. My job was to coordinate visits to my school by the music, art, and crafts teachers, and to organize sporting activities and games for the kids to play. I enjoyed the work, and it paid well enough to enable me to save a few hundred dollars to pay for room and board, books and supplies at Stanford in the fall.

1968-1969, My First Year at Stanford

In 1968, tuition at Stanford was $1,770. The cost to live and eat in one of the dormitories was $1500. Since the tuition fee was waived, my only big financial worry was the cost of living in a dorm and books and supplies. I decided to try to not work part-time during the school year. I wanted to spend as much time as possible on coursework and the inevitable distractions of being a college student. I applied for a dorm room and was assigned to Toyon Hall, a beautiful, historic dormitory originally built in 1923 in the Romanesque and Mediterranean revival architectural styles. Next door to Toyon Hall was an L-shaped building that housed five eating clubs where residents of Toyon Hall ate their meals. Also, students who lived off campus could join one of the clubs and pay to eat their meals there. Toyon Hall residents got to choose which eating club they wanted to join. I joined Los Arcos. I ate meals there for two years, and met many great fellow students who became good friends. About 2015, the eating club building was torn down to make room for a residence hall for the business school. I was surprised the eating club building lasted as long as it did. It was an old unattractive building of simple wood construction. I always thought it was a fire hazard. It was clearly blocking the path of planned campus expansion. But I was sad to see it go. Toyon residents and students residing off campus now eat their meals at other dining halls on campus.

For the first time in my life, I was living away from home. Like most people going through that experience, I felt liberated and happy. I had two roommates in Toyon Hall. We got along okay, but neither of them became good friends. One roommate was a physics major named Pierre. About eight weeks into the academic year Pierre had some sort of a mental breakdown. For about ten days he sat on the floor of our room not speaking to anyone nor responding when someone spoke to him. He must have somehow eaten food while I was attending classes, but I never saw him eat. Eventually, he snapped out of it and returned to life, a somewhat quieter, more troubled version of himself. I took Pierre's collapse as a warning to me. I vowed to make sure my Stanford experience included time and opportunities to relax, enjoy fun times, and release pressure that might build up due to course assignments and exams. My friends at Los Arcos helped with this enormously. Some of my best friends included David Myers and Roy Woolsey. We went on weekend trips to the mountains, where I learned to ski. I played on the club's softball team. Dave and I played golf together on Stanford's magnificent golf course. The daily conversations over meals were fun and filled with laughter. I also continued going to Mass every Sunday at St. Thomas Aquinas Church in Palo Alto and started becoming friendly with one of the priests, Father John Duryea. I never felt depressed at Stanford.

At the beginning of the 1968 fall quarter I declared my academic major to be sociology. I identified the courses I still had to take in order to meet the university's requirements for obtaining an undergraduate degree, required core courses for my sociology major, additional "foundation" courses for my major, and elective courses I might like to take. During the 1968-69 academic year I took courses in economics, anthropology, introduction to social theory, foundations of social research, small groups research, organizational theory, and psychology. I went to all the home football games, Sunday night movies in Memorial Auditorium, and parties organized by Los Arcos and Toyon Hall. I also volunteered in a Stanford-organized program to tutor disadvantaged students in local high schools. I tutored a Latina high school student who was having trouble in her chemistry class. She was flunking chemistry. We met twice a week for two months. I remember some of what I learned from the chemistry class I took at West Valley College. But the most important way I helped her was to teach her how to learn: how to read a textbook, what to do when she didn't understand something, how to learn something well enough that you can teach it to someone else. She was so proud of herself, and rightly so, when she got an "A" grade at the end of her semester. I discovered I liked being a teacher.

I quickly learned that the Stanford Sociology Department strongly emphasized sociological theory. All of my courses taught the theories or conceptual frameworks used by researchers to study behaviors in groups, organizations, communities, or larger social structures. Several of the department's senior faculty members (Joseph Berger, Bernard Cohen, and Morris Zelditch, Jr.) were working in the sociological subfield of group behavior. They collaborated on a program of research to develop and test a set of ideas called expectation states theory. This theory is an approach to understanding how people evaluate other people's competence in small groups and the amount of credibility and influence they give them as a result. Central to the theory is the idea that we evaluate people on two criteria: the specific skills and abilities they have related to the task at hand, such as prior experience and training; and their status characteristics such as gender, age, race, education, and physical attractiveness. People's evaluations of others based on these characteristics are predicted to form the basis for the social hierarches that form in small, task oriented groups. So, the assumptions we make about people – especially those we do not know very well or with whom we have limited experience – are largely based on social cues that are often guided by the stereotypes of race, gender, age, class, and looks. Because this happens, people who are already privileged in society in terms of social status end up being favorably assessed within small groups, and those who experience disadvantages due to these characteristics will be negatively assessed. Eventually this set of ideas would be expanded to apply to social assessments outside of small work groups. These ideas helped me to at least partially understand the social structures I observed in everyday life and the efforts by so many disadvantaged and oppressed groups to make more visible the pernicious nature of the origins of those social structures and to organize social movements to break them down. I wanted to learn more about expectation states theory, and I took a number of related courses. It was exhilarating to learn about these ideas and to read about the research studies that tested whether the hypotheses derived from the theory were empirically supported. I thought this work was interesting and helped me understand aspects of social life that were troubling to me, and it was fun to use my mind in this way.

Unfortunately, I had been only able to save enough money from my summer job to afford living in Toyon Hall for two of the three academic quarters. At the end of the winter quarter, I had to move out. I was out of money. In April 1969, I commuted from my parents' home to Stanford for a couple of weeks. But, that made life too difficult. Through Stanford's financial aid office I applied for a National Defense Education Act (NDEA) student loan. At first, the loan officer told me that I should ask my parents for the money I needed. After I firmly told her that Mom and Dad didn't have any money to give me, she approved a loan for $1,700. The loan saved me. I rented a room in a large house in Palo Alto, close to campus. I still took my meals at Los Arcos, studied in the Undergraduate Library (affectionately called UGLY), and went to my rented room only to sleep. This worked pretty well. I found I could concentrate on my studies in spite of living off campus. NDEA loans had generous repayment terms. Payments were suspended as long I was in school or serving as a VISTA volunteer. Also, if I became a teacher 10 percent of the loan was forgiven for each of the first five years I taught. I started repaying this loan in 1981, and only had to repay half of the original amount. It was an amazingly good deal for me.

The Vietnam War

The anti-Vietnam War movement was a constant part of life and learning at Stanford, and it clearly affected my personal growth. Opposition to the war at Stanford began in the mid-1960s, but the intensity of the anti-war movement increased greatly while I was a student. The Vietnam War was a long, costly war that pitted the government of North Vietnam against South Vietnam, and eventually South Vietnam's ally the United States. Vietnam had been under

French colonial rule since the 19th century. During World War II, Japanese forces invaded Vietnam. To fight off the Japanese occupiers and the French colonial administration, political leader Ho Chi Minh, inspired by Chinese and Soviet communism, created a strong opposition force to regain Vietnamese control of their country. After the Japanese surrender, Ho's Viet Minh forces immediately rose up, taking over the northern city of Hanoi and declaring a Democratic Republic of Viet Nam (DRV) with Ho as president. Seeking to regain control of the region, France backed French-educated Emperor Bao Dai in the south and set up the state of Vietnam in July 1949, with the city of Saigon as its capital. Up to a point, both sides wanted the same thing, a unified Vietnam. But while Ho and his supporters wanted a nation modeled after other communist countries, Bao and his supporters wanted a Vietnam with close economic and cultural ties to the west. Bao was a corrupt, ruthless leader, who was eventually assassinated by his own army officers. But South Vietnam forces continued to engage the North's Viet Cong. The war was intensified by the on-going cold war between the United States and the Soviet Union. In the U.S. the foreign policy goal of supporting Bao Dai and his successors was to "contain" communism in North Vietnam. The prevailing thought in political and military circles in the U.S. was the "domino theory," which held that if one Southeast Asian country fell to communism, many other countries would follow. Through manipulative and dishonest reports falsely claiming that U.S. Navy ships had been attacked by North Vietnamese forces, President Lyndon Johnson got the U.S. Congress to approve the Gulf of Tonkin Resolution, which gave Johnson broad war-making powers. Bombing by U.S. forces and a land war with the North Vietnamese army began shortly thereafter. More than 3 million people (including over 58,000 Americans) were killed in the Vietnam War, and more than half the dead were Vietnamese civilians. Opposition to the war bitterly divided Americans, even after President Richard Nixon ordered phased withdrawal of U.S. forces in 1973. Communist forces ended the war by seizing control of South Vietnam in 1975, and the country was unified as the Socialist Republic of Vietnam.

In the late 1960s I was increasingly troubled by what I learned about the war, and the deadly reality of the war struck home to me

Off To A Good Start

as I sat in my parents' house one December day in 1967 and read the newspaper article reporting that Carl Edward Albert, a friend I called Eddie since the sixth grade, was killed in Vietnam. He was killed just 18 months after graduating from high school. Why was Eddie killed? What was the purpose being served by his death? Were the purpose and the means South Vietnam and the U.S. were using to achieve that purpose moral? Were the stories I read about atrocities being committed against civilians true? Why did the fact that I was in college qualify me for a draft deferment? I had a lot of serious questions about the war. Over the next two years, as I learned more about the Vietnam War and the means being used to fight it, I concluded that the war was neither legitimate nor moral. The U.S. government, which had been widely trusted by its citizens throughout the 1950s, had become committed to an immoral war and was routinely lying to its people about it. This dishonesty destroyed many Americans' confidence and faith in their government, an effect of the war that persists to this day. Eventually, l decided that I would not allow myself to be drafted into the Army to support the war.

The Summer of 1969

During the summer of 1969 I again lived at my parents' house on Weston Dr. It was great to be with Mom, Dad, Cathy, Sue and Wayne again. But I had grown and changed in ways that even I didn't fully understand. My Stanford experiences, normal teenage psychological growth, and the Vietnam War were affecting my personality and my values. I felt a little awkward, a bit like a stranger to them. But I also understood how generous and loving they were being. Given how small the house was, I felt their willingness to have me fill up a bedroom again was terrifically supportive. I ate most of my meals at home. Mom and Dad also continued to let me use their "second" car. I think they were proud of what their son was doing, and they helped me in the ways they could.

That summer I was hired as a physical therapy aide at the Kaiser Medical Center in Santa Clara. The job paid well, enabling me to save a lot of money for Stanford expenses the following year. I also got to learn what work as a physical therapist involved. Being a physical therapist was of interest to me since high school when I underwent physical therapy for my knee. Working as an aid in the Physical Medicine Department (which included physical therapy) clarified my feelings about possibly becoming a physical therapist. While the work clearly helped people, which was intrinsically rewarding, I also observed that the daily routine of a therapist involved a lot of repetitive tasks: putting heat pads or ice packs on patients' injured body parts, using ultrasound to treat patients, setting up whirlpool baths, assisting patients as they exercised. Each patient's doctor ordered the specific therapy to be applied, somewhat like an order sent to a pharmacy for a prescription drug. Therapists had very little ability to modify the physician's order. I suspected there were other settings in which the work of the therapist would have been more varied and challenging. But from what I saw in this department, I concluded that I would not be happy working as a physical therapist. I thought it was a little boring. I started thinking about what other kind of work would make me happy and productive.

1969-1970, My Second Year at Stanford

I returned to Stanford in the fall of 1969 for my second undergraduate year. I had saved enough money during the summer so that, when combined with the money available from my NDEA loan, I was just able to pay for my room and board costs for the entire academic year. I was reassigned to my old room in Toyon Hall. My roommates were David Ortmeyer and David Damassa. We had instant camaraderie and became good friends. Dave Ortmeyer taught me the basics of playing the guitar. I was enjoying the college experience I had always heard about, living in a dorm with two great roommates, with lots of studying, football games, and social events. But the experience was being overshadowed by the protests, marches, and violence in opposition to the Vietnam War.

To earn a little extra money, I applied to be a research assistant at the Social Research Laboratory in the Sociology Department. I was hired to work on a study that Professor Bernard Cohen (whom everyone called Bernie) was doing that tested some of the hypotheses derived from expectation states theory. Bernie hired me, and I spent most of the academic year recruiting high school students to participate in the study, organizing and scheduling the small group meetings that were required for the manipulation of the individuals' expectations of others in the group, and doing data compilation and analyses. These studies involved what at the time was state-of-the-art electronic technology that allowed us to provide video images and communication among the group members. The work was fun, and I continued to be interested in the ideas within the theory.

In late 1969, the U.S. government announced that it was no longer allowing draft deferments for being enrolled in college. Even though this change exposed me to the risk of being drafted, I thought this was the correct policy. On December 1, 1969, the government instituted the first draft lottery since World War II, and broadcast it live over radio and television. Based on his birthday, every draft-eligible man would be randomly assigned a number. The Army would proceed to draft men starting with those assigned number 1. They would continue drafting men until they reached the quota set for that year. To assign the random numbers, the 366 days of the year (including February 29) were printed on slips of paper. These pieces of paper were then each placed in an opaque plastic capsule, which were then mixed and dumped in a glass jar. Capsules were drawn from the jar one at a time and opened. The first date drawn was September 14 so all registrants with that birthday were assigned lottery number 1. The process continued until all 366 numbers had been drawn and assigned a draft number. After each birthdate was drawn, I could hear men moaning and screaming from within Toyon Hall and nearby dormitories. It was an awful night. My birthday of September 13 was drawn as the 175th capsule, so my draft number was 175. Over the next few days there was much speculation among my friends about how high into the numbers the Army would have to go before their draft quota for 1969-1970 was filled. My guess was that I was not safe. It turned out that the highest number called for induction was 195. Although it did not happen until well into 1970, I got drafted.

During 1969 and 1970 I continued my studies in sociology and working part-time for Bernie Cohen. Bernie and I got along well. I was reliable and thoughtful in my small groups research work. I enjoyed doing this type of research. I earned a solid "A" in his famous course on research methodology. We liked working together. In 1969, I decided that I loved academic life, and I wanted to go to graduate school and study for a doctor of philosophy degree in sociology. I investigated several departments in universities around the country, and I applied to four of them. One day I was discussing the alternatives with Bernie, and he asked me if I had applied to Stanford. I was a little surprised by the question. I said no. He suggested I apply, saying something like "you are competitive for admission." So I applied. On March 11, 1970, I received a letter from Lincoln Moses, Dean of the Graduate Division, saying he was happy to inform me that the Committee on Admissions had admitted me for graduate study in the Department of Sociology. I'm sure Bernie's support helped me get admitted. On April 1, 1970, I received a letter from Professor Paul Wallin, Chair of the Sociology Department's Admissions and Fellowships Committee offering me a Graduate Fellowship for the 1970-1971 academic year in the amount of $2,000 plus full tuition. Saying a little prayer of gratitude, I immediately accepted admission and the fellowship.

On May 13, 1970, Cathy married Craig Goodell, They had one child, Carla Marie. Of course, Cathy moved out of Mom and Dad's house, leaving only Sue and Wayne at home. Years later, Cathy would marry a second time to Mark Merrill. Cathy and Mark would have a son, Patrick.

Graduation Day

Stanford's graduation ceremony for the class of 1970 was held on Sunday, June 14, in Laurence Frost Amphitheater. My whole family came to see me graduate. I was happy and proud beyond words that I was graduating from this great university, the first person in my family to graduate from college. During the awarding of degrees, some students introduced a little whimsy into the proceeding. One student walked up to receive his degree dressed as Captain America, complete with red, white, and blue tights and shirt, and a garbage can lid as a shield. The Vietnam War was never far from anyone's mind. Some students raised signs of protest. The most direct and impressive attack on the war was delivered by our graduation speaker, U.S. Senator Charles Percy. Percy was a Republican from Illinois, and the father of one of the graduating students, Roger Percy, who was a friend of mine. In one part of his speech against the war Senator Percy called for redirecting "ourselves to bringing an end to American involvement in Indochina. We must have the grace and the fortitude to admit now that this war was a tragic error without military or moral justification." I joined thousands of students and guests in giving Percy a standing ovation.

When it was my turn, I walked up to the stage and was handed my diploma by President Kenneth Pitzer. Afterwards I gathered with my family and took a few pictures with them and some of my best college friends. It was a beautiful, sunny June day, and I was filled with pride and satisfaction in what I had accomplished. I still had not received a draft notice. The Army had not yet reached my draft number of 175. I had a summer job nailed down working at SRI (Stanford Research Institute) on an evaluation of the Federal Government's educational program called Follow Through. I would start my doctoral courses in the fall. I took a few moments to savor what had happened. I reflected on how I got here. A boy who grew up on a dirt road on the outskirts of Yuma, who had anxiety about his future while living in Campbell, was now a man who had just graduated from Stanford University believing he had a very bright future indeed.

1970-1971, My First Year as a Graduate Student

When I returned to Stanford in the fall of 1970, Roy Woolsey, a friend I had met in the Los Arcos eating club, managed to get me invited to live in the dormitory where he lived, Eucalipto House in historic Lagunita Court. The theme of Eucalipto House was "international," and it combined undergraduate with graduate students, and students from the U.S. with those from many countries around the world. Lagunita Court was a beautiful complex of buildings built with Mediterranean-inspired architecture around a tree and flower filled courtyard. The street on which Lagunita Court was located, Santa Teresa Street, came to a dead end about one hundred yards past the dormitory. There was little automobile traffic. Across this quiet street was a swimming pool. Next to the pool were a volleyball court and a large grass-covered field that was perfect for playing Frisbee or throwing a football around. Behind the field were six tennis courts. Inside Lagunita Court, there were lounges where students could hang out and talk with each other. The dining room was large and elegant. For breakfast and lunch we got our food cafeteria style. But there was seated service for dinner, and on Sunday nights we ate dinner by candlelight. Sometimes after dinner one of the students would start playing the grand piano that was in a corner of the dining room. To top it all off, I had a "single" bedroom: no roommates. To me, this was the height of luxury.

I loved living in Lagunita Court. I made many friends there. In addition to Roy Woolsey, my friends included Mary Hewlett; Walter Hewlett and Esther Ball (who would later marry); Inder Sud and Peg Duff (who would also marry); Ian Smith; Jed Hepworth and Lee Schubert (also to marry); Gursharan Sidhu who married another resident, Elvira; Heather Hudson; Elaine Tennant; Ron Levine; Mel Malinowski; Suzy Argenti (our house mother); and Rob Creighton who became my tennis teacher, fellow adventure seeker, and best friend. For some reason Rob started calling me "Tommy R," and it stuck. I've stayed in touch with my friends from Lagunita Court, and to this day they all call me Tommy R.

Another great aspect of Lagunita Court was that it was located just a block from the Stanford Press where my dad worked. Dad was still working the late afternoon/night shift. After dinner, I would often go to the door near the room where the linotype machines were located and pound on the door. I had to pound the door because it was noisy inside and Dad was hard of hearing. He would eventually hear the pounding and come out to see me. We would just chat a while. I would tell him how school was going for me. He would tell me any family news. Then Dad would go back to work. I loved those chats. I think they brought us closer together.

In early December of 1970 I received a Christmas card with a letter from Grandfather Earl Rundall, whom all the family called Gramp. After his wife Edna died, Gramp lived alone in Anaheim for several years, but in the early 1960s he moved into Aunt Wilma's apartment at 2306 #2 Union St. in San Francisco. He and Wilma routinely came to our house in Campbell for holidays, and we made trips to visit them. When I was 15 years old, I spent a week during the summer living with them, which I thought was a great adventure. Gramp was a wonderful man, kind and supportive, and I loved him very much. In his Christmas letter Gramp said he would not be able to come to Campbell for Christmas because he was in poor health, and he asked that none of his grandchildren buy him Christmas presents. He was excited about Jim Plunkett and the Stanford football team playing Ohio State in the Rose Bowl, and he predicted Stanford would win 21-14 (he was close, Stanford won 27-17). He wished me a merry Christmas. Sadly, in January Gramp had to go into a nursing home. I visited him there, and we had a nice long talk. I promised to come back soon. That was the last time I saw him. Gramp died of congestive heart failure on January 21, 1971. He is buried next to his wife, Edna, at Melrose Abbey Memorial Park and Mortuary in Anaheim, California. Rest in peace, Gramp.

One night in April 1971, Walter, Rob and I were sharing a pitcher of beer at our favorite bar/restaurant, the Oasis (no longer in existence). Walter, who had run cross-country when he was an undergraduate at Harvard, told us about the upcoming second annual Golden Gate Marathon, to be held on Saturday, May 29. I had never run a race of any sort in my life. It's amazing what a little alcohol can do to one's judgment. Walter, Rob and I told each other we were going to run that marathon. We started training. Both Walter and Rob had to stop because of injuries. I was determined to run the race, and could be seen running all over campus trying to get in shape. The marathon course started at Paradise Beach in Tiburon, wound its way through Mill Valley, and then down through Sausalito, up the impossibly steep grade from Sausalito to the Golden Gate Bridge, then down past Chrissy Field to the finish line at the Marina Greens. I started off strong, and for the first ten miles I was doing well. Rob and Roy were my support team, giving me water and encouragement at various spots along the way. I've been told that most normal humans who run a marathon hit a "wall" at the twenty-mile mark. The twenty-mile mark for this marathon was at the steep grade from Sausalito up to the Golden Gate Bridge. As I slowly jogged up this grade I saw dozens of runners on their backs with their feet up in the air. They had hit a very solid wall. I managed to continue, but I admit I walked about half the length of the Bridge. Once across the Bridge, the course was generally downhill or flat. I arrived at the finish line completely exhausted, but I made sure to sprint the last 100 yards for effect. It took me four hours and thirty minutes to run the marathon, but I was very happy that I did it. It was the only marathon I ever ran. There was never to be a third annual Golden Gate Marathon. There were too many complaints about the difficulty of the course, and the event was never held again.

My doctoral courses in the 1970-71 academic year included advanced courses in sociological theory, social stratification, qualitative research methods, and multivariable statistical analysis. All was going well until one fall day when I received a letter notifying me that I was drafted into the Army.

Becoming a Conscientious Objector

Starting in 1968, I was a committed antiwar activist, going to teach-ins and marching against the war. I thought the immorality of the war was going from bad to worse. The last straw for me was the U.S. massacre at My Lai, where in March 1968 U.S. forces murdered about 500 Vietnamese unarmed civilians. Victims included men, women, children, and infants. The massacre happened amid a campaign of U.S. search-and-destroy operations that were intended to find enemy territories, destroy them, and then retreat. When my draft letter arrived, I was faced with the decision of whether to fight being drafted into the Army. I was concerned that if I did resist being drafted my parents would believe I was bringing shame upon the family. After some deep thought and reflection, I decided to start the process of being considered a conscientious objector (CO), which would allow me to perform alternative service instead of going into the Army. But before I could be considered for CO status, I had to get an Army physical, which I passed with flying colors. The only test I ever felt sorry I aced.

For my application for CO status I had to write an essay explaining and justifying my moral objections to serving in the Army and in Vietnam. I was a practicing Catholic. I wrote an essay based on Saint Thomas Aquinas' 13th century Just War Theory. His argument was that to be considered a just war, a given war needed to satisfy three criteria: the war needed to be waged by a legitimate authority, have a just cause, and have the right intentions. I argued that the Vietnam War, especially at the time I was drafted, failed to meet all three of these criteria. I had to have letters of support. Father

Off To A Good Start

John Duryea, a priest at the Catholic Church in Palo Alto, and the Chair of the Sociology Department, Sanford Dornbusch, each wrote a letter confirming the sincerity of my beliefs. These materials were considered acceptable by the local draft board, and I was asked to go through an interview with a three-person panel that would challenge my arguments and beliefs. In the spring of 1971 I traveled to San Jose and went through the interview, answering each question calmly and with confidence. A few weeks later, I got a letter officially assigning me conscientious objector status. I had to quickly identify what alternative service I was going to propose. One of the acceptable options was to join Volunteers in Service to America (VISTA). VISTA was known as the domestic Peace Corps. Volunteers were assigned to qualified projects designed to improve living conditions for people residing in low-income communities. I chose to join VISTA and completed the necessary paper work. Since I was already in the spring quarter of my academic year, I was allowed to finish the quarter before beginning my alternative service.

As the spring quarter was winding down, I received a letter from the Chair of the Sociology Department, Morris (Buzz) Zelditch, Jr., notifying me that the faculty had approved a leave of absence in order for me to complete my two years of alternative service. I would be re-admitted in good standing if I chose to return to the department.

Also in the spring I received a post card from VISTA informing me that I had been selected to serve for the next two years on a project sponsored by Child and Family Services in Waianae, Hawaii. I was shocked. I didn't believe this was true. I had never heard of Waianae, but if it was in Hawaii I had just become one of the luckiest people on earth. I looked up Waianae. It was a small community consisting mostly of families of Hawaiian and Samoan heritage on the west coast of Oahu, about 31 miles from Honolulu. Was this some kind of a joke? Was I somehow misreading the rather cryptic way the information was conveyed on the card? To find out, I called the VISTA office and asked them to confirm that I had been assigned to this project in Waianae. The person I spoke to checked some files and said that was correct. It was true. I was going to Hawaii!

Toyon Hall, my dormitory during my first two years at Stanford University

Lagunita Court, my dormitory during the 1970-71 academic year

The 1970 Los Arcos Eating Club softball team;
I'm on the lower left

Running the Golden Gate Marathon in 1971,
Rob Creighton and Roy Woolsey as support team

During my senior year at Stanford, 1970

Off To A Good Start

Graduation day picture with my friend Mary Ann Tracy,
June 14, 1970

5

Two Years as a VISTA Volunteer

At the outset of this chapter I note that there is some confusion in both the public and private spheres about how to spell Hawaiian words. Until the 19th century, Hawaiians had no written language. In 1820, American missionaries arrived and soon formulated a written language based on the sounds they heard. The Hawaiian alphabet was adapted from the English alphabet. It contains five vowels and seven consonants: A, E, I, O, U, H, K, L, M, N, P, W. Due to words with different meanings being spelled alike, use of the `okina (`), a glottal stop, became necessary. Similarly, the macron, or kahakō, was used to mark heavy syllables (e.g. Mākaha). Hawaiians quickly learned the written form of their language following the introduction of printed bibles, grammars, and other textbooks. However, as Hawaii became increasingly Americanized, the use of Hawaiian spellings with the `okina and the kahakō was discouraged. Up until 1978, almost everyone used English spellings of Hawaiian names. But in that year, the State Legislature modified the Constitution of the State of Hawaii to add Hawaiian as a second official state language. Both Hawaiian and Standard English spellings are proper and legal. For example, in various government and private sector documents, one can find Hawaii or Hawai`i, Lahaina or Lāhainā. The English spelling of Hawaiian (which is an explicitly English word for which no `okina is used) place names is generally acceptable. But I think the Hawaiian spellings reflect more respect for the Hawaiian culture and the struggle Hawaiians have experienced as their land and culture have largely been taken over by Americans. In the following pages, I predominantly use Hawaiian spellings of people and place names.

The Beginning of My Time in Hawai`i

The Child and Family Services social work organization in Honolulu had requested VISTA volunteers with backgrounds in social science and teaching to help the organization's staff establish two group homes for troubled teenagers on the Wai'anae Coast and in another community, Waimanalo, on the other side of Oahu. In addition to me, VISTA assigned Jon and Bonnie McCluskey, a married couple from Wisconsin, Steve Rickard from California, and Bob Ozaki from Honolulu to work on these projects. Jon, Bonnie, Steve and I would work in Wai'anae. Bob would work with some other local volunteers in Waimanalo, which was behind the Wai'anae project in its planning.

In July 1971 we gathered at San Francisco State University for about two weeks of training. We learned all about VISTA, what it meant to be a VISTA volunteer, what the bureaucratic rules were, and we went through a lot of simulated work situations to strengthen our problem management and interpersonal communication skills. We also learned how to do a community needs assessment. A few days before we left for Honolulu, Bob knocked on my room door. It was ten o'clock at night. He said, "You want to go to the Doggie Diner for a hot dog?" Of course, I said yes. We ate hot dogs and talked late into the night. It was the beginning of a life-long friendship.

When we completed our training, we boarded a United Airlines plane and flew to Honolulu. As our plane approached the Honolulu airport we flew past Perl Harbor, and I thought of my Dad and Uncle Wayne spending time there while they were in the Navy during World War II. I couldn't help but note the irony of another Rundall coming to Honolulu as a conscientious objector. Upon arrival, the soft, warm air and breathtakingly beautiful joining of land and sea along Oahu's coast was magical. I think l was besotted with Hawaii at that moment, and I have loved the islands ever since. John, Bonnie, Steve, and I were taken to Wai'anae. Bob went home to his wife, Bonnie, and his children Becky and Holly. He would soon be working in Waimanalo, and we would see each other frequently in the coming months.

The Director of the VISTA program in Hawai'i at the time we arrived was a woman named Marti Polen, a former VISTA volunteer who grew up in St. Louis. Marti was actually the Interim Director, and shortly after we arrived, Mike Gale, who had been a Peace Corps volunteer and had worked for many years in government service programs, arrived to take on the director role. We also met Patti

Lyons, a social worker who worked for our project's sponsor, Child and Family Services. All three of these people were committed and very good at their jobs. I enjoyed working with them.

Learning about Wai`anae and Hawai`i

The Wai`anae Coast is about 13 miles long, stretching from Barber's Point to Kaena Point on the leeward side of Oahu. Wai`anae is the largest town on the coast with a population of about 13,000 people. Others include Nānākuli and Mākaha, where the famous surfing beach is located. The towns are squeezed between the ocean and the Wai`anae Mountain Range. The Farrington Highway, the coast's main road, connects the towns. The highway ends before Kaena Point, so there is no thru-traffic on the Wai`anae Coast. Most residents feel somewhat isolated from the rest of Oahu. The people who live on the coast are mostly Hawaiian and Samoan families with strong ties to their ethnic cultures. The families are typically large and live in simple wood constructed homes. The weather is spectacular, warm and dry. With beautiful beaches, majestic valleys, and abundant marine life, one might think the Wai`anae Coast would be a favorite spot for tourists. But in 1971 tourists rarely visited the Coast, partly because to many visitors it appeared remote and uninviting. Some residents did not welcome tourists. Also, many of the residents were unemployed and lived in or near poverty. Many tourists felt uncomfortable vacationing in the midst of such an economically depressed area.

As part of our training and preparation for work, we four Wai`anae VISTA volunteers were required to live with a local family for two weeks. Steve and I lived with a Hawaiian family in Nānākuli, and Jon and Bonnie lived with a Samoan family in Wai`anae. Steve and I shared a bedroom and ate meals with our host family. We asked them many questions about their lives and the opportunities and challenges they encountered living on the Wai`anae Coast to understand what their day-to-day life was like and to listen to what they wanted to tell us.

Our work preparation also included doing a community assessment to identify the resources available in the community to help children in difficult family circumstances and what services the community needed. We met with anyone who would agree to talk with us: parents, teachers, church leaders, storeowners, drug rehabilitation workers, physical and mental health providers, and others. The most important thing we learned was that the present circumstances on the Wai'anae Coast were closely linked to Hawaii's history. The story of the settlement of Hawai'i and its religious, social, political, and economic development is long and filled with drama. Here is a brief summary of some important history we learned as we started our VISTA work.

The Hawaiian Islands were first settled around 400 C.E. when Polynesians from the Marquesas Islands, 2000 miles away, traveled to Hawai'i's Big Island (which is officially named the Island of Hawai'i) in canoes. They were highly skilled farmers and fishermen, and in time populated small communities ruled by chieftains who battled one another for territory.

The first European to set foot on Hawai'i was Captain James Cook, who landed on the island of Kauai in 1778. Cook would return a year later and was killed in a confrontation over a small boat with Hawaiians at Kealakekua Bay, on the Big Island. In 1795, King Kamehameha's army united Oahu under his rule. The fierce battle claimed hundreds of Oahu men who were defending their island, many of whom were driven up a valley and forced over what is now called the Pali Lookout, a sheer drop of over 1,000 feet. By 1810, Kamehameha conquered all other rulers and united the islands into one kingdom. It has always been odd to me how often brutal, conquering military leaders become revered in the land they conquered. King Kamehameha died in 1819 and is still celebrated today with a large statue in downtown Honolulu and floral parades every June 11, King Kamehameha Day.

The first Americans in Hawai'i were early 18th century traders who came to exploit the islands' sandalwood, which was very much valued in China at the time. In the 1830s, cane sugar was planted in Hawai'i, and the sugar industry became a major part of the economy. Many American planters and missionaries had arrived in Hawai'i by the mid-19th century, and they brought about great changes in Hawaiian political, cultural, economic, and religious life. In 1840 a constitutional monarchy was established, stripping the Hawaiian monarch of much of his authority. During the next forty years, Hawai'i entered into a number of political and economic treaties with the United States, and in 1887 a U.S. naval base was established at Pearl Harbor as part of a new Hawaiian constitution. Sugar exports to the United States expanded greatly in the 1880s, and U.S. investors and American sugar cane planters on the islands broadened their control over Hawaiian affairs.

However, in 1891 Lili'uokalani, the sister of the late King Kalākaua, ascended to the throne, and refused to recognize the constitution of 1887. She replaced it with a new constitution increasing her personal authority. In January 1893, a revolutionary "Committee of Safety," organized by Sanford B. Dole, the son of an American Protestant missionary, staged a coup against Queen Lili'uokalani with the tacit support of the United States. On February 1, 1893, U.S. Federal Minister John Stevens recognized Dole's new government on his own authority and proclaimed Hawai'i a U.S. protectorate. Dole then submitted a treaty of annexation to the U.S. Senate, but most senators opposed the annexation, especially after it was revealed that most Hawaiians didn't want annexation. President Grover Cleveland sent a new U.S. minister to Hawai'i to restore Queen Lili'uokalani to the throne under the 1887 constitution, but Dole refused to step aside. Queen Lili'uokalani was deposed, placed under house arrest, and forced to abdicate the throne. Dole convened a constitutional convention, and on July 4, 1894 the Republic of Hawai'i was declared with Dole as president. President Cleveland was unwilling to overthrow the government by force, and his successor, President William McKinley, negotiated a treaty with the Republic of Hawai'i in 1897. In 1898, the Spanish-American War broke out, and the strategic use of the naval base at Peal Harbor during the war convinced Congress to approve formal annexation. Two years later, Hawai'i was organized into a formal U.S. territory and in 1959 entered the United States as the 50th state.

Queen Lili'uokalani, the last Hawaiian ruler, was a truly remarkable woman. She did all she could to safeguard Hawaiians as American political and military forces took over. In 1909, the Queen created the Queen Lili'uokalani Trust into which she placed several thousand acres of land that she owned. The financial proceeds from these lands were (and still are) used to provide for orphan and destitute children in the Hawaiian Islands, with a preference for Native Hawaiian children. Queen Lili'uokalani was also a brilliant songwriter. She was the composer of over 150 songs, including "Aloha 'Oe," Hawai'i's signature song and one of the most beautiful melodies ever written. She is a Hawaiian heroine. Many times I have visited Honolulu's Iolani Palace, where the Queen lived during her reign and where she was held captive after the coup. It has been fully restored and is an emotionally stirring reminder of the dark role Americans played in Hawai'i in the late 19th century.

The Queen Lili'uokalani Trust is an important part of Hawai'i's educational and social service system for children. The motto of the Trust is "Thriving Hawaiian Children," and its mission statement is, "We believe in the resiliency of our Hawaiian Children. We advocate for their well being and build them pathways to thriving lives." The trust serves about 10,000 children annually through direct services and reaches thousands more through collaborations with community partners. In 2002, after holding executive positions at The Queen's Health System and at Amfac, Inc., Bob Ozaki was appointed the President and CEO of the Lili'uokalani Trust (LT). He is a beloved leader of the Trust. In 2021, Bob will leave his position as President and CEO and join the Trust's Board of Trustees. About Bob's contributions to the Trust, Claire Asam, Chair of the Board of Trustees, said, "Mr. Ozaki has successfully orchestrated the transformation of LT in both financial and program areas through a culture of innovation and excellence, positioning LT to achieve significant outcomes and transform the lives of our most vulnerable Hawaiian children." Congratulations Bob, and well done!

From 1850 to 1940, Hawai'i's economy was largely based on sugar cane and pineapple plantations and, to a lesser extent, cattle ranches. To tend the fields and ranches, Hawaiian business owners actively recruited laborers from China, Portugal, Spain, Japan, the Philippines, Korea, Puerto Rico, Samoa, and Okinawa. This immigration permanently changed the face of Hawai'i. In 1853, indigenous Hawaiians made up 97 percent of the islands' population. By 1923, their numbers had dwindled to 23 percent. In general Hawaiians did not do well during this period of growth through immigration, with many of the immigrants climbing the economic ladder and most native Hawaiians being left behind. However, native Hawaiians used many of the materials and goods immigrant groups brought with them and brilliantly adapted them to fit with Hawaiian culture and traditions. One notable example is the Hawaiian quilt, similar to quilts missionaries brought with them but using beautiful images of native flowers and plants as decoration. Jane and I have several Hawaiian quilts, including one particularly beautiful one that covers our bed every day. Another example is Hawaiians' adaptation of the tuning of the guitar, brought by Portuguese and Spanish cowboys (paniolos), to suit Hawaiian traditional melodies. Hawaiians created new musical keys by slackening the guitar strings. Several different Hawaiian families created their own "slack key" guitar tuning. Combining the slack key tuning with traditional Hawaiian musical styles and melodies was a huge success. Slack key guitar music is the most beautiful music I have ever heard. Over many years Jane and I have followed the work of slack key guitarists and attended their concerts in Hawai'i and California. Some of our favorite performers are Gabby Pahinui and his son Cyril Pahinui, Dennis Kamakahi, Ledward Kaapana, George Kahumouku, Keolo Beamer, and Jerry Santos.

In 1920, the Hawaiian Homes Commission Act was enacted by the U.S. Congress to try to protect and improve the lives of native Hawaiians. The act created a Hawaiian Homes Commission to administer certain public lands, called Hawaiian home lands, for use as homesteads. Individuals having at least 50 percent Hawaiian blood could lease homesteads on Hawaiian home lands, to which they could receive 99-year leases, with annual lease rent of $1.00 per year. Many native Hawaiians moved to houses on Hawaiian homestead properties. In 1971, there were two parcels of such land on the Wai'anae Coast where about 2,400 native Hawaiians lived.

On December 7, 1941, more than 2,300 Americans were killed in the Japanese attack on U.S. military bases on Oahu, including the Naval base at Pearl Harbor. The USS Arizona was sunk and many other ships were damaged. The U.S. immediately entered World War II, and Hawai'i, particularly Oahu, became an essential base for launching military operations in the Pacific. By the time the war ended on September 2, 1945, many Army, Air Force, Marine, and Naval bases had been built or expanded on Oahu, an island roughly 25 x 40 miles in size. In the late 1940s and 1950s, thousands of men and women who served in the military on Oahu returned as civilians to live.

After the war, to a great extent the culture of the transplanted white mainlanders (or Haoles as they are known in Hawaiian) became dominant, gaining advantage through political activities and economic power. The U.S. military was still a major presence across Oahu, and many native Hawaiians worked for the military in various support roles, absorbing cultural beliefs that worked on military bases but not in Hawaiian homes and communities. The names of the streets were all Hawaiian words, but the government changed the street names to eliminate the kahakō and the ʻokina. Schools were forbidden to teach the Hawaiian language.

All of these changes, and the physical, psychological, and economic effects they wrought, were part of what we had to be sensitive to in our VISTA work. For example, in the early 1970s there was the beginning of a revival of slack key guitar playing and traditional Hawaiian music, as well as of the hula and many traditional Hawaiian crafts and activities. One of my friends on the Waiʻanae Coast, Millie Allen, was a leader of the hula revival movement. Native Hawaiians were also demanding their children be taught the Hawaiian language in public schools. These movements have created a lot of positive change in Hawaiʻi. Today, there are slack key guitar festivals that draw thousands of listeners. The hula is widely practiced and a part of all major events. The street signs have been changed back to correct Hawaiian spellings, including the kahakō and ʻokina. Hawaiian culture, history, and language are now taught in public schools. The revitalization of Hawaiian culture was largely a grass-roots movement to restore Hawaiian culture and language, and for Hawaiians to regain a prominent role in Hawaiian political, social, and economic life. Hawaiians wanted their culture and their state back. In 1971, the Waiʻanae Coast was one of the centers of this movement.

The Group Homes

Through her previous work over many years in Waiʻanae and other low-income communities on Oahu, Patti Lyons understood the challenges many families faced. She had great credibility with native Hawaiians, Samoans, and their community leaders. One of the needs often mentioned by local residents was help with their children during their teenage years. Many children ran away from home. Others committed crimes and were under court supervision. Working with the Wai'anae community, Patti and her colleagues at Child and Family Services developed a plan to acquire two homes large enough to house up to ten children each. One home would be for boys, the other for girls. The children would receive counseling, social support, and assistance in managing family-related problems. It was expected that most of the kids living in the homes would benefit from the break in their cycle of destructive behavior, gain life skills from the counseling they were provided, and return home. For a few, it was anticipated that the group home staff would help them find jobs or enter the military, becoming independent of their families. Just before our VISTA team arrived, two large homes had been acquired on Auyong Homestead Road in Nānākuli. In many cases local families would ask Patti Lyons if their child could stay at one of the homes. In other cases the family court referred children to the group homes.

After our training period, Steve and I were assigned a vehicle from the island's Federal General Services Administration (GSA) office. It was a panel truck, big enough to transport lots of people, furniture, equipment, and surfboards. We began helping with all the tasks required to set up and house children. We sought out and transported furniture, drove staff and kids to meetings in Wai'anae and Honolulu, organized outings for the kids, and held meetings with parents and politically powerful people on the coast to explain what the group homes were all about. Each home usually had eight to ten kids living in it, and we became friendly advisors/counselors to each of them. We often had to attend meetings at Child and Family Services in Honolulu. We also connected with other similar programs in other locations on Oahu and went to meetings with their staff to learn from their experience and learn what they knew about child development programs around the state that we might be able to use. We were quite busy with this work. This was in a time before computers, email, the Internet, and cell phones. All our communications with others were either in-person or over a land-line phone call. We all had pocket calendars to keep track of our appointments. On some days, we made multiple round trips between Wai'anae and Honolulu in order to attend meetings. I think I set the record with four such round trips in one day.

Steve was also a conscientious objector assigned by VISTA to this project. He was tall and good looking. Steve got a lot of attention from women in Hawai'i. He was smart and funny to be around. He also could establish rapport with anyone very quickly, which made him good at solving problems that might come up in the group homes. We both played the guitar and enjoyed playing and singing with friends in the evenings. We liked working together and quickly became best friends. Steve was also the luckiest person I ever met. For example, one time he drove our GSA truck to a local beach He put the keys to the truck in a pocket in his swimsuit. While he was swimming in the ocean he noticed that the keys had fallen out of his pocket. He had parked the truck on the beach at low tide. The tide was now coming in, threatening to wash the truck away. In a panic, Steve walked up and down the water line feeling with his feet for the keys in the sand. Miraculously he felt the keys, picked them up, and quickly drove the truck to safety. Only Steve could do something like this, and he did it all the time.

The group homes shared a counselor/psychologist named Mel Takahara. Mel was an immensely gifted man. He was not only a mental health counselor; he was an excellent pianist, a great chef, and a published poet. When it was time for Steve and me to move out of our host family's home, Mel joined us in looking for a home to rent. We rented a house in Wai'anae for several months, but later moved to a newer house in Mākaha. The three of us lived together for about eleven months, one of the most enjoyable periods of my life.

Each group home was under the daily supervision of house parents. Usually house parents were local married couples hired to live in the homes, cook meals, and provide the structured guidance, communication, and support that parents would provide. It was a difficult, often emotionally draining job. It required a special ability to connect with and help troubled adolescents. From the perspective of most community residents, it was best if the house parents were local Hawaiians or Samoans. Many house parents quit after a short period of time. Finding good house parents was frequently an issue.

Some friends on the coast recommended Jim Chiddix for the job. Jim was about 25 years old. He had gone to Cornell University and majored in electrical engineering. In the Army Jim taught electrical engineering to soldiers maintaining nuclear warhead missiles. He was now out of the Army and living on the coast. In partnership with an old friend, Bob Khlopin, he was taking care of and renting out to tourists a trimaran boat named the Seraphim, which was anchored in Pokai Bay in Wai'anae. Against his better judgment, Jim agreed to be a houseparent. I think we all knew he was not a good match for the position, but we were desperate. Jim didn't last long as a house parent. He knew very quickly he was not prepared for this type of work, and he was not really a member of the local community. But Jim would continue to live on the coast, and we became great friends.

In time Jim would turn his electrical engineering expertise to fixing television monitors for the local cable television company, Wai'anae Cablevision. That was a very modest beginning to a career that would transform the cable television industry. During his career, Jim led the development of many of the technologies that have shaped modern cable television services. He spent fifteen years as Chief Technology Officer and in other senior posts at Time Warner Cable, overseeing research and development, engineering, and construction activities. He pioneered the use of optical fiber technology in cable systems that enabled video on demand, DVR applications, and high speed Internet access through cable modems. In 1994, Jim accepted a Technical Emmy Award for his team's work improving the transmission of cable television. Jim is also one of the nicest people I have ever met. We have been good friends for nearly 50 years.

Adventures

Steve, Jim and I often enjoyed adventures together. One example of the good times and trouble we got into involved a December 1971 sailing trip on the Seraphim from Pokai Bay to Lāhainā on the island of Maui. One weekend Steve and I were invited to join Bob Khlopin and Jim on this sailing trip. Bob was a very experienced sailor. He and his wife Andrea were living on the coast with their two children and had sailed on the Seraphim many times. Our plan was to sail from Pokai Bay past Moloka`i Island to Lāhainā, a distance of 104 miles. We put our gear on the Seraphim and set sail, cruising past Honolulu at sundown. It was a beautiful sight. Then we started crossing the Moloka`i Channel, the water channel that separates Oahu from the island named Moloka`i. This channel is famous for its high winds and rough waves. We were beating into the wind and fighting the waves all night. It was a little like riding a roller coaster with speed bumps. We took turns at the wheel, and tried to sleep in shifts. I was anxious about whether the Seraphim could handle this brutal crossing. But I grew exhausted and eventually fell asleep. Suddenly, at dawn I and everyone else were rocked awake. The Seraphim had hit something. In the early morning hours Steve had taken his turn at the wheel, and as we reached the calm waters on the leeward side of Moloka`i he fell asleep. Currents brought the boat toward shore, and we hit an offshore shoal. The collision punched a hole in one of the Seraphim's hulls, and water was slowly pouring into the hull. This was a disaster. None of us owned this boat, and it was in some danger of sinking. We turned on the bilge pump and took turns swimming under the boat to paste a temporary patch on the hole. We then sailed to Lāhainā, where we bought marine supplies and put on a better patch. We were exhausted. I suggested we go to the Lāhainā Yacht Club, a members only club for sailors. I knew the club had a policy of allowing people sailing to Lāhainā from outside the State of Hawai`i to be given a temporary free membership, which allowed them to shower and buy meals. I explained to the man at the bar that we had just arrived from the Marquesas Islands and were exhausted from our tough crossing of the Moloka`i channel. It was the biggest lie I ever told, but it worked! We showered, ate, and returned to the boat excited to complete our trip.

The next morning we sailed to the Island of Lanai, and the following day set sail for home. But Moloka`i was trouble again. We stopped at a small harbor on Moloka`i for an hour or so. We returned to the Seraphim excited to now sail the Moloka`i Channel toward Honolulu downwind during daytime. We would reach a tremendous speed, and this time the roller coaster ride would be fun. As we pulled away from the dock, the clip holding the halyard to the mainsail somehow separated from the grommet on the mainsail and was immediately pulled up to the top of the boat's mast. The mainsail fell to the deck. Since we were now already being tossed about by wind and waves, no one was allowed to climb the mast to retrieve the halyard. All we had to catch wind was a small secondary sail and the tiny jib. Instead of flying across the Molokaʻi Channel, the Seraphim slowly limped along, with many people on other sailboats staring at this weird sight and no doubt wondering how we could have messed things up so badly. Perhaps because of this ill-fated adventure, Steve, Jim and I bonded even more strongly. We spent a lot of time together on other adventures on Oahu and the other islands.

Other trips with Steve, Jon, Bonnie, and Mel were also adventures, including two trips to the Big Island of Hawaiʻi to see the Kilauea volcano while it was active. The first time we watched from about a quarter of a mile away as Kilauea spew a fountain of lava about two hundred feet into the air. The second time was after the volcano had calmed down a bit. We walked up a designated path to join a park ranger at the edge of the volcano and looked down to see the molten lava bubbling about 250 feet below us. It was as if we were watching the origins of the earth. In fact, we were. Over the years that volcano added quite a bit of land to the Big Island. They don't let visitors look over the edge of the volcano any more.

There were many other happy days spent at local beaches, in Honolulu with its magnificent Waikiki Beach, and hiking through the mountains. We took our VISTA work seriously and never shirked our duties. But during our off days we enjoyed being in one of the most beautiful places on earth.

Three Special Projects

During the summer of 1972, as my first year in Hawaiʻi was winding down, it became apparent that there was not much work for the VISTA volunteers to do for the group homes. The community seemed to accept the homes. Their operations had been stabilized. Each home had solid house parents, and Mel was making progress with the kids. Patti Lyons asked me if I would be willing to help with some special projects. Of course I agreed.

For one special project, Patti asked me to team up with Bob Ozaki and function as the eyes and ears of the Group Homes project at the State Legislature in Honolulu. She asked us to identify any legislative bills that might affect the group homes, especially any legislation that might affect the compensation the group homes received from the State. Bob and I leaned into this work. Several days a week we would meet at the capitol building. The Governor of Hawai'i was John A. Burns and the Lieutenant Governor was George Ariyoshi. On our first day, Bob said, "let's pay a courtesy call on the Lieutenant Governor." This brashness and what I considered "out of the box" thinking were some of the reasons I admired Bob so much. On my own I would never have thought of doing that. We were wearing T-shirts, jeans, and sandals. We walked upstairs to Mr. Ariyoshi's office. The receptionist looked a long time at us, but didn't give a hint of disapproval. Bob explained that we were VISTA volunteers and would be tracking legislation that might affect group homes on Oahu. He asked if we might pay a courtesy call on Mr. Ariyoshi. She smiled, excused herself, and went into the Lieutenant Governor's personal office. When she came out, she said. "Mr. Ariyoshi will see you now." I was a little dazed, but followed Bob into the office. Ariyoshi greeted us warmly. We explained the situation with adolescent group homes on Oahu and what our roles were. He asked a few questions and thanked us for our service to the State. I liked George Ariyoshi and was happy when he was later elected Governor of Hawaii. Bob and I spent the summer tracking the movement of any pieces of relevant legislation, going to public committee meetings, and talking with staff of legislators to gather information. We reported regularly to Patty Lyons. I wrote up a guide for how we did our work that Patty used in training someone to do this work the following year.

With time on my hands, I was also asked to help a local woman in Wai'anae who wanted to learn how to drive a car and get her driver's license. She wanted the freedom to go shopping and on other trips without having to rely completely on her husband. Her husband could not, or perhaps would not, help her. I started teaching her to drive a car. At first she was fearful of hitting something and drove very slowly. Each day her confidence improved. We practiced in all kinds of driving circumstances, and I taught her how to parallel park. In about three weeks she was driving at speed with confidence. She was ready to take her test. We both were more than happy that she passed her test on her first try. She invited me to join her family for dinner one night as a way of thanking me. I was happy to join them but I was a little bit worried about how her husband would react to me. I had never met him, and I wasn't sure he approved of his wife learning how to drive. I worried for nothing. He was very happy his wife now had a driver's license. He thanked me several times for helping her. We had a wonderful dinner together.

Another special project was initiated by a phone call from a member of a Samoan family, most of whom were immigrants from American Samoa. Over the past few months he and I had met at various events, and I had visited his home a couple of times. He asked if he could meet with me, as there was something he wanted to talk about. When we met, he told me that his grandfather, Ala Fuimaono, the patriarch of his clan, was having some problems with the Internal Revenue Service over taxes and with the federal office that processed passports. He had tried to sort out the problems, but he couldn't get it done. He didn't understand the problems and didn't know how the bureaucracies worked. I said I would look into it. I took all the relevant documents and started going to the respective offices to explain the problems Fuimaono was having and ask for advice. It turned out that the problems could fairly easily be solved. Fuimaono had to complete some forms, sign some documents, and submit them to the respective offices for review. Getting this information and completing the paperwork took a modest amount of my time over a month or so, but once everything was submitted, Fuimaono got letters from the IRS and passport offices that the issues had been resolved.

Several weeks later, after I had moved from Waiʻanae to Honolulu to start my second year of VISTA activities on another project, I again got a call from my Samoan friend. He said there was something very important that his family needed to talk to me about. Could I come to Waiʻanae for a meeting that day? It turns out I had a date with a girlfriend that evening starting about six o'clock, but the meeting was going to start in the afternoon, so I thought I could go without canceling my date. When I arrived at Ala Fuimaono's home there was a group of about twenty Samoans in his living room. We were all asked to sit down on the floor mats. The men in the room started speaking in Samoan, each man speaking in earnest with dramatic exclamations. After about an hour, I had no clue what was going on. I now realized that I was going to be late for my date. This was before cell phones. I had no way of contacting her to explain my situation. I could see there were still six or seven men who were going to speak, and Ala Fuimaono was clearly going to be the last speaker. My friend was sitting next to me. I leaned over to him and explained that I would have to leave soon. He said, "Tom, you don't understand. You are being made a Talking Chief of our clan." I was shocked. This was an incredible honor. I told my friend I was sorry I misunderstood, and of course I would stay for this ceremony as long as needed. The gratitude and respect this family was giving me was overwhelming. At the end of the ceremony I did my best to thank Ala Fuimaono and the others for this honor. I was truly surprised and grateful for what had just happened. Once the meeting was clearly breaking up, I excused myself and rushed to the nearest pay phone and called the woman I had stood up. She amazingly understood, and we went out together many times in the coming months. Although I did not stay in touch with Ala Fuimaono after I left Hawai'i, I like to think that being a Talking Chief is a lifetime appointment. I am proud to say that I am Thomas Rundall, Talking Chief for the Ala Fuimaono clan.

The End of My First Year in Hawai'i

July of 1972 marked the end of my first year in VISTA. Since Jon and Bonnie had no obligation to stay a second year, they returned as planned to Wisconsin. Samoan families all over the Wai'anae coast were sorry to see them go. So was I. There are no finer people anywhere. Jon became a special education teacher, working with kids that have learning disabilities. Bonnie became a nurse. They continue to live in Wisconsin near their children and grandchildren. They are still good friends, and we communicate regularly via email and Christmas letters.

Through some bureaucratic rule that came into play when Steve was late filing some paperwork, he was released from his two-year alternative service obligation after serving only one year. I said that he was a lucky person. Steve stayed on Oahu for a while, and after moving back to California, he returned a few times for visits. We continued our friendship when we both returned to the mainland, and he was my best man when Jane and I married in 1975. Steve became a chiropractor, practicing in Watsonville for many years. Eventually, Steve and his wife, Cathleen, moved to the Big Island, where he continues to practice.

My Second Year in Hawai`i

For my second year in VISTA, I was released from my working arrangement with Patti Lyons and Child and Family Services. I was asked by VISTA Director Mike Gale to fill a different kind of role. An architecture firm in Honolulu was requesting VISTA to send some lawyers, architects, and city planners to Hawai`i to work as VISTA volunteers on the design of low-income housing and community buildings. VISTA had already identified the volunteers who would come. For some reason, the architectural firm decided that they could not be the host organization for this project. Mike and the leaders of the firm then hit upon the idea of creating a separate non-profit organization to serve as the host organization. Mike asked me to become what was called a VISTA Supervisor, a promotion of sorts, and to create the non-profit company and oversee the work of the volunteers when they arrived. I quickly agreed, sensing I would learn a lot and help the volunteers do some good work on low-income housing. I moved to Honolulu and rented a small basement apartment on Wilhelmina Rise. The owners of the house above had a beautiful view of the back of Diamond Head.

I went through the process of incorporating a non-profit organization, which I named the Neighborhood Action Corporation (NAC). I established a business bank account for NAC and arranged for a free office at the headquarters of the Salvation Army in Honolulu. VISTA sent two lawyers, two architects, and a city planner, and when they arrived I managed their stipend payment and tax withholding as well as all other aspects of running a small non-profit business. I spent the year working on this project. Of course the work encountered many obstacles. There were objections to low income housing in many communities. Building low-cost housing units that met building codes was more challenging than we had anticipated. An architecture professor at the University of Hawaii helped a great deal in thinking about these problems. But the work proceeded slowly. By the time my second year was complete there were architectural plans for housing units, but we had not yet been able to overcome community resistance. No houses were under construction. In July of 1973, I turned over my responsibilities to a new VISTA supervisor, who was to carry on the work of the Neighborhood Action Corporation.

During the 1972-1973 year, I became very close with Bob Ozaki and his family. Bob's one-year commitment to VISTA had been fulfilled, and he was now working and looking for his next adventure. I spent a lot of time with them at their house and on day trips to the beach and other places. Over the many years since, Bob, Jane, and I have remained close, and Jane and I have also become close with Bob's second wife Becky, who has a doctoral degree and spent many years as an associate professor in the Center on Disability Studies at the University of Hawai`i. I'm glad I have been able to enjoy so many adventures with the Ozakis, including many rounds of golf with Bob, his father, and his daughter Holly. Jane and I always visit Bob and Becky on our trips to Hawai`i. Now, Owen, Mananya, and Genevieve are part of the friendship circle. We all had dinner together in the summer of 2019 at the Side Street Inn in Honolulu, and we look forward to our next visit.

Leaving Hawai`i

I was sure I could stay in Honolulu after my two years of VISTA service were finished and find a job without too much trouble. Since I loved living in Hawai`i so much, I gave the idea some serious thought, but in the end I decided I wanted to return to graduate school at Stanford. The opportunity I had there was something I simply could not let go. In July of 1973, as I was making arrangements to leave, I reflected on my time in Hawai`i. In every possible way, my two years as a VISTA volunteer exceeded my expectations. I did meaningful work that contributed to several of Hawaii's communities. I made life-long friends: wonderful, talented people who went on to make important contributions to society throughout their lives. I enjoyed the stunning beauty of Oahu and all the other Hawaiian Islands. I had gone through remarkable personal growth, now much more clear about where I wanted my doctoral education to take me. But what was most unexpected was the deep appreciation I gained of the most important part of Hawai'i, the spirit of aloha.

The Spirit of Aloha

The spirit of aloha is the heart of Hawaiian culture. It is a complex concept that can only truly be understood by living in a community in which aloha is practiced. It is common in Hawai'i for people to say aloha as a way of saying hello or goodbye. But aloha is much more than a word of greeting or farewell. Aloha is a way of living and treating each other with love and respect. According to the old kahunas (priests), being able to live the spirit of aloha is a way of reaching self-perfection. To improve ourselves, we must send and receive positive energy. There are many ways to do this. Aloha is living in harmony with nature and other people. Aloha is an approach to living that emphasizes good will towards others. The spirit of aloha is felt when someone is creating positive feelings and thoughts and sharing their love for others. Inspired by the philosophy and wisdom of the spirit of aloha, many institutions and businesses in Hawai'i carry its name: Aloha Tower, Aloha Stadium, and Aloha Airlines, for example. Many Hawaiian singers write and perform songs about aloha as well. The spirit of aloha is one of the things that make Hawai'i so wonderfully different from any other place I know, and why I have been returning to Hawai'i regularly for forty-seven years.

Off To A Good Start

Millie Allen dancing the hula

This is the Seraphim, the trimaran my friends and I sailed
from Pokai Bay to Lahaina, December 1971

Off To A Good Start

Ala Fuimaono, who made me a Talking Chief of his clan, 1972

Me with Samoan and Hawaiian children in Waianae, 1972

Me watching the Kilauea Volcano erupt, 1972

Steve, Bob, and I saying goodbye to Jon and Bonnie
at Honolulu International Airport, 1972

Off To A Good Start

6

Returning to Stanford

I flew from Honolulu to San Francisco in August of 1973. I was feeling sad to be leaving Hawai'i, a place I had grown to love, but also happy to be coming home and restarting my graduate studies at Stanford. I stayed at my parents' home in Campbell for a week. We were all thrilled to be together again. I had come home twice during my two years in Hawai'i, but the stays were brief. Now I was able to visit at length with Dad and Mom, Sue and Wayne, who were still living at home, as well as Sandy, Carol, Cathy, and their families. I told them all about Hawai'i, the work I did there, and my adventures with Steve, Jon, Bonnie, Jim, and Bob. It was great to be back home. But after a week or so, I started focusing on my return to Stanford.

My Return to Stanford

Classes at Stanford would be starting in September. I had lots to do. I went to the Sociology Department and met with the Department Chair, Sandy Dornbusch. I had written to him months earlier letting him know I would be returning to the department for the 1973-74 academic year. He welcomed me back warmly and said he had processed the paperwork to get me reenrolled. I also met with my mentor, Bernie Cohen. We were happy to see each other. We talked about the work going on in the department's social research laboratory, where I had done so much work with Bernie in previous years. My time in Hawai'i had changed my thinking about my future research. I was no longer interested in doing small groups research in an artificial social laboratory setting with contrived groups of study subjects that were manipulated in ways that allowed testing of some hypothesis. My Hawai'i experiences had made me even more of a do-gooder than I was before. I wanted my work to be more directly connected to solving real world problems, to making the world a better place. That meant my research had to be accessible not only to other scholars, but also to practitioners. Besides this, my early interest in the health care field, wanting to become a physical therapist, had been transformed into a much broader interest in doing research that would be helpful in improving the performance of healthcare organizations. I held off talking to Bernie about all of this. It was too soon, and my ideas were not fully formed. But I knew I would have to explain to him my new research and career interests as I got closer to identifying my dissertation topic. I knew Bernie would be disappointed. I hoped he would support my decision.

I also started re-establishing myself in Palo Alto. I reconnected with my friends, including Roy Woolsey, Rob Creighton, Walter Hewlett and Esther Ball. While I was away Walter and Esther had married. With good friends, even two years apart is unimportant. We all were happy to see each other, and we picked up right were we left off. I started playing tennis again with Rob. He was the best player I ever played. Every part of his game was strong. I was sure he could have played on the Stanford tennis team. Over the years we played together dozens of times. I managed to win sets off of him, but never a match. I found a very small house to rent. I lived there for three months until Roy asked if I was interested in looking for a place to live together. Roy and I found a two-bedroom house at 161 Bryant Street that we rented. The house was on a quiet street, but only a few blocks from downtown Palo Alto, and an easy bike ride to campus. This would be my home for the next two years. The last piece in getting myself ready to return to student life was buying a car. Dad and I went to an auto dealership, where I saw a previously owned blue Volkswagen Beetle that was in good shape and would be ideal for my modest travel needs. I bought the car. It was cheap to drive, reliable, and easy to park anywhere. I kept it until Jane and I were married. My reinstatement to the sociology doctoral program included a scholarship that paid for tuition and provided me with a stipend for living expenses. The stipend was not enough to pay all my expenses, but I could resume working part-time as a research assistant in the social research laboratory to make ends meet.

There were several doctoral students in the Sociology Department that I remembered from 1971, and several students who had been admitted to the department over the last two years and were new to me. I reentered the graduate student social circle pretty easily. Knowing how to play bridge helped. In 1970, while I was living in

Toyon Hall, Roy Woolsey taught me how to play bridge. Roy was a master bridge player. After I learned the basics, he asked me to be his partner at the weekly contract bridge contest that was held on campus. We had great times playing bridge. Roy was able to remember every card played and to figure out what cards other players were holding. Whenever possible I bid in ways that allowed Roy to play the hand; not the best strategy overall, but it allowed our team to use its best player most often. Everyday during lunch some doctoral students and faculty would play bridge in the Sociology Department lounge. These were riotous affairs, with a lot of teasing each other. I fit right in and quickly established friendships with many of my fellow students and faculty members.

Academic Course Work

During the fall 1973 quarter I was taking course work in social theory and research methodology. I was especially impressed with learning how to think about research design as presented in a course taught by Professor Mike Hannan using Donald Campbell and Julian Stanley's brilliant book *Experimental and Quasi-Experimental Designs for Research*. I would use the ideas I learned in this course in my research and teaching for the rest of my career.

I continued my course work throughout the spring of 1974 and all of 1975. I took several courses in organizational sociology. With regard to organizational theory, this was an exciting time to be at Stanford. In the Sociology Department, Mike Hannan was developing organizational population ecology theory. John Meyer and W. Richard (Dick) Scott were independently making major contributions to the institutional theory of organizations, and in the Business School Jeffrey Pfeffer was formulating the resource dependence theory of organization-environment relations. All of these theories and related concepts have been widely used in organizational research since the early 1970s. I had a front row seat to their development. I also took a sociology of medicine course in the medical school taught by Diana Dutton. Since that was the only course available in that field, I also took an independent study course that allowed me academic credit for doing extra reading in this area.

Off To A Good Start

Moving Away from Research in the Social Laboratory

During the spring of 1974, it was time to have my heart-to-heart talk with Bernie Cohen. I explained how my research interests had changed, that I no longer wanted to do work in small group dynamics in the social research laboratory. I told him I was still interested in social psychology to the extent that it would help me understand organizational behavior, and I said I had developed an interest in studying health care organizations. I could tell he was disappointed. He had hoped I would do my dissertation research as part of his research group. But as always, Bernie was supportive. He said he understood why I wanted to change my career path, and he knew I had given it a lot of thought. He said he would continue to support me in any way he could, and if I would find it helpful he would be happy to serve on my dissertation committee. Bernie was an exemplary role model of a mentor, and I never forgot the lessons I learned from this conversation.

My Qualifying Examination

At the end of the 1974 spring semester, I was required to take a qualifying exam. All doctoral students were required to pass their qualifying exam before they were allowed to continue on to their dissertation research. On the day of the exam, the student is given a piece of paper with three research questions related to three different sociology subfields. Two of the research questions were from the major subfields, although the subfields were alternated from exam to exam, so a student never knew which of the subfields would appear on their exam. The third question was drawn from a field that the examiners knew was of special interest to the student. Students were given four hours to write out answers to the three questions (on paper in longhand; this was before desktop computers had been invented). For each question students could receive a grade of Fail, Pass, or Pass with Distinction. My three questions were drawn from the fields of organizational theory and behavior, social stratification, and the sociology of medicine. I wrote furiously for four hours, citing as many relevant books and research articles as I could remember, and even including some relevant research I did in my answer to the medical sociology question. A couple of days later I got the results. For the organizational theory and behavior and social stratification questions, I received a pass grade. For the sociology of medicine question, I passed with distinction.

Joining Dick Scott's Research Team

Not long after my qualifying exam, Dick Scott asked to meet with me. He invited me to join his research team studying the organizational factors that affected patients' outcomes from surgery. This research was stimulated by the observation that some general anesthetics, such as halothane, had surprisingly high mortality rates among the surgical patients on whom they were used. To clarify what was going on, a research study on the effects of general anesthetics on surgical outcomes, controlling for other factors that could also affect patients' outcomes was required. Dick and colleagues at the Medical School had received a grant from the National Science Foundation to do this research. They were collecting huge amounts of clinical data on adult surgical patients at 17 U.S. hospitals selected by a stratified random selection procedure. But the team was also collecting data on the social characteristics of the patients and the organizational characteristics of the hospitals, such as the extent to which surgeons operated with the same surgical team over their many surgical procedures (working within established teams). I was amazed by what Dick was telling me. This was exactly the type of sociological research I wanted to do. I quickly said yes and became a research assistant at the Stanford Center for Health Care Research (SCHCR) located at the Medical School. From that time on, Dick Scott would be my primary mentor.

In the summer of 1974, I went to work at the SCHCR and began learning about the data sets that had been collected. The current phase of the research involved a lot of checking the validity of the data, tracking down why certain data items were wrong, and correcting the error. All of this had to be done very carefully with detailed documentation of what was changed and why. For example, Ann Flood, another sociology doctoral student working on the project, found a patient in our data set that was a 103-year-old man who had a hysterectomy. It took a little work to track down the source of the error and fix it.

I worked long hours at SCHCR. Computers were just starting to be used in this type of research, but the equipment and software were not very good. The work we were doing proceeded slowly. We were making progress, however, and eventually some of the clinically oriented manuscripts appeared. Ann and others had already claimed many of the interesting organizational variables that might be used in a dissertation study before I arrived. But there was a set of variables collected from the patients prior to their surgery that identified which of 14 life changes they had experienced in the last three months, including marriage, divorce, marital separation, death of a spouse, new child in the family, job promotion, moving a distance greater than 100 miles, fired or laid-off work, unemployed more than two months, retirement, legal problems, jail term, and substantial increase in personal debt. Trained technicians stationed at each hospital collected data on whether the patient had experienced any of these fourteen life changes within the three months prior to surgery, the patient's preoperative stage of disease (severity of the disease at the time of surgery), postoperative morbidity and mortality (at seven days after surgery), postoperative length of stay in the hospital, and the patient's perception of his or her recovery from surgery at forty days postoperatively. Data were also collected on a number of control variables, such as the patient's age, sex, marital status, income, education, ethnic origin, and insurance coverage. Current social-psychological theory and empirical research argued that the accumulation of life changes, whether positive or negative changes, adversely affected people's mental and physical health. There were several psychological and physiological causal mechanisms proposed by researchers that could cause such effects. I decided to push this line of research forward by examining the relationships between life changes and patients' recovery from surgery for different types of surgical procedures.

My dissertation research proposed to test two models of the relationship between life change and illness behavior in a prospective study of surgical patients in six disease-operation categories. The sensitization model hypothesized that higher levels of life change experienced prior to surgery would be related positively to the number of problems perceived by patients with their postoperative recovery. The physiological reaction model predicted that life change would be positively related to the patient's actual morbidity.

I asked three faculty members to serve on my dissertation committee: Dick Scott (of course), Bernie Cohen, and Patricia Barchas. I developed my research proposal and had it reviewed by my committee members and a few other people. After making revisions, I was ready for my dissertation proposal defense, what everyone called the dissertation exam.

My Dissertation Exam

My dissertation exam was scheduled for the spring of 1975. I was to be examined by my dissertation committee members and a member of the Stanford faculty from another department who was chosen by the Graduate Division. The role of the "outside" member of the dissertation exam committee was to insure that the broad intellectual standards of the university were met by the proposed dissertation, and that the student could articulate and defend those ideas adequately. For my dissertation exam committee, the Graduate Division chose Joshua Lederberg, Ph.D., a molecular biologist who had won a Nobel Prize at the age of 33 for discovering that bacteria could mate and exchange genes. When word got out that Lederberg was the Graduate Division appointed member of my committee, Buzz Zelditch, the Chair of the Sociology Department, said he would also come to the examination. Dr. William Forrest, Jr, M.D., the co-director of the Stanford Center for Health Care Research and on the faculty of the School of Medicine, also told me he was going to attend the examination.

I was nervous about all this, but I had no choice but to be examined on my dissertation ideas by this committee. A date, time, and place were chosen, and that information was sent to all the committee members and me. On the morning when the exam committee and I gathered in a room in the Sociology Department, Joshua Lederberg was not present. We waited about 15 minutes, and he still was not there. Someone called his office at the Medical School. An assistant said she would contact him. We waited another 15 minutes and Lederberg still had not arrived. We received a message that he was on his way. Lederberg arrived forty minutes after the scheduled time. He gave his abject apologies for being late. He said he had forgotten to bring his copy of my research proposal and asked if there was an extra copy available. I slid him my copy across the table, and we began.

My mind was racing during the forty minutes that we waited for Lederberg. At first the delay made me nervous. Then at some point I understood from how all the others were reacting that this delay was violating important university norms regarding attendance at such examinations. I began to relax. I figured they would have a very hard time voting to fail me after such a long delay. I calmly gave an introduction, explaining the motivation for this research, the current state of evidence regarding the effects of life changes on health, my hypotheses, and the data I was going to use to test the hypotheses. While I was doing this, Lederberg was scanning my proposal. I then answered questions for about ninety minutes, with each member of the committee asking questions. As I walked out of the meeting room I had to shake my head in wonder. Joshua Lederberg, who clearly had not read my proposal before coming to the meeting, had asked the most relevant and interesting questions.

I passed the dissertation examination. A few days later, Dick Scott gave me a letter that Joshua Lederberg had written him saying that my exam was one of the most interesting he had ever attended, and to please pass on his congratulations to me. This was my proudest moment in academic life to date. A Nobel Prize winner liked my work!

Completing My Dissertation Data Analyses

For the remaining months of 1975 and the first seven months of 1976, I carried on with my data analyses, examining the relationships among different indices of life change that I created on measures of patients' recovery from surgery for various types of surgery. The results showed mixed support for the theory, but there were some clearly supportive findings. For example, undesirable life events had a deleterious effect on physiological recovery of hysterectomy patients. In August 1976, I handed in my dissertation, *Life Change and Recovery From Surgery*, and my committee members signed it. The long and winding road to being awarded my doctoral degree was complete.

During this journey, I met Jane and we were married. There is much more about all that in the next chapter. Here I just note that we were about to start our lives together no longer being tied to Stanford. We were a bit sad about this. We loved Stanford, but we were excited about moving on and where the future would take us.

A Little More on Joshua Lederberg

In 1978, while on the faculty at Cornell University I published an article in the *Journal of Health and Social Behavior* summarizing my dissertation research findings. To my amazement, Joshua Lederberg sent me a note asking for a copy of my article. I sent him a copy of that article, and a few other related ones, with a note thanking him for his interest in my work. In 2005, I received a letter from the National Library of Medicine requesting permission to digitize our correspondence, "which will help provide valuable historical context for other items in the Joshua Lederberg Collection." I would meet Lederberg once more during my career. He came to U.C. Berkeley to give a speech at the School of Public Health. When we met, I reminded him that we had met years earlier at Stanford at my dissertation defense. He recalled the meeting and even referred to some of the committee members by name. Lederberg was a brilliant scientist and provided excellent academic leadership as President of Rockefeller University. He received the Nobel Prize, the National Medal of Science, and the Presidential Medal of Freedom. Lederberg died in New York City in 2008 at the age of 82. He will be greatly missed.

The Stanford Main Quadrangle;
the Sociology Department is under the far right arch

Sailing on San Francisco Bay, 1973

House I shared with Roy Woolsey,
161 Bryant St., Palo Alto, 1973-1975

Me at Stanford, June 1974

Off To A Good Start

7

Meeting and Marrying Jane Tiemann

The winter quarter of 1974 was just beginning when I got invited by one of my doctoral student friends, Pat Lauderdale, to go to a party on Sunday, January 13, to watch Superbowl VIII. The party was going to be held at the house he rented with one of his friends, Steve Figler. I didn't know Steve, but I was happy to go. There were about 30 people at the party. The Minnesota Vikings were playing the Miami Dolphins to decide the National Football League champion for the 1973 season. I only knew a few people at the party, but as the game progressed I met and chatted with several of Steve's friends. At halftime Miami led 17-0 (and eventually won the game by a score of 24-7). It was a beautiful January day. The sun was shining brightly. I went outside with a few other people to sit on the front porch to enjoy the warm sun. Jane joined us. I had noticed Jane earlier, but had not met her. We said hello to each other and started to talk. Jane had long, straight blonde hair and blue eyes. She was pretty and had a fit figure and warm smile. She laughed easily. We talked about the game, but also about our connections to Stanford. Jane graduated in 1967, had moved to the Chicago area for a few years, and then returned and was working as an administrative assistant in Dr. Frank Stockdale's laboratory at the Stanford Medical School. We were so focused on each other, we didn't say much to anyone else. Then, Jane said the sun was making her too warm and returned to the house. I was completely smitten. I asked Pat if he knew if Jane was dating anyone. He said that until recently the guy he shared the house with, Steve, had been Jane's boyfriend. But he thought they had broken up. He wasn't sure what their status was now. Since Jane had so abruptly returned to the house, and there was the possibility she was still involved with Steve, I decided the best course was not to pursue her. I needed a clue that Jane was available and interested in dating me.

Off To A Good Start

Jane Asks Me to Go On a Date

Miraculously, as if she was reading my mind, a few days later I found an envelope from Jane in my sociology department mailbox. In the envelope was a letter saying how much she enjoyed meeting me at the party. She had tickets to an upcoming performance of the San Francisco Symphony and asked if I would be interested in joining her. I was stunned that Jane would ask me out. Women did not ask men out very often in 1974. Later, I learned from Jane that she had been trying to send me signals of her interest through some of our mutual friends. I clearly wasn't getting the signals, so she decided to take things into her own hands. I was very happy and excited that with this one brief note Jane had answered my two questions. She was not in a relationship with someone else, and she was interested in me. Jane included her phone number in the note. As soon as I got home I called her. After saying hello, I told Jane how happy I was to find her note in my mailbox and that I would be delighted to go to the symphony with her. Jane had been bold in putting that note in my mailbox, and I felt I needed to be bold in return. I said "Why don't you come to my house for an early dinner before we go to the symphony." Jane thought that was a great idea, and we agreed on a time. I was over the moon!

The concert was Wednesday evening, January 23, at the War Memorial Opera House in San Francisco. The featured piece was Brahms' Piano Concerto No. 2 in B-flat major. Rudolf Serkin was the pianist, and Seiji Ozawa conducted the orchestra. Jane arrived at my house wearing a cream colored sweater, a mostly tan and cream-colored long skirt, and brown shoes. I have no idea what I wore. She was just as attractive as I remembered. While we were both nervous, we gave each other a hug. I broke the ice by telling her I was making Czechoslovakian chicken for dinner, and I told her about my mother with her Czech ancestry. The meal I prepared was actually just fried chicken cooked the way my mom cooked it, with a simple salad. Jane said she loved the chicken, and I had to admit to her it had only a weak familial tie to Czechoslovakia. She said again that the meal was good and that I got extra credit for cooking on our first date. We told stories, shared a little about our lives, and laughed a lot through dinner. When it was time to leave I drove us to San Francisco in my blue Beetle. We enjoyed the concert, joining the others in the audience in applauding Serkin and Ozawa.

I drove us back to my house. We talked so easily all the way to Palo Alto. Jane came in the house and we continued talking about our favorite things to do, our Stanford experiences, and other "getting to know you" topics. We were both a little shy and reserved, Jane more than I. But we eventually shared a hug and kissed. I sensed this was the beginning of something big.

Jane and I started calling each other almost daily. I started spending a lot of time at Jane's house. I met Elaine Davis, Jane's best friend and the woman with whom she shared a house at 4 Perry Lane in Menlo Park. Elaine started dating Lee Pinto (who she would eventually marry), and the four of us had a lot of fun doing things together. Jane and I continued to date throughout the spring and summer of 1974. Even though she didn't like to swim, Jane joined me to relax in the sun at the pool across the street from the Lagunita Court residence, where I used to live. She came to my softball games. Jane became friends with all of my sociology department friends, and I did the same with her medical school friends. Jane's constant support helped me deal with the pressure of my doctoral qualifying exam. We shared the same values and political beliefs. I liked how smart she was and that she had a better, more classical education than I. I learned a lot from her. We both wanted to have a family. Jane understood and appreciated the journey I had taken to get to graduate school and was committed to the same type of life I aspired to. She valued the contributions academics made to the world as much as I did. We had become best friends.

Jane Moves (Temporarily) to Charlottesville, Virginia

I was thinking we were in a long-term relationship. I believe Jane was thinking the same thing. But there was an unexpected twist. Before she met me, Jane had applied to graduate school in the English Department at the University of Virginia. Of course she was accepted and offered admission in the fall of 1974. She was clearly upset about having to make a choice between continuing to work at Stanford Medical School while waiting for me to finish my doctoral degree, and moving to Charlottesville to start her own graduate degree program. We talked about our options a lot. We certainly wanted to be together and were worried about what would happen if we tried to maintain a long-distance relationship. Also, we didn't know how long either of us would take to complete our degrees. But there were several reasons we thought Jane should go to Virginia. The English Department at the University of Virginia was world-renowned, and the chance to study there was a terrific opportunity. Also, the idea of turning down such an opportunity so she could stay in place while her boyfriend finished his degree ran against Jane's feminist beliefs. She should be pursuing the life that gave her opportunities and satisfied her own career interests. I didn't hate those ideas even though they meant Jane would go away for a long time. But I had to admit to myself that, having passed my qualifying exam, I would be working very long hours on my dissertation research work. It might be a good idea not to introduce stress in our relationship by being an absentee boyfriend, unable to spend as much time with Jane as both of us would like. We decided that Jane would move to Charlottesville and start her graduate program. We would maintain a long-distance relationship. Then Jane would return to Palo Alto for Christmas break and if we still felt the same about each other, we would get engaged.

In early August of 1974, Jane and I set out in her little Ford Pinto to drive across the country. We stopped in St. Louis, where Jane's parents lived. I had met Jane's mother, Ruth, once before when she was on a trip to the Bay Area. She invited Jane and me, Elaine, Lee, and Jane's brother Bob (who lived in Palo Alto) to dinner at an upscale Chinese Restaurant in San Francisco. But this was the first time I met her father, Robert. I also met Jane's brother Jonathan, who was still living at home. We all got along well. I told the Tiemanns a bit about my life and about my doctoral research. Jane and I shared stories of our meeting and becoming a couple. We went out to dinner at a restaurant along the Mississippi River. Robert and Ruth were among the most polite and courteous people I have ever met. When we returned to their house, Ruth made up a bed for me on the couch in the family room. The Tiemanns seemed to like me. Even though I was poor as a church mouse, they saw that I had excellent prospects, which I think helped them relax some about my relationship with Jane.

Robert and Ruth Tiemann were staunch Republicans. Jane and I were not. During August of 1974, the Watergate break-in scandal was coming to a head. The scandal stemmed from the President Richard Nixon administration's attempt to cover up its involvement in the June 17, 1972, failed break-in of the Democratic National Committee headquarters at the Washington, D.C. Watergate Office Building. During the Congressional investigation of the break-in, witnesses testified that President Nixon had approved plans to cover up administration involvement in the break-in, and that there was a voice-activated audio taping system in the Oval Office of the White House. As information from witnesses and the tapes about Nixon's involvement in the cover-up became public, he lost most of his political support. The House of Representatives Judiciary Committee approved articles of impeachment against Nixon for obstruction of justice, abuse of power, and contempt of Congress. To avoid being impeached by the full House of Representatives and being removed from office by a trial in the Senate, Nixon chose to resign. On the evening of August 8th Nixon announced he would resign from office the next day. We sat in the Tiemanns' living room and watched the resignation announcement on television. Jane and I were very quiet. There was some tension in the room. At the end of Nixon's brief speech, a reporter started recounting some of the popular things Nixon had done during his presidency, such as ordering the phased withdrawal of troops from Vietnam. Jane's Dad reacted to all this by saying "And now the press will be generous." Sensing that he had been spiteful, Robert turned a to us and said "I'm sorry."

A couple of days later Jane and I continued on our drive to Charlottesville. When we arrived, we booked a room at a hotel. We took a tour of the University of Virginia campus, the famous serpentine brick wall, and Thomas Jefferson's house on a hill overlooking the campus. Charlottesville is a beautiful college town. Jane had many things to do to get settled in, including finding a place to live. Her mother had agreed to come to Charlottesville after we arrived to help Jane. It was time for me to go. Jane drove me to the airport, and we took some time to say our goodbyes, promise to write and call, and say how much we were going to miss each other. I flew back to San Francisco hopeful, but not sure our relationship would survive this separation.

Off To A Good Start

Jane's December Visit and Our Wedding Plans

For the next four months Jane and I regularly wrote letters to each other. Less regularly we made telephone calls (long distance calls were expensive at that time), and talked about how our studies were going and how much we missed each other. When Christmas came we were excited to see each other, and realized how much in love we still were. I also learned that Jane was not happy with some of her professors in the English department and their approach to critical analysis of books and other literary texts. She had decided not to pursue a doctoral degree there. She would finish her masters degree, then leave. I was not sorry to hear that she would be leaving Charlottesville. We started talking about our long-term plans. One evening a few days before Jane had to return to Charlottesville, Jane asked "Are we going to get married?" I said, "Yes, I would love to marry you." Once again, Jane led the way in our relationship. But I was one hundred percent glad that she did. I was too poor to buy an engagement ring, and so I did not kneel down to ask for her hand. We just committed to getting married and started talking about how we could do it. It was at this point in time that Jane and I simply joined hands, turned, and starting walking through life together.

Jane knew I was a practicing Catholic, and she agreed to be married in a Catholic ceremony. But there was a problem with that idea. Jane had been married once before. Right after she graduated from Stanford, she married her college boyfriend. But the relationship did not last, and after only three and a half years they divorced. Catholic doctrine does not allow for divorce. In the eyes of the church, married couples are believed to be married for life. I had a good relationship with Father John Duryea, a priest at the church I was attending. He had a reputation as a liberal, compassionate priest. He had written me a letter of support when I applied for conscientious objector status. I thought he would be able to find a way for us to get married in the Church. I made an appointment for Jane and me to meet with Father Duryea one morning. We explained our situation. Father Duryea asked Jane if there was any possible justification for having her marriage annulled. He explained what those justifications might be. Jane said none of those applied in her case. Father Duryea then took a very hard line. He said we could not be married in the Catholic Church. In the eyes of God she was still married to her ex-husband. She should have worked harder to save her relationship with him. If Jane and I married, we would be living in sin, and I would go to Hell. Both of us sat stunned by what he said. I never expected such an attack on Jane. He gave us no hope. I left his office angry and depressed. When we got back to our car, Jane burst out crying. She was afraid I was not going to marry her now. I promised her that I did not believe the things that Father Duryea said and that I was completely committed to marrying her. As soon as we drove home we began thinking of another plan, a non-Catholic wedding.

As a follow-up note, it turned out that Father Duryea was, himself, a person living in sin. Shortly after Jane and I were married, we read a newspaper article reporting that John Duryea had been excommunicated. For years he had been in a romantic relationship with a woman, a non-Catholic, who was 24 years younger and had two daughters from a previous marriage. Duryea received his official letter of excommunication on his wedding day. The anger we felt about how Duryea had treated Jane exploded. We concluded that he, in part, was harshly reacting to us out of the frustration, anger, and guilt he felt about his own romantic life. I don't know if it was justified by the actions of one hypocritical, shamed priest, but on that day I became much less of a Catholic, and Jane and I felt justified in being married outside the Church.

Jane and I Get Married

After visiting Father Duryea, Jane and I continued our wedding planning. We picked the date of May 24, 1975. Neither of us had any money, so I decided to sell my Volkswagen Beetle to pay for wedding expenses. Still, we had to find ways to put on a wedding ceremony as inexpensively as possible. We checked if Memorial Church on the Stanford Campus was available. It was not. In fact, it was already booked for all possible dates in May or June. But someone at the church told us that some couples that could not reserve the church had their wedding ceremony in a beautiful grove of trees on the grounds of Frost Amphitheater, the site of our undergraduate graduation ceremonies. We looked at the grove, and although it was next to the amphitheater we decided it would work nicely. A small clearing was beautifully surrounded by trees and had a serpentine path from near the parking lot that could be used for our entrance. The amphitheater was maintained in a natural state, it had grass covering the ground with a small stage in front that we could use for serving food. We reserved the grove for our wedding day.

Jane returned to Charlottesville and I returned to my doctoral work. Over the next few months we made all the arrangements for the wedding, relying heavily on family and friends. One of our friends offered to make me a wedding suit. Jane's father, who was Director of Labor Relations at the beer company, Anheuser Busch, arranged to have barrels of beer sent. Some of our friends offered to bake the wedding cake (carrot cake) and prepare other food dishes. In the second week of May I flew to Charlottesville and Jane and I drove back to California together. Before we left, Jane bought two Virginia hams that would serve as the main course at the reception. We somehow squeezed them into Jane's already over-packed Ford Pinto. Steve Rickard agreed to be my best man, and Elaine agreed to serve as Jane's Ms. of honor. My dad printed the invitations, which included some lines Jane selected from *Emma* by Jane Austen: "…the wishes, the hopes, the confidence of the small band of true friends who witnessed the ceremony, were fully answered in the perfect happiness of the union."

On Saturday, May 24 the weather was sunny and warm. Steve was a little late arriving to my house on Bryant Street. In his absence, Jim Chiddix, who flew in from Honolulu for the wedding, took on the role of my best man for the morning. We went to Frost Amphitheater to pick up bits of paper and generally clean the place. We had some food, and we talked about how Jane and I met and the story of our romance. Jim helped create the mood for a wonderful wedding day. Fortunately, Steve showed up in plenty of time for the ceremony.

At one o'clock friends and family gathered in the grove at Frost Amphitheater. Jane and I walked up the path to the grove of trees together. She looked stunningly beautiful in a long floral patterned cream-colored dress. About fifty family members and friends gathered in a circle around a brightly colored carpet I had purchased for us to stand on. Wendy Smith, one of the first women Episcopalian Deacons, presided, and Jane and I said our wedding vows. We exchanged rings and kissed for the first time as a married couple. It was an outdoor wedding, closely resembling a "hippie" ceremony, and one of the guests sun bathed in the nude at the back of the amphitheater during the reception. But everyone enjoyed the ceremony and reception, with their wishes and hopes fully answered.

Our First Honeymoon in San Francisco

For our honeymoon, I wanted to take Jane to Hawai'i. But all we could afford was a one-night stay at the Hyatt Regency Hotel in San Francisco. The Hyatt Regency was a fairly new, beautiful hotel with a dramatically designed inner courtyard. Rooms were arrayed on floors across one side of the courtyard going up the entire height of the building. We were happy we could afford to stay there, even if for only one night. We ate dinner at the hotel restaurant in that dramatic courtyard. It was also prom night for some high school, and the event was being held at the Hyatt Regency. We were still in our wedding clothes. Some people looked at us a long time, trying to figure out if we were part of the prom group. When I booked the room weeks earlier, I told the reservationist that the booking was for our wedding night. The hotel sent us a bottle of champaign, which we enjoyed with our dinner. The next morning we watched the Golden State Warriors, led by Rick Barry, defeat the Washington Bullets 96-95 to sweep the Bullets and win the NBA Championship. I had to call the front desk to request a late checkout time so we could watch the ending of this close, exciting game. If Jane wasn't aware of my love of sports before our wedding, she was now. I was very relieved to see that Jane was interested in the game and was not at all upset that I wanted to watch it. While our stay at the hotel was short, and featured a basketball game, we both felt it was a beautiful start to our lives together. But I promised Jane we would have a "proper" honeymoon in Hawaii before long.

Our Second Honeymoon in Hawai'i

In fact, ten months later during spring break, we took advantage of a Stanford charter flight to Honolulu and spent about eight days there on our "second" honeymoon. We stayed several days with Jim Chiddix at his apartment in the Mākaha Towers. Jim was now involved in expanding and modernizing the cable system along the coast. Jim showed us around Wai'anae and Oahu. He took us on a tour of all the places I lived and worked when I was a VISTA volunteer, including the group homes. We also showed Jane some of our favorite spots on Oahu, including the sugar cane and pineapple fields, the small towns and surfing sites on the north shore, the Nuuanu Pali Lookout and its views of the sheer Koolau cliffs and the lush windward coast. We visited Honolulu and its famous Waikiki Beach with its spectacular view of the Diamond Head volcanic cone. We had a great time.

We also spent time with Bob Ozaki and his first wife, Bonnie. Bob and Bonnie left their two girls with relatives and flew with us to Maui. We traveled around the island for several days. We saw the lush Iao Valley and the famous "needle" volcanic rock formation that rises above the valley. We also visited Lāhaniā, and we walked past the Lāhainā Yacht Club, which gave me a chance to recount the story of my ill-fated sailing trip from Pokai Bay with Jim and Steve in 1972. We returned to Honolulu, and the next day flew back to San Francisco. It was a great trip in every way. I was especially happy that Jane had bonded so well with Jim, Bob, and Bonnie. Importantly, Jane fell in love with Hawai'i. She sometimes teases me by saying that if she didn't fall in love with Hawai'i our marriage would not have lasted. I don't think that's true, but I'm glad we didn't have to find out. Jane and I have returned to visit Hawai'i many times over the years.

In August of 2019, we took Owen, Mananya, and Genevieve to Hawai'i, and stayed at the Ko Olina resort, which was built in the early 2000s on a former sugar cane plantation only a few miles from Wai'anae. They also fell in love with Hawaii, and we plan to return there for family vacations many times.

Cutting the wedding cake, May 24, 1975

Jane at our wedding

Our first kiss as a married couple

Ruth Rundall de la Forest and her cousin, my aunt, Wilma Rundall Zavoral at our wedding

Off To A Good Start

Mom and Dad at our wedding

Dad and Mom Rundall, Jane and I, Ruth and Robert Tiemann
at our wedding

8

My First Academic Job: Cornell University 1976-1980

After our wedding, Jane and I moved into a rental house at 1025 Florence Lane in Menlo Park. It was one of four small houses clustered around a common driveway. We loved living there. For the next thirteen months Jane worked as an administrative assistant in the Dean's Office of the Stanford Medical School, and I continued working on my dissertation, extracting the variables I needed from our project's master data set and doing data analyses. I was making steady progress and thought I could finish in the spring or summer of 1976.

We spent Christmas at my parents' home, a huge family gathering that included all my siblings, nieces, nephews, and Aunt Wilma. In January, Jane brought up the possibility of finishing a master's degree in English at the University of Virginia by returning for the summer semester and completing the few courses she had not yet taken. As much as I disliked the idea of being separated from Jane again, I knew I was going into "crunch" time with my dissertation and would be working more than full time to get it done. The thought of being able to work as long on any day as I needed without worrying about Jane being neglected was appealing to me. We agreed she would complete the summer courses at the University of Virginia and earn her master's degree. On June 11 she flew to St. Louis to spend a couple of days with her parents. On June 13 She flew to Charlottesville, and started classes that week.

By the time Jane left, I had nearly completed my data analyses and was writing the dissertation. In addition to working on my dissertation, I was working nearly full-time doing analyses of data for the other studies being done at the Center. I was also on the job market, and I expected to be doing some traveling for job interviews. It became clear to me that I would not finish writing my dissertation by July. I explained this to my dissertation committee members, promising to complete the work by August. They were fine with my new delivery date and promised to read and sign off on the dissertation soon after I handed it in.

Choosing the Academic Job at Cornell

The job market in 1976 for healthcare related academic and research positions was generally acknowledged to be weak. I wound up interviewing for two jobs: a researcher position at Abt Associates in Boston, and a faculty position in the Sloan Program of Health Services Administration in the School of Business and Public Administration at Cornell University in Ithaca, New York (years later the name of the school would be changed to the Johnson School of Management). The position at Abt Associates paid considerably more, but Jane and I agreed that we were academics at heart and would be much happier in a university environment. I accepted the Cornell faculty position.

On July 15, Jane and I met in Ithaca. It was primarily a house-hunting trip. We met with our agent, Ms. Warren, on Saturday, July 17. She knew her business well, and told us we would probably like Cayuga Heights, "where many Cornell faculty members live." She showed us a house at 425 Cayuga Heights Road that was more modern in style than most of the neo-colonial houses in the area. It had three bedrooms, two bathrooms, a fireplace, a large kitchen, and it was furnished. It was a long, but doable walk to campus. We were ready to get settled and decided to rent this house. The next day Jane flew back to Charlottesville, and I flew to San Francisco.

Finishing My Dissertation

I was due in Ithaca in mid August, which meant I had to hand in my dissertation in early August. Each night, after working all day at the Center, I would bring home a six-pack of Coca Cola, and sip Coke while I wrote my dissertation chapters. It was an awful lifestyle. But it worked. I delivered my dissertation, *Life Change and Recovery From Surgery*, in early August as planned.

Moving to Ithaca

Jane's courses ended in the second week in August. We agreed I would drive the Ford Pinto to St. Louis and meet her at her parents' home. We would then drive to Ithaca together. I packed up our things at our house on Florence Lane and arranged for a moving van to transport our packed boxes and furniture. On August 9, I drove to Campbell to say goodbye to my family. I was moving to the other side of the country and we would not see each other very often. Aunt Wilma had been diagnosed with breast cancer and was now living at Mom and Dad's house. She wasn't doing well. We both knew we would never see each other again. Wilma and I had a special bond. Somehow she knew more about my ambition than anyone else. For Christmas one year she gave me a Webster's dictionary, which I regularly read. I tried to tell her I was sure her chemotherapy would put her cancer in remission. It made parting a little easier, but neither of us believed what I said. Saying goodbye was very difficult. I realized this was the downside of having ambition: the pain of parting from your family and friends and a life you knew so well to pursue something else. I drove away with very mixed emotions. Sadly, Wilma died on August 30, 1976, only two weeks after Jane and I arrived in Ithaca. Her body was laid to rest in a mausoleum at the Lima Family Santa Clara Mortuary at 466 North Winchester Boulevard in Santa Clara (Garden Crypt, Section 35, E4). I was devastated that I could not attend her funeral. Wilma was born in 1915 near the town of Philip, South Dakota, the first child of my grandparents, Earl and Edna Rundall, who were pioneers homesteading on land in that state. Her first playmates were children of the Sioux Nation, as the Rundall family land was close to the Rosebud Indian Reservation. When she was 13 years of age the family moved to Cedar Rapids, where she and her two brothers grew up. When later in life she moved to San Francisco, Wilma had me occasionally stay with her at her apartment at 2306 #2 Union Street. She took me to the first restaurant I remember eating in, Alioto's on Fisherman's Wharf. At her memorial service, my dad said, "May we all present here have the courage and the dignity that Wilma had in illness and death." I loved her more than I can say.

This was now the Ford Pinto's third trip across county. But it didn't fail us. It was a pretty amazing little car. I drove to St. Louis and met Jane at her parents' house on August 12. Two days later, Jane and I continued on to Ithaca. We arrived in Ithaca on Sunday, August 15, and picked up the key to our house the next day.

Ithaca was (and is) a small city in the Finger Lakes region of New York. It is named after the Greek island of Ithaca. It's located on the southern shore of Lake Cayuga, in central New York, about 45 miles southwest of Syracuse. The region around Ithaca is known for its farming and dairy industries. In 1976, Ithaca had about 25,000 permanent residents. The town is home to Ithaca College and, of course, Cornell University, a highly respected Ivy League University. Ithaca had many of the businesses characteristic of small American university towns: bookstores, movie theaters, craft stores, and local restaurants with a range of ethnic foods. The region is exceptionally beautiful. Most areas are heavily wooded. There are many gorges and waterfalls delivering water to Cayuga Lake. Many people love Ithaca for its scenic beauty and small town atmosphere. But Ithacans have to put up with cold, snowy winters; hot, humid summers; and the isolation that comes with living in a rural region. Over the next four years, Jane and I would come to experience all these aspects of Ithaca, the good and the bad.

Life in Ithaca 1976-1977
Joining the Faculty of the School of Business and Public Administration

A day or so after we picked up our house keys I went to the School of Business and Public Administration (BPA), which at that time was housed in Malott Hall, and visited with the Dean, H. Justin Davidson, the Associate Dean, David Thomas, and the Director of the Sloan Program of Health Services Administration, Roger Battistella. I was walked around the building and introduced to faculty members and staff. Among others, I met Joe Thomas, who worked in operations management, Harold Bierman from finance, Tom Dyckman and Bob Swieringa from accounting, Bob Smiley from marketing, and John McClain, who was in operations management and health services administration. I was especially happy to meet the other first-year faculty member in the health administration program, Jack Wheeler, a health economist from the University of Michigan. We would grow into our jobs together during our first year at Cornell.

An interesting additional comment about Bob Smiley: from 1989 to 2003, Bob was the Dean of the U.C. Davis Graduate School of Management. Our daughter-in-law, Mananya Chansanchai, received her MBA in 2009 from that school and knew our friend Bob when he was no longer Dean but still on the faculty. Sort of a small world.

As I got to know more about BPA, I realized I had been educated in a theoretical sociology department and had relatively little practical knowledge to bring to the students in this professional school. After getting settled into my office, one of the first things I did was to find out the days and times of the monthly research seminars held by the finance, accounting, marketing, and operations management departments, and I marked them on my calendar. To be successful at BPA, I had to learn at least a little bit about these fields and find out how my knowledge of organizations, research methodology, and health care systems would add value for the students. I attended as many of these seminars as I could over the next four years, essentially treating my professorship as a long post-doctoral training program in business management. It was one of the best things I have ever done.

I was asked to teach business-related courses I had never taken as a graduate student. But my courses at Stanford had provided a lot of foundational knowledge that I could adapt and use in the more applied courses for business school students. For example, I was asked to teach a course in health program evaluation. While I had never taken such a course before, I had taken many research design and methods courses at Stanford, and I could fairly easily adapt those ideas, with the help of a relevant textbook, to doing research to evaluate a health program. In this way, I adapted what I had learned and added to my knowledge base for each course. I enjoyed teaching, and I invested a lot of time in it. Students liked my courses, and the word spread that I was a committed teacher. Other faculty members noticed, too, which helped me build credibility and respect with them.

One of my first publications was a book, *Health Care Policy in a Changing Environment*, which I co-edited with Roger Battistella. This was a collection of readings on current issues in U.S. health care policy. But I knew I had to begin publishing research articles. I started by writing an article reporting the results of my dissertation research, Life Change and Recovery from Surgery, which was published in the *Journal of Health and Social Behavior*. I also did a study, Factors Associated with the Utilization of the Swine Flu Vaccination Among Senior Citizens in Tompkins County, which appeared in the journal *Medical Care*. But the best research I did while I was at Cornell was in collaboration with Jack Wheeler and John McClain.

Jack only stayed at Cornell for one year. He then returned to his alma mater, the University of Michigan, where he eventually became Chair of the Department of Health Management and Policy. But we continued to work on research projects for a few years after he left. I learned a lot of health economics from Jack. We published The Effect of Income on Use of Preventive Care: An Evaluation of Alternative Explanations in the *Journal of Health and Social Behavior*, and Secondary Preventive Health Behavior in *Health Education Quarterly*.

Working with John McClain

When I first arrived at BPA, John McClain and I quickly became friends. I had an idea for a research study, but it required more mathematical modeling and statistical expertise than I had, and John was great at that kind of work. The idea was to use the theory of the population ecology of organizations to predict the responses of general practitioner and specialist physicians to population growth and decline in their counties. The study not only used a relatively new set of theoretical ideas, but it also pooled cross-sectional and time-series data on population size and the numbers of primary care and specialist physicians for all counties in the State of New York, a fairly new approach to research design and data analysis. It was an elegant assessment of how different types of physicians responded to population growth and decline, showing that specialists tended to leave areas that were going through population decline much faster than did general practitioners. This had implications for physician workforce planning, recruitment, and retention. We submitted the manuscript, Environmental Selection and Physician Supply, to the very prestigious *American Journal of Sociology*, and it was accepted.

This research project was a turning point in my life in several ways. Working together solidified my friendship with John, and publication of this article in such a prestigious sociology journal established my credentials as a strong academic. The article also was the launching pad for my eventual move to U.C. Berkeley.

Owen's Birth

Shortly after arriving in Ithaca, Jane and I agreed we wanted to start our family. Within two months she announced the happy news that she was pregnant. We were happy that it happened so quickly. Jane's due date was in late June, so we could look forward to spending our next summer with our baby.

As the months rolled along, we went through one of the coldest winters in Ithaca's history. In the winter of 1976-1977, the temperature was frequently below 10 degrees. One morning the outdoor thermometer at our house read - 27 degrees. Cayuga Lake was frozen solid for the first time in 50 years. I learned all about snow tires. We emerged from winter, a little like hibernating bears, happy to see the sun again.

During the spring of 1977, our close friend Jim Chiddix traveled from Hawaii to visit us and reconnect with his alma mater. It was the first time Jim had been back to Cornell since he served in the Army. Jim showed us some of his old hang outs, and we went to Taughannock Falls to see the spectacular show during the spring runoff. Jim's career in the cable television industry was taking off, and he would soon become a corporate leader in the industry, working in offices in Denver, Connecticut, and New York City. It was great to see Jim again.

In time Jane and I started attending Lamaze classes. These classes helped a great deal. After I started learning how to be a coach and help Jane control her breathing, I felt much more a part of what was going on. Until then, Jane's pregnancy and our unborn baby's growth were happening to them, not me. The Lamaze classes made me feel a part of the pregnancy experience. I just felt more like it was happening to me, too.

Off To A Good Start

In June of 1977, my distant cousin, Ruth de la Forest visited us. I had known Ruth many years. She was the daughter of Clyde Rundall, one of my grandfather's brothers. She was born July 11, 1912, so was close in age to her cousin, my Aunt Wilma. In fact, Ruth and Wilma were great friends and had made plans to do a lot of traveling together after Wilma retired. After Wilma died in 1976, Ruth still traveled to visit relatives and friends. Not having Wilma as her travel buddy made her trips not as much fun for her. But we were very glad to have her come to Ithaca. Ruth timed her visit to coincide with Jane's due date, hoping to see our new baby and to help in some way. But the due date came and went. Ruth stayed as long as she could, but she had a commitment to arrive at another family member's home in Minnesota in early July, and she left before our baby was born.

Over several months Jane and I had done a thorough review of possible names for our child. We had trouble agreeing on names. We decided to independently list our favorite ten names for boys and girls. We compared the lists. The only name for a girl common to both lists was Laura. The only name on both lists for a boy was Owen.

In the early morning of July 10, Jane went into labor. Jane said she wanted to take a shower before we went to the hospital. I was a little terrified that this delay could mean that I would end up delivering our baby. But Jane showered, which made her feel much better, and we drove to Tompkins County Hospital. Jane was attempting to have a drug-free birth, but as the contractions got stronger, the pain became overwhelming. She was in labor for a total of 12 hours. After about 10 hours, at a nurse's suggestion, Jane took an injection of some pain medication. But the major effect of the shot was to numb Jane's left leg. Then, when she needed to go to the bathroom and put weight on her foot, she couldn't feel her foot, and she stepped awkwardly, seriously spraining her ankle. She had pain in her left foot for months afterward. At one point Jane pleaded with me to just take her home. She was certain she would feel better there, and maybe all the pain would go away. I used all the knowledge and skills I learned in our Lamaze classes to convince her to stay and help her with her breathing.

As Jane got near to giving birth she was moved into the delivery room. I was allowed to join her, a somewhat unusual thing in those days. At two o'clock in the afternoon on July 10, 1977 our baby was born. We had never known what sex our baby was going to be. In fact, when the doctor held our baby up, I was so focused on Jane and hoping she was feeling all right, I was a little startled when he said: "It's a boy!" I would have been overjoyed regardless of the sex of our child. But it did now sink in that Jane and I would be raising a boy. It was a wonderful feeling. Our boy had reddish hair, which suited the name we gave him, Owen Tiemann Rundall.

A nurse brought a telephone with a long extension cord into the delivery room (no mobile phones in those days). This allowed us to call our parents to tell them the good news. Given the time difference between Ithaca and St. Louis, Jane's mom was initially confused about why we waited a whole day to call them. But that was quickly clarified, and there were cheers from the Tiemanns and some guests they had visiting. My parents were also overjoyed at the news. Jane told Mom how difficult and painful the labor had been. My mom, who had given birth to six children, wisely said: "It will fade in time."

I went home, feeling exhausted. I couldn't imagine how tired Jane must have felt. The next morning I went to see Jane in her hospital room. I told her, "I have been an athlete all my life, and I have seen people push their bodies to the limit many times. But I have never seen anyone exert themselves the way you did in giving birth to Owen." Jane smiled and laughed a little. She understood the compliment.

Three days later we took Owen home to 425 Cayuga Heights Road, and Ruth Tiemann was on her way from St. Louis to help.

We would continue to live on Cayuga Heights Road for only another month. Earlier that summer, Jane and I had purchased a home at 432 Mitchell Street, and in August the house was available for us to move in. We would live on Mitchell Street for the next three years. About ten days after we came home with Owen, Mom Tiemann returned to St. Louis. On August 1, we moved into our new home. Moving was a lot of stress for a new mother, but Jane took things slowly and did not over exert herself. After the birth of our baby and the move into our own house, I felt an immense wave of gratitude and responsibility sweep over me. I recall walking the upstairs floor of our house with Owen in my arms one afternoon while Jane was napping. I quietly whispered to Owen, "I will never leave you, you can always count on me."

Life in Ithaca During 1978-1980

In 1978, Richard Thaler joined our faculty. Richard was an economist who had previously served for four years on the faculty of the Graduate School of Management at the University of Rochester. I liked Richard very much. He had a sharp mind and a great sense of humor. He was one of the regulars in a monthly poker game established by some of us on the BPA faculty. Richard was doing very interesting work in a new field called behavioral economics. He was collaborating with Daniel Kahneman and Amos Tversky at Stanford to develop and test the basic principles of behavioral economics. Their work challenged the essential principle of classical economics, that humans were rational decision makers. Rather, they argued humans were often irrational decision makers, and there were predictable circumstances under which humans would demonstrate irrationality. It was fun and challenging to talk with Richard (actually, we all called him Dick). In 1995 he moved to the University of Chicago, ironically the long established home of classical economic theory. For his work developing the field of behavioral economics, Richard was awarded the 2017 Nobel Prize in Economic Sciences. In its Nobel Prize announcement, the Royal Swedish Academy of Sciences stated Thaler's "contributions have built a bridge between the economic and psychological analyses of individual decision-making. His empirical findings and theoretical insights have been instrumental in creating the new and rapidly expanding field of behavioral economics… by incorporating psychologically realistic assumptions into the analyses of economic decision-making. By exploring the consequences of limited rationality, social preferences, and lack of self-control, he has shown how these human traits systematically affect individual decisions as well as market outcomes." A few days after Richard was awarded the Nobel Prize, I sent him an email congratulating him and suggesting that at least some of his ideas about irrational economic behavior must have been stimulated by our monthly poker games at Cornell. Richard wrote back, saying that indeed that poker game was highlighted in his new book: *Misbehaving: The Making of Behavioral Economics*. What an interesting guy he is.

Deciding to Leave Cornell

I enjoyed the next two years. We made occasional trips to California to visit my parents in Lucerne on the shores of Clear Lake in northern California (where my parents moved at the end of 1976 when Dad retired), and to Peoria, where Jane's father had taken a job as the plant manager at the Pabst brewing plant (the Peoria plant would soon be closed, and Robert and Ruth would move to Milwaukee, where he would take a similar position). Owen became a toddler, and we enjoyed taking him to parks and playgrounds. As he grew older we played many games together. He especially liked Monopoly, which we played for hours at a time. We liked living on Mitchell Street. It was about a half-mile walk to Malott Hall, which I enjoyed even in the winter.

But the Ithaca weather took its toll. After our first winter set record cold temperatures, the second winter set snowfall records. During most of the year, and especially during winter, we rarely saw the sun. The summers were hot and humid, and the sky was almost always filled with clouds. It was gloomy much of the time. It bothered Jane more than me. She got seasonal affective disorder, and became depressed during the worst of the gloomy periods. After Owen was born, Jane started working as a paper grader for a class taught in the Agriculture School, which led to more teaching responsibilities. These jobs and the activity around them helped. But Jane never adapted to the gloomy environment. The weather was terrible for Jane's health.

While I was less affected by the weather, I was becoming restless at BPA. There were not many faculty members who taught and did research on health care issues. Jack Wheeler returned to the University of Michigan after only one year. John McClain was the only colleague I worked with, and as much as I enjoyed working with John I felt we were isolated in the school, and the school was isolated in rural upstate New York. There was no major hospital or medical school nearby that might provide opportunities for doing organizational or health-related behavioral research. Jane and I decided that we could not stay in Ithaca for the long term, and talked about moving somewhere else, preferably on the west coast. I started paying attention to academic job openings in California, Oregon and Washington.

The Call from U.C. Berkeley

Then a miracle happened. I was sitting in my office on a dark, cold afternoon in the spring of 1979 when I got a phone call from Professor Joan Bloom, who was on the faculty of the School of Public Health at U.C. Berkeley. Joan was an old friend. We had gone to graduate school at Stanford together. She told me that the School of Public Health had received permission to start a search for a new faculty member, and the position description sounded a lot like me. Was I interested in applying for the position? I tried not to sound too excited, but in fact I was extremely excited. Once again, as when Dad was hired at Stanford, I felt my world shift a little. I said yes, I would be pleased to apply.

I completed the application materials and made copies of my publications. I wrote a little essay on why this position and the School of Public Health were a good fit for me, and sent the packet of materials off to the search committee. A month or so later, I received a letter inviting me to travel to U.C. Berkeley in June of 1979 to give a presentation on my research to the search committee and other faculty members in the School of Public Health. The timing was perfect. John and I had completed work on our study, Environmental Selection and Physician Supply, which was the strongest research I had done to date. Also, we had been invited to give a presentation on this work at the combined annual meeting of the Operations Research Society of America and The Institute of Management Science, which was to be held in the middle of June in Honolulu. Our preparations for this annual meeting would serve to make me very prepared for my U.C. Berkeley job talk.

Everything went as I had hoped. My presentation at the School of Public Health displayed my strengths in sociological theory, research methodology, and statistical analysis. It also showed I could contribute to discussions of important health policy issues. My topic was of interest to many faculty members since there was a great deal of concern at that time about the supply of physicians, especially in rural areas. I was confident I had given a top-notch presentation. But I knew a faculty position at U.C. Berkeley would attract the best candidates from all over the country. I was certainly competitive, but I had no idea who the other candidates were. So I just had to wait.

While on our trip to Honolulu and Berkeley, Jane, Owen, and I also went to my sister Susanne's wedding. On July 7, 1979, Sue married Mike Hawk at Sanborn Park in Saratoga. It was a beautiful outdoor wedding on a warm, sunny day. Owen was just three days short of his second birthday. He could walk quite well. At one point during the post-wedding reception we saw him going from table to table drinking beer from almost empty glasses. When we got to Owen he was trying to drink directly from the spigot attached to the beer keg. I can say that my little son was a happy drunk. Sue and Mike eventually moved to Gilroy, California, and they have a son and a daughter, Michael Allen and Jamie Lee.

By coincidence, in the summer of 1979 Dick Bailey, a senior faculty member of the School of Public Health, came to BPA to spend six months on a sabbatical leave. Dick had some relatives living in upstate New York, and he sought out the opportunity to be a visiting scholar at BPA so he could spend some time with his relatives. Dick knew I had applied for the faculty position at the School of Public Health. We liked each other and became friendly. But I knew that I should not try to "sell" myself to him. I let him watch me over the summer and fall months to see how the BPA students and faculty felt about me and learn how I would fit in with the faculty at Berkeley. In the end, I think Dick was influential in the U.C. Berkeley faculty's decision to offer me the job. He gave very positive reports about me from his first hand experience with me as a colleague at BPA. In the winter of 1980, I received a letter offering me the faculty position at Berkeley, indicating that it would be effective July 1, 1980. Jane and I were overjoyed. Our hopes came true. We would be returning to the Bay Area, I was joining the faculty of one of the world's great universities, and Owen would grow up close to at

Off To A Good Start

least some of his extended family. I accepted the job offer, and we started planning our move.

John was the first person I told about accepting the U.C. Berkeley job. He was sorry I was leaving, but understood the decision. I waited a little while to tell my other colleagues. But I did so after only a couple of weeks. It was important for them to know in time to go through the process of looking for my replacement. At first my colleagues tried to dissuade me. The Dean of the School offered me a raise and a job for Jane. But we were so happy about returning to the Bay Area I didn't reconsider our decision for a second. My only real regret was that I would no longer be in such a close working relationship with John. We had become great friends with him and his wife Donna. Fortunately, in spite of the distance between us, our friendships have remained strong for over forty years.

Moving Back to California

The first six months of 1980 were spent getting ready to move. We agreed to rent a house in Orinda at 45 Ardilla Road, just over the Berkeley Hills from the U.C. Berkeley campus. My new colleague, Dave Starkweather, and his wife Faye owned the house and had offered it to us to rent. It was a much-appreciated offer. The house was next door to their house, and they had a son, Brad, who was about Owen's age. I finished teaching my last classes. Jane, who had started teaching writing courses at Cornell in late 1977, now unplugged from those duties. We sold our house. The Ford Pinto would not have to make another trip across the country. In 1979, we bought a new car, a yellow Volvo sedan. When Owen first saw the car, he walked up to one of the wheels, which had a hubcap with the letter "V" on it. He shouted out "V!" Forever after that car was known as the V Volvo. We packed our belongings and arranged for a moving van to transport our boxes and furniture. On July 10, we celebrated Owen's third birthday with a party for all his friends. Three days later, after saying our goodbyes to many friends, we drove out of Ithaca and headed for California.

Our trip across country was during a heat wave. Our V Volvo did not have air conditioning. When we stopped for the night in Denver, about to head across very hot desert country, we decided to stay a couple of extra days and have air conditioning installed. It was a great decision. Two days of comfortable driving later across Colorado, Utah, and Nevada, we crossed the border to California. We all cheered, even three-year-old Owen.

Our first home in Ithaca, 425 Cayuga Heights Rd., January, 1977

Our home at 432 Mitchell St., Jane and Jim Chiddix in the foreground

Malott Hall, Cornell University circa 1976;
photo credit Edward Tremel, reproduced with permission

Owen at three years old

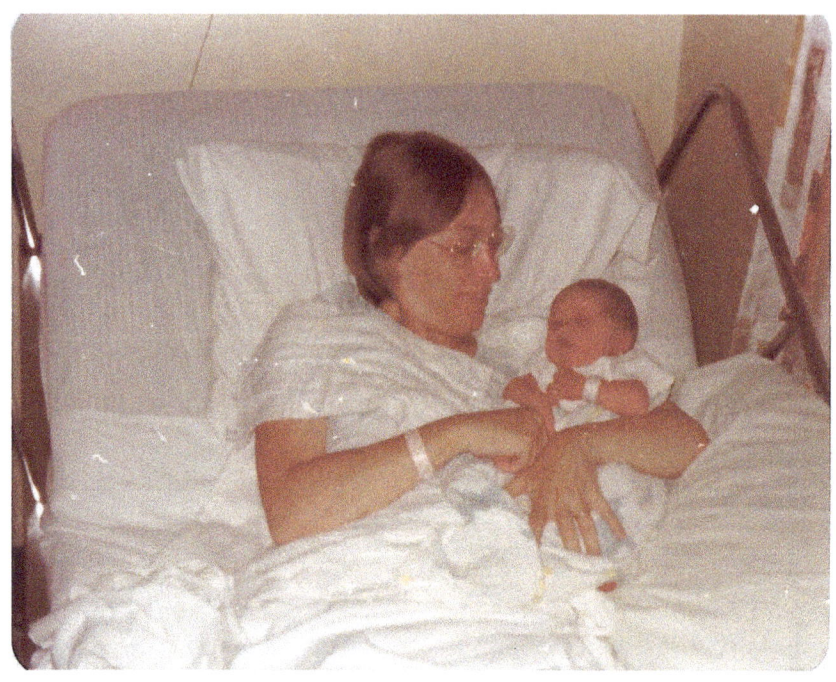
Jane and Owen at Tompkins County Hospital; Owen one day old

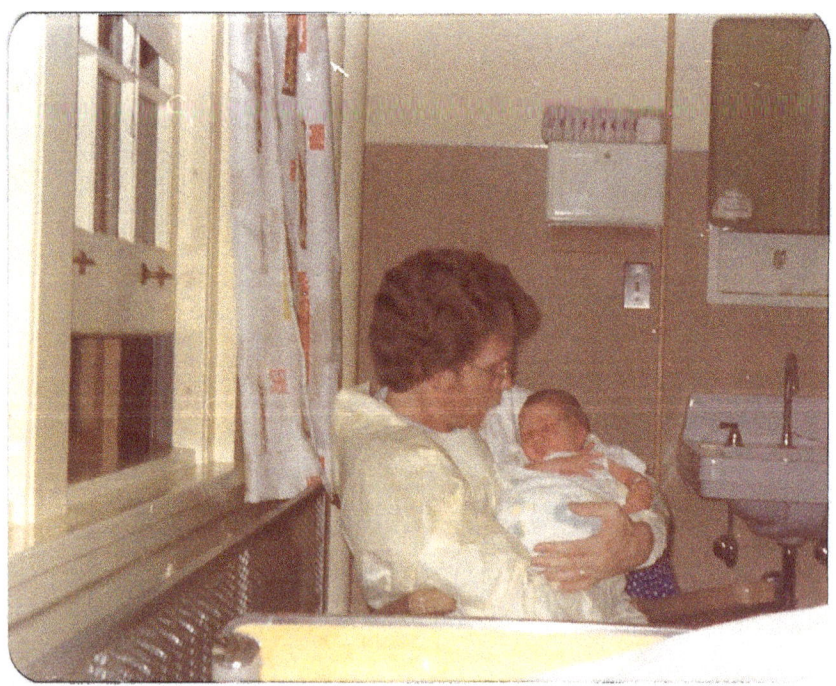
Holding Owen at Tompkins County Hospital; he is one day old

Jane's father, Robert Tiemann, holding Owen at six months old

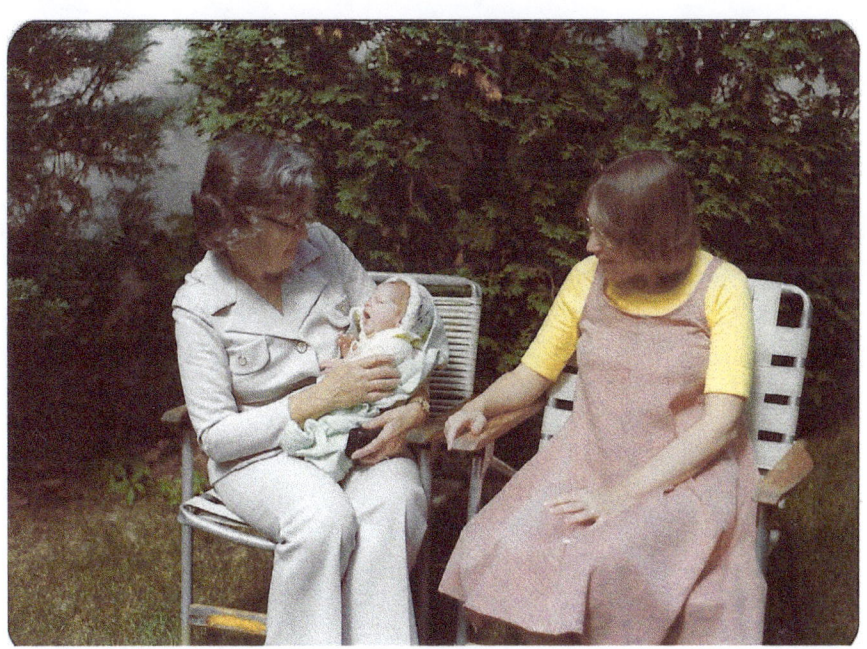

Jane's mom, Ruth Tiemann, holding Owen when he was three weeks old

Off To A Good Start

Owen getting ready for a hot day in Ithaca, 1980

Carol and Sandy at Sue and Mike's wedding, July 7, 1979

Rundall and Hawk families at Sue and Mike's wedding, July 7, 1979

My dad with Owen at Sue and Mike's wedding

My sister Cathy Rundall Goodell, 1980

Jane, Owen, and I on a visit to Elaine and Lee Pinto
in Los Altos, 1979

Thomas Rundall

9

A U.C. Berkeley Professor's Life: Three Decades of Family, Work, Friends, and Community

Recounting the details of my life over thirty years is challenging. There were so many positive, fun and rewarding activities and events. But there also were heartbreaking events, mostly the deaths of much loved family members, which are difficult to write about. Many of my professional activities, such as being department chair or director of a research center, unfolded over several years, and other important events occurred at the same time I was engaged in those activities. It is impossible to draw a strictly linear timeline of activities and events. Rather, I have divided this chapter into three decades, and written about especially meaningful events and related activities while doing my best to keep things straight when activities were overlapping. I have provided as many beginning and ending dates as I could as a way to bring some clarity to the chapter, and, hopefully, make it easier for my beleaguered reader to follow along. I start this chapter with the events of 1980-1989, beginning with the story of Jane and me buying our home at 68 Ardilla Road in Orinda.

1980-1989

Orinda is located in a small valley in Contra Costa County, just east of the Berkeley hills. Through the center of the valley runs San Pablo Creek, which flows north into San Pablo Bay. Residential roads wind through the hills above the valley floor. Orinda is semi-rural. In most of the town there are no streetlights or sidewalks. There is one commercial street, Orinda Way, which has small shops, restaurants, banks, and the Orinda Theatre with its bright vertical neon sign that displays ORINDA. The town has a "village" feeling about it. But it also has a BART train station to allow people to commute to the nearby cities of San Francisco, Oakland, Berkeley, and Walnut Creek and other places in the Bay Area. Orinda has a Mediterranean climate characterized by warm, dry summers and cool rainy winters. There are many parks and trails in the hills around Orinda. The schools are exceptionally good. The overall crime rate is quite low, and there is virtually no violent crime. In 1980 Orinda had only 16,500 residents. Today, nearly 40 years later, the town still has only 17,643 residents, and the town's long-range plan is designed to maintain Orinda's small-town character. Orinda has all the charm and advantages of a small town, but it has easy access to larger cities nearby. For all these reasons, Orinda is a highly sought after place to live, with many affluent families.

During our year renting the Starkweathers' house at 45 Ardilla Road, Jane, Owen, and I quickly fell in love with Orinda. We also fell in love with Ardilla Road, a narrow, winding road that rises up from Camino Pablo on the valley floor, then it joins North Lane and a circle is completed as North Lane turns downhill and rejoins the main road. Many beautiful old oak trees, bushes, and ground ivy line both sides of Ardilla Road. In Spanish, the word Ardilla means squirrel, and the oak trees lining Ardilla Road are filled with them. The houses, many of which were originally cottages used since the 1930s by wealthy San Francisco families to get out of the summer fog, were charming. Over the years, the cottages had been expanded and remodeled. Each home is unique and many have views of the countryside. As the end of our one-year lease on 45 Ardilla Road approached, Jane and I started looking for a house to buy. We wanted to live on Ardilla Road, but the typical price for a home there was well beyond what we could afford to pay. One afternoon, Jane, Owen, and I went out for a walk around the Ardilla Road/North Lane loop. At the corner of Ardilla Road and North Lane we saw a new "For Sale" sign on a house, 68 Ardilla Road, that we had walked past many times.

The house was a single story "ranch" style construction with wood siding painted three different shades of green and a red tile roof. It was in bad need of restoration. The garage door was nailed shut. Instead, the owner drove her car into the garage through an opening in a side of the garage where someone had removed the wall with a power saw. The original structure dated from the mid-1930s, and it looked like very little had been repaired or replaced since then. Still, it was on a beautiful piece of property about a third of an acre in size. Jane and I asked for a tour of the house. We were disappointed to learn that none of the exterior doors fully shut. Most of the windows did not work properly either. The foundation had settled in one corner, causing about a ten-inch drop from the high corner of the house to the low corner. I thought this house was a pile of dirty boards. Seeing how much work would be required to make the necessary repairs, I wasn't very interested. But on the positive side, we could afford this house. In fact, it was the least expensive home for sale in Orinda. Jane presented a persuasive case. The house was exactly in our preferred neighborhood. We could make essential repairs now, and as our incomes grew we could expand and modernize the house. It would, in time, be a lovely family home for us. We bought 68 Ardilla Road, and it has proven to be everything Jane said it would be. For nearly a decade Jane and I did little fixes for the worst of the house's problems. Owen was very patient about the sorry state of his room. But with a couple of waves of remodeling construction (1991 and 2003), we now have a two-story, three-bedroom, two-and-a-half bath modern home with many features drawn from the work of Frank Lloyd Wright. Our home is beautiful to look at and interesting and comfortable to live in. We have happily lived here for 39 years. Thank you, Jane!

In many neighborhoods, homeowners meet each other and become friends through their children. That was certainly true for us. In 1981, there were many children on Ardilla Road and North Lane who played together. As Owen built relationships with these children, we built friendships with their parents. In addition to the Starkweathers, we became friends with Betty Ann and Dan Craven and their son Chad; Tom and Chris Anderson and their three boys, Mark, Brett, and Reed; John and Ann Shumaker and their children Peter and Katie. Although, they did not live in our neighborhood, through being connected at school Owen became friends with David and Greg Callaham, and we became good friends with their parents, Lee and Mike. Owen has remained close friends with David and Mark for nearly forty years. One of our neighbors, Fran Smith was the director of the preschool at St. Marks Church, which Owen attended until he started elementary school at Sleepy Hollow School, and she always paid a little special attention to Owen. We were lucky to live in a community to which we felt connected and that enabled us to build friendships that enriched our lives.

We also reestablished friendships with people that Jane knew when she was a student at Stanford. Jane's roommate during freshman year was Ann Hallberg. They were friends throughout their college years. Right after graduating from Stanford, Ann married another of Jane's Stanford friends, Nelson Shelton. Over the next few years, Jane lost contact with Ann and Nelson. She knew they lived somewhere in the East Bay. Shortly after moving to Ardilla Road, Jane was looking through the phone book for something and noticed the name of Ann's brother, Ross Hallberg, with an address in Walnut Creek. Jane called Ross, and learned that Ann and Nelson lived in Concord, about twelve miles from Orinda. When Jane called Ann, they were delighted to learn we now lived so close to them, and we soon met. Since then, we have been friends with Ross and his wife, Pat, and very close friends with Ann and Nelson.

Soon after arriving in Orinda in August 1980, I went to the School of Public Health to connect with my colleagues and start getting organized to teach my fall classes. Among others, I met with my old friend Joan Bloom, Department Chair Henrik Blum, a behavioral science colleague, Bill Bruvold, and a few others. Everyone was happy to see me, and I was excited to start my career at U.C. Berkeley. Some people think that the life of a university professor is somewhat slow and contemplative. Nothing could be further from the truth. All full-time faculty members are expected to teach, conduct and publish research that will move their field forward, and perform university and community service. Doing all of these things well is challenging and requires an enormous amount of time, including many evenings and weekends. U.C. Berkeley requires all its professors to undergo peer reviews of their performance regularly, every two years for non-tenured, and every three years for tenured faculty members. Since promotions, the tenure decision, and the amount of one's salary depend on these reviews, there is constant pressure to be productive. It was important to get off to a good start.

During my first few years at Berkeley, I taught courses in program evaluation; hospitals, health systems and managed care; and healthcare organization and behavior. I published work I did with colleagues on social networks and help seeking among the elderly; hospital care for the aged; and hospital contract management, the management of publicly owned hospitals by private, for-profit management companies. I served on various faculty committees within the school and on the boards of directors of the Health Services Research Foundation, the Hospital Council Foundation, and the Network for Healthcare Management. In 1983, I was reviewed for tenure. To be awarded tenure means that a faculty member has demonstrated they have conducted high quality research that has contributed to the development of their fields of study, demonstrated they are an effective teacher, shown leadership in university and community service, and demonstrated professional maturity and judgment in all their work. The main purpose of tenure is to allow professors who have demonstrated all of those things the independence to pursue controversial research questions and report findings without fear of being pressured by the university or outside interests to support a particular position. Professors who are awarded tenure cannot be fired except in very unusual circumstances, such as committing moral turpitude. Because the tenure decision could result in essentially a lifetime appointment, the review is very thorough and typically takes several months. I was confident about my qualifications for tenure, but I was, of course, relieved when in the spring of 1984 I received the letter from Chancellor Ira Michael Heyman congratulating me for being awarded tenure. I was also promoted from assistant professor to associate professor. Jane, Owen, and I celebrated!

An important family event happened in 1983. My brother Wayne married Cathy Demers on June 8, 1983, at the Courthouse in Honolulu. Wayne and Cathy met while they were in the Air Force and stationed on Oahu. Before long, they were both discharged from the service, and Jane and I were happy to meet Cathy when they returned to the mainland. The following year their son, Corey, was born. Wayne's Air Force training in "ground radio electronics" and experience with the installation and maintenance of telecommunication equipment prepared him well for his career working for Electronic Data Systems (a company founded by Ross Perot), where he worked in mainframe operations, data communications, and general raised floor operations for the State of California's Medi-Cal Program. Wayne eventually took a position with an e-commerce start-up in April of 2000, managing their help center. Through acquisitions and spin-offs, Wayne eventually worked for EBay, PayPal, Magento, and Adobe before retiring in 2019.

In 1985, I decided I wanted to strengthen my understanding of national health policy and the policy-making process in Washington, D.C. The Robert Wood Johnson Foundation Health Policy Scholars program was designed to provide this kind of opportunity for academics working in health sciences schools. The faculty members awarded one of these fellowships would have all their expenses paid to move to Washington, D.C., and the Foundation would help them get invited to join the staff of a U.S. Senator, member of the House of Representatives, or a senior leader in a federal department. The Robert Wood Johnson Foundation (RWJF) was an influential organization and very well connected in the nation's Capital. The RWJF fellowships were very competitive, and being selected was considered a positive indicator of one's status in the field and one's potential to make important contributions in the future. Jane and I talked over the possibility of my applying for one of these fellowships. We decided it would be good for my career and an interesting adventure for our family to live in Washington, D.C. for a year. I applied, flew to Washington, D.C. for an interview, and was selected. I arranged a leave from U.C. Berkeley, and in the summer of 1985 Jane, Owen, and I moved to a townhouse in a neighborhood known as Fairlington in Virginia, near the Pentagon and just across the Potomac River from the Capital. I was one of six RWJF Health Policy Fellows that year. After going through several weeks of educational sessions and visits to the offices of many prominent people, we were asked to identify the health policy leader we would like to work for. I asked to be considered by the offices of Ted Kennedy, Senator from Massachusetts, and David Durenberger, Senator from Minnesota and the Chair of the Senate Finance Subcommittee on Health. Senator Kennedy's chief of staff interviewed me. It was clear he would like to have me work there. I would be a free additional member of his staff. When I asked what he wanted me to work on, he said, "anything you want." Next, I was interviewed by Charles (Chip) Kahn, Senator Durenberger's senior health aide. When I asked what he wanted me to work on, Chip gave me a short list of specific pieces of legislation the Senator hoped to have passed. I joined Senator Durenberger's staff.

In 1978, Dave Durenberger was elected to the United States Senate in a special election to complete the unexpired term of Senator

Hubert Humphrey, whose position had been temporarily filled by Humphrey's wife Muriel. He was reelected twice, and served in the Senate through January 3, 1995. Durenberger was a centrist Republican who supported the Medicare Catastrophic Act, the Americans with Disabilities Act, President Clinton's National and Community Service Act, the Safe Drinking Water Act, the Women's Economic Equity Act, and he voted for the bill establishing Martin Luther King, Jr. Day as a federal holiday. Durenberger was also personable, and had a decency about him that I admired. I liked working for him, and I learned a lot during my year in his Senate Office.

My work for Senator Durenberger focused on preparing proposals to change the Medicare payment formula to shift some Medicare funds from urban, teaching hospitals to rural hospitals. I thought it was a noble idea to help save struggling rural hospitals. Predictably, the political power of the nation's teaching hospitals pushed back against our proposals, and they were defeated. But in the process I learned an enormous amount about health policy making, including how to lose.

My family had a great year in Washington, D.C., exploring the many sights in the region, including all the museums on the Mall, the White House, George Washington's home, and Civil War battlegrounds. Owen was in the third grade in a school system that had more money to spend per student than California schools, and he played baseball on the Red Top Cab team. He seemed to adapt well to our temporary home and made several friends. During the year, many friends and relatives visited us. When our friends, Ann and Nelson, visited we took a special trip to Gettysburg, Pennsylvania, the site of the famous Civil War battle. Lee Callaham and a former student, Lucky Ehigiator, came to visit as well. The entire Tiemann family came for Christmas week, and we enjoyed showing them around.

One day in the summer of 1986, I got a call from my sister Sandy. She said that Dad had suffered a stroke and part of his face had been paralyzed. A local doctor was recommending that Dad have surgery to clear his carotid arteries. He was currently doing well, but it was possible that he would have another stroke or other problem in the future. Dad had surgery on his left carotid artery, and it seemed to go well. Several weeks later, he had surgery on his right artery, and it did not go well. He began to have serious signs of cardio-vascular problems.

My year as a fellow was up in August, and Jane, Owen, and I returned to the Bay Area and went to see my dad. He looked tired and I noticed a slight slur in his speech. Jane and I talked a lot about our year in Washington, D.C., and he enjoyed hearing our stories. When we left, I hoped he would continue to recover and gain some strength back. We settled back into our Orinda home, which we had rented out for the year. Owen started the fourth grade, and I returned to my work at U.C. Berkeley. In late October, Mom called me to say that while he was in his doctor's office Dad had a heart attack. The doctor put a tab of nitroglycerin under his tongue, and irresponsibly told him to walk across the parking lot to the urgent care center. Dad somehow managed to do this, and after the physician at the urgent care center saw Dad, he was airlifted by helicopter to Adventist St. Helena Hospital in Napa County. I immediately drove to the hospital. Dad was in bed in a single-patient room. He was in bad shape. A lifetime of smoking and a high-fat diet had taken its toll. He was able to talk, and I asked him to tell me what had happened and what his doctors were going to do. The plan was to keep Dad in the hospital, let him rest and recover until his heart was strong enough for coronary artery by-pass surgery. After a long time, I said goodbye and started to leave. As I approached the door, Dad called after me and said, "Take care of your mother." I was shattered.

Eventually Dad had surgery. I was obliged to continue teaching my classes, but I made the 60-mile drive to the hospital every other day to visit him. For many days Dad had a variety of tubes in his mouth, and he was unable to talk. So we would just sit together, and I would tell him news of our family and work life. He seemed to enjoy my company. At that hospital children were not allowed to visit patients in the cardiac care rooms. Since he was only nine years old, Owen could not visit Dad in his room. So, he made a large sign that said, "Get Well Grampa!" One Saturday when the three of us visited my Dad, Owen stood outside the window of Dad's hospital room and held up the sign so Dad could see it, smiled broadly, and raised his fist. Dad loved that. It was typical of Owen to think of doing such a nice thing.

Dad was in the hospital about seven weeks. He was gaining strength, and his doctors were encouraged. In mid-December they arranged for Dad to leave the hospital and go to a nursing home not far from Lucerne. I came to the hospital and drove Dad to the nursing home. He was breathing oxygen through a tube attached to a small portable oxygen cylinder. I tried to encourage him by saying I thought he was in much better shape now than when he entered the hospital. I don't think he agreed with me. It was the last time I saw him. Dad died in the nursing home on December 22, 1986. Mom was, of course, heartbroken. But she had weeks to prepare herself for this. At least in front of family and friends she was very strong. Mom arranged to have Dad cremated and his ashes spread over the water at Shelter Cove, a beautiful place on the northern coast of California. Dad started his life in a sod house near Philip, South Dakota. He went through the depression and lost a brother during World War II. But he found a life partner in Mom, and they raised six children, first in Yuma, then in Campbell. He never shirked his responsibilities, and he worked hard all his life to support his family. He was a good man. His children loved him dearly. I'm glad that even though he died too soon, Dad had nine years of retirement in Lucerne, where he could enjoy his life as he wanted to live it.

At the time of Dad's death, Stanford University was building the Evelyn Lloyd Dees Cardinal Plaza. This was a large, shaded brick plaza with picnic tables and benches located near the football stadium. It was designed to give families a place to eat a meal and relax together before or after football games. It's a lovely, park-like setting protected by beautiful, large oak trees. As a way to defray the cost of constructing the plaza, Stanford was selling individual bricks that they would have inscribed with any text that the purchaser wanted that would fit on the brick. Dad and I had a special relationship with Stanford. He had a great career working at the Stanford Press, and his employment by Stanford enabled me to attend the university tuition free. I decided to buy a brick and have it dedicated to him. The inscription on the brick reads:

RICHARD RUNDALL

THANKS DAD TGR

While Dad was suffering from cardio-vascular disease in late 1986, it became apparent that my sister Sandy also was not well. She had persistent pain in her back, and she was losing weight. She was diagnosed with cancer. This was unbelievable! Everyone in the family was devastated by this terrible news. I have forgotten the name of the specific type of cancer Sandy had. It appeared to be breast cancer that had metastasized to other parts of her body. It was an aggressive form of cancer. Sandy was only 42 years old. One day she called me at my office and asked me to do some research. She wanted me to find out what was the life expectancy for patients with this type of cancer at her stage of disease. I went to the Public Health Library and searched through medical journals. The answer I found was awful. The data showed that the average life expectancy was nine months. Most of the patients who were afflicted with this type of cancer were much older than Sandy. I hoped her relatively young age would be an advantage. I could not bring myself to call her back that day. I was in shock.

The next morning Sandy called me and asked if I had learned anything. This was the hardest conversation I have had in my life. I told her what I had learned as gently as I could, emphasizing that the patients used to calculate this average life expectancy were much older than she was, and that was probably an important factor. She was young and did not have any co-morbidity. I told her these things would work in her favor. Sandy listened quietly, then she thanked me for being honest with her, and she hung up. Sandy fought against her disease with all her might, but it took a devastating toll. In the spring of 1987, all of my siblings and I gathered at a photography studio in San Jose. We took pictures of the six of us together. Sadly, it would be the last time we were all together. One day in August, Jane, Owen, and I drove to San Jose to visit Sandy. She was emaciated and confined to a hospital bed that had been put in her living room. Sandy's appearance would have frightened anyone, let alone a ten-year-old boy. But once again Owen's kindness and empathy for others shone through. He calmly sat down next to the bed and talked with Sandy easily and without fear. He and Sandy talked for a long time, and then she needed to rest. Jane and I have never been more proud of our son. Sandy died on August 31, 1987, nine months after our phone conversation. She is buried at Oak Hill Memorial Park, located at 300 Curtner Avenue in San Jose.

In time, even though they were never far from our thoughts, my family came to accept that Dad and Sandy were no longer with us. We resumed our normal activities and tried to get on with our lives. We knew Dad and Sandy would want nothing less. I published some articles with Bill Bruvold, meta-analyses of evaluations of smoking and alcohol prevention programs. I extended my previous work on hospital care for seniors with some research I did with a college friend, Connie Evashwick, on hospital-based services for older adults. I extended my previous work using population ecology theory to examine the growth of different types of physician practices. I also wrote some book chapters, including one on uncompensated care in hospitals. I was serving on the Editorial Board of the *Journal of Health and Social Behavior* and several other publications. In the spring of 1987, I accepted an invitation to be the Editor of a journal named Medical Care Research and Review. At that time the journal was published by Health Administration Press (HAP) in Ann Arbor, Michigan. For seven years I worked closely with Laura Rodwan and other HAP staff members on publishing and marketing the journal.

I was a little surprised when in 1989 the faculty of my department and the Dean of the School asked me to become Department Chair. I was still just an associate professor, and department chairs were almost always full professors. I decided to accept their offer and served as Chair of the Department of Social and Administrative Health Sciences from 1987 to 1990. Being chair of a department in which there are many professors at a more senior rank is tricky. Fortunately, in 1988 I was reviewed for promotion to full professor. I was awarded this promotion, effective July 1, 1989, at the age of forty years. I felt like my career was just beginning.

By the late 1980s, I realized I had to focus what leisure time I could find on one sport. I gave up softball and tennis, and decided to only play golf. In 1987, Jane and I joined the Moraga Country Club (MCC), primarily so I could easily play a round of golf when I had the time to do it. Our neighbor, Dan Craven, and I joined at the same time, and we enjoyed playing a lot of golf together over the years. I was a better than average golfer, but nothing special. I would usually shoot in the 80s, with a couple of rounds a year in the high 70s. In my best year, I lost in the semi-final round of the

Club Championship. Playing golf is challenging and relaxing at the same time. When I was playing golf, the only thing I could think about was golf. Over the next twenty years, I had a lot of fun playing with friends at MCC. I also played golf with Owen and friends at some of the world's great golf courses, including the Old Course at St. Andrews, Scotland; Pebble Beach, Torrey Pines, La Quinta, and Harding Park in California; Colonial Country Club in Fort Worth, Texas; and Ko Olina on Oahu, Hawai`i. These were all memorable rounds of golf, and getting to play them with Owen and other good friends made the experiences even better. But in time I played less often, and Jane and I decided we needed to join an athletic club where we could exercise even in cold winter weather. We sold our MCC membership in 2007 and joined the Oakwood Athletic Club in Lafayette, which Jane and I continue to use (Jane more regularly than I). I continued to play golf at MCC for a few years as a guest of my member friends, and in time I would play a lot of golf with Nelson Shelton and friends at the public courses, Franklin Canyon and Diablo Creek.

Throughout the 1980s, Owen was growing into a wonderful boy. He was busy with school, playing with friends, and riding his bike around our neighborhood. Jane was home every afternoon to welcome Owen home from school, sometimes with a milkshake in hand to restore his energy. He and I competed in tense games of Monopoly and chess. We became members of Park Pool, and Owen loved to go there during our long, warm summers to swim and hang out with friends. During summers he also loved playing organized baseball in Orinda, and Jane and I went to every baseball game he played. Owen loved all sports, especially baseball. He became a huge fan of the Oakland A's. In 1988 he started attending Orinda Intermediate School. We made sure his friends understood they were welcome to come to our house. He was a happy boy who always seemed to bring joy to whatever he was doing. I don't remember many instances of Owen causing trouble or misbehaving. He was a reliable, problem-free boy, who was remarkably thoughtful of others. Owen was a great kid.

1990-1999

In 1990, Jane got a surprise call from an old friend, Joanne Ingwall, a professor at Harvard Medical School who was the current President of the Society of Magnetic Resonance in Medicine (SMRM). Joanne asked Jane if she would be interested in serving as the Publications Director for SMRM, which had its offices in Berkeley, not far from the School of Public Health. Up until then Jane had worked only occasionally and part-time helping to teach a writing class at Saint Mary's College in Moraga. She was ready to take on more responsibility and work full time. We were sure Owen could handle this. She accepted the job.

In 1991, we started the first of our two house remodeling projects: leveling the foundation, tearing down the kitchen, bathroom, utility room, and family room, and adding a new kitchen, bathroom, family room, dining room, and a second floor with a bedroom, bathroom, laundry, and office. We also rehabbed the existing living room (the second project in 2003 would remodel the two bedrooms and bathroom on the east side of the house). We could not live in our house while the work was under way, so we rented an apartment in the nearby town of Moraga. That was convenient, because in the fall of 1991 Owen started his first year at Miramonte High School, which sits on the border of Orinda and Moraga. The apartment was close to Owen's school. For the next ten months we lived in the apartment, then in June 1992 we returned to a beautiful, well-designed, house on Ardilla Road. We loved the house.

Also in 1991, Owen started working during the summer months for SMRM, helping the staff organize and put on their annual meeting. He would continue working part-time with Jane, now the Executive Director of SMRM, for the next eight years. In 1994, SMRM was merged with another similar society. The new organization was called the International Society for Magnetic Resonance in Medicine (ISMRM), and Jane was appointed the Executive Director. Every third year SMRM/ISMRM's annual meeting was held outside the U.S. For years I tagged along with Jane and Owen on trips to terrific places, including San Francisco (1991), Berlin (1992, after which we went to Prague and Paris), New York (1993), Dallas (1994), New York (1996), Vancouver (1997), Sydney (1998), and Philadelphia (1999).

We had wonderful times traveling together and learning about the cities we visited. Jane and her staff were turning their society into a much-admired professional organization. Owen was also learning a great deal about hotels and conference planning and management.

In 1993, to celebrate their fiftieth wedding anniversary, Mom and Dad Tiemann took all their children and grandchildren on a trip to Germany and Switzerland. Our trip included a couple of days at Bad Laer in northwest Germany, where there was evidence the Tiemanns lived in the sixth century. We also drove the Romantische Strase, the Romantic Road. The Tiemanns had hired a small bus and driver who drove us through the Bavarian forests and mountains to King Ludwig II's iconic Neuschwanstein Castle. We also went a very short way into Switzerland to tour Schleitheim, which we believed was the ancestral home of Mom Tiemann's family. We visited many other cities and villages. We had a wonderful, memorable trip. Jane, Owen, and I still talk about it.

The Rundall family was very happy in 1993 when Wayne married his second wife, Julie Sathe, and Julie's two daughters, Heather and Jennifer, from her first marriage came to live with them in their home in Elk Grove, near Sacramento. We have grown very close with Julie, Heather and Jenn, and Owen and his family are now very close with Corey, Heather, and Jenn's families. Since Owen is an only child, Jane and I are especially happy that he is a close friend with many of his cousins.

By the fall of 1993, it became apparent that Owen had a group of about 10 guys from Miramonte High who he spent time with after school and on weekends. We were always happy to come in our house and find a huge pile of sneakers on the floor of the foyer. Owen and his friends would be watching something on television. They were all great kids. David Callaham, Brad Davis, Greg Flandermeyer, Eric Greathouse, Andy Elliott, Dave Hoppock, Dave Bercovich, Mike Gleason, and Ryan Zeiger were the core of the group. We knew teenagers were strongly influenced by the friends they hung out with. We felt Owen was in very good company. One day, one of the guys told us the name they called the group: the "O" Gang. We found out Owen was the glue that held the group together. We liked that very much.

Owen graduated from Miramonte High School in 1995. Influenced largely by the fact that his friend Chad Craven was attending Colorado State University, Owen decided to go to college there as well. He applied and was accepted for the fall 1995 class. Owen and I could not attend the 1995 ISMRM meeting (in Nice, France!) because we were driving to Colorado State in Fort Collins for the start of his freshman year. Jane flew to Fort Collins after the meeting and stayed a few days with Owen before returning to our "empty nest" in Orinda. We were both sad not to have him at home. Owen continued to work part-time for ISMRM throughout college, helping Jane and her staff put on their annual meeting (then held in the spring), and each summer he worked as an intern in the Sales and Marketing Department of the Hilton Hotel in San Francisco. In 2000, Owen graduated from Colorado State with a major in economics and a minor in history. He soon accepted a full-time position at the Hilton Hotel.

In 1994, the School of Public Health went through a re-organization, and the Division of Health Policy and Management was created (at U.C. Berkeley it is called a division; in most other universities it would be called a department). The Division's mission was to educate both high-impact practitioners in health care policy and management as well as researchers with a focus on the healthcare industry and policy. The students took courses in health policy and policy analysis, economics, finance, management, organizational behavior, and law. They specialized in policy or management, and prepared for careers in research, health policy analysis, or management of healthcare organizations. I was asked to serve as Division Head (Chair) over the period 1994-1995. This was followed by service from 1994-1999 as the Director of the MBA/MPH Graduate Program in Health Services Management, which the School of Public Health ran jointly with the Haas School of Business. My five years as Director of the MBA/MPH program were possibly my most enjoyable years at Berkeley. The students were smart, committed to making a positive difference in the world, and we all got along very well. It was fun and I got a chance to use in my teaching some of what I learned when I was at the School of Business and Public Administration at Cornell University. In 1997 the School of Public Health awarded me the Outstanding Teaching and Mentoring Award to acknowledge the good work I was doing with students. In 1996, I founded a new research center, the Center for Health Management Studies, and served as its Director from 1996-1999, helping to develop research projects that I and other faculty members worked on.

In 1994, Dave Starkweather and I were selected to work with an Australian colleague, Mary Harris, to evaluate the National Program of Management Development for Australian Clinicians. This was the beginning of my working relationship with Dr. Jennifer Alexander, one of the Australian faculty members in the management development program. Jennifer is a physician who has also acquired training in management. She has served as a leader in several prestigious Australian organizations, including as President of the Royal Australasian College of Medical Administrators, the Chief Executive of the Australian Institute of Management, and Council Member of the University of New South Wales. Jennifer is also a superb cook and has great knowledge of food and wine pairings. Jennifer and I became great friends. Over the next few years we planned and carried out several educational tours of U.S. health care systems for Australian and New Zealand clinicians and senior healthcare managers. The participants were always interested in visiting Kaiser Permanente, as well as other U.S. health systems. One year we reversed the flow, and I accompanied several U.S. healthcare executives to Australia. Jennifer also invited me to give presentations on my research to various audiences. I loved Australia, and working with Jennifer was fun and worthwhile for all involved. I started traveling to Australia once or twice a year. In all, I have been to Australia nine times, including other trips with Jane and Owen and my brother Wayne and his wife Julie. I've visited Sydney, Melbourne, Adelaide, Brisbane, Perth, and a handful of other smaller cities. I like them all.

Throughout the 1990s I continued to publish strong research articles, with several related to healthcare quality improvement, development and performance of integrated delivery systems (such as Kaiser Permanente), and community-based health organizations serving AIDS patients. Some of my favorite articles from this period include: The Health Care Quality Improvement Initiative: Insights from Fifty Cases of Serious Medical Mistakes, published in *Medical Care Research and Review*; Impact of the Ryan White Care Act on the Availability of HIV/AIDS Services, in *Policy Studies Journal*; and Type of Health Care Coverage and the Likelihood of Being Screened for Cancer, in the journal *Medical Care*. With coauthors Dave Starkweather and Barbara Norrish, I published a book based on a study we did of restructuring nursing governance (the way in which nursing work is planned and managed) in hospitals: *After Restructuring: Empowerment Strategies at Work in America's Hospitals*. In 1997, the most senior researchers in my field honored me by voting in favor of appointing me a Fellow of the Association for Health Services Research.

Since joining the U.C. Berkeley faculty in 1980, I listened to classical music in my office nearly continuously. I enjoyed the music, and it helped me relax. I was happy when Ann and Nelson asked Jane and me if we wanted to join them in purchasing season tickets for six performances of the San Francisco Symphony (SFS). We bought our first season ticket in 1997. The SFS now performed in Davies Symphony Hall instead of the War Memorial Opera House, the site of our first date in 1974. We have been going to symphony performances with Ann and Nelson for twenty-three years. We also have a great time vacationing with Ann and Nelson. Every year we take a trip together. We have explored Paris, Normandy, and other parts of France; Finland; England; Hawaii; Charleston and Savannah; Palm Springs; Los Angeles; Santa Fe; Vancouver, British Columbia; and Pasadena. These trips are always fun and educational. I learned a lot from Ann, Nelson, and Jane recounting stories of when they lived in various Stanford in Europe campuses, and from their knowledge of history, the arts, and social life in other countries. The vacation in Palm Springs was extra special because afterward Jane and I visited Joanne and Dick Ingwall at their winter home in Borrego Springs, then we drove to Yuma, where for the first time Jane saw the town in which I spent my youth.

A transformative change for the School of Public Health and me occurred in 1998: our School's successful recruitment of Professor Steve Shortell. Steve was the pre-eminent health services researcher in the U.S., and probably in the world as well. He was on the faculty at Northwestern University in Chicago. Steve and I were friends, having met at research conferences, and we enjoyed going to dinner together at these meetings and talking about our work. In the mid-1990s the Blue Cross of California Foundation gave the School of Public Health three million dollars to endow a "Distinguished Chair" in the field of health policy and management. The campus administration allocated a faculty position to go with the endowed chair, and the School formed a committee to lead the search to recruit a new faculty member worthy of such a chair. I served on the search committee. One morning I called Steve and explained the opportunity we had to recruit a world-class colleague, and I asked if he would consider this position. I was thrilled when he said he might be interested. Steve was happy at Northwestern, and he was not seeking to leave. But he and his wife, Susan, had a vacation home in Sebastopol, about 65 miles from Berkeley, they liked the Bay Area, and he was intrigued by the possibility of joining the U.C. Berkeley faculty. The other members of the search committee were equally thrilled that Steve was interested in learning more about the chair and the school. Steve talked to several of the school's faculty members, including the Dean of the School. He made a visit to the campus and gave a research presentation. Steve and his wife Susan ultimately decided that the School, and the San Francisco Bay Area were well suited to their professional and personal interests. In due course the School announced that Steve would be joining our faculty. Steve and Susan moved to Berkeley. Steve and I have similar research interests and extensive backgrounds in organizational theory and management science. For the first time in my career, I had a colleague to work with who did research on integrated delivery systems and other organizational and health system topics that overlapped with my interests. Steve and I have enjoyed working together on many research projects and, later, in the administration of the School. Jane and Susan are in the same book club. We have become the best of friends

In 1987, Robert Tiemann retired and he and Ruth moved from Milwaukee to Fearrington Village, just outside of Chapel Hill, North Carolina. They enjoyed living in Fearrington very much. It was a former farm that had been transformed into an upscale housing development with a "village" character about it. For years Robert suffered from poor circulation and related problems. In 1998, as his health grew worse, Robert and Ruth invited the entire family to join them on a vacation in Jamaica. Robert was visibly weak and we all sensed that his health was ebbing away. All their children and grandchildren made sure to spend time with him. On November 20, 1998, only a few months after we returned from Jamaica, Robert passed away in a hospital in Chapel Hill. The family had him transported to St. Louis, where we gathered for his burial in the family plot in St. Paul Churchyard (7600 S. Rock Hill Road, St. Louis). Robert Tiemann was a fine man. He was a World War II veteran who, with his wife Ruth, raised five wonderful children, including his namesake, Robert Tiemann, Jr., who was accepted into West Point but refused to fight in Vietnam. He was greatly missed by all his family, including me. Mom Tiemann returned to her home in Fearrington, but eventually sold her house and moved to an assisted living facility, Galloway Ridge, also at Fearrington. She loved living in that community, and her oldest son Tom Tiemann and his wife Eileen McGrath lived nearby in the town of Carrboro.

The following year, my sister, Carol, died unexpectedly. Carol struggled with numerous challenges throughout her life, including two failed marriages. Her two sons, Rick and Ron, suffered from Wilson's Disease, an inherited disorder that causes too much copper to accumulate in the body's organs. Eventually Rick would die from complications associated with this disease, and Ron would struggle for years with the effects of Wilson's Disease on his nervous system. Carol worked for several years as a glass blower for Watkins-Johnson, a company in Scotts Valley, California that made laboratory supplies. She was very good at her job, and she used her glass blowing skills to make beautiful glass art as well. For some reason, that job ended, and Carol never recovered financially. In the late 1990s, she was living in San Jose in a mobile home with a roommate. On November 27, 1999, Carol had a brain aneurysm and died immediately. She was only 53 years old. On the day Carol died I was home alone. Jane was attending a meeting in Chicago. My sister, Sue, called and told me the awful news. I fell to my knees in shock. I felt like everyone in my family was dying. It was a terrible time. We held a memorial service for Carol. Ron and I both spoke about her and cried over how much we were going to miss her. For the first time in my life I heard my mom sobbing in grief. Sue asked the managers of the Oak Hill Memorial Park if it was possible for Carol's ashes to be placed in the same grave site where her sister, Sandy, was buried.

They said, "Yes, of course." Carol was not a member of any church, so there was no priest or minister to lead her burial ceremony. I was asked to do that. All of us gathered at her gravesite. I talked about her life and how much she loved her children. Then, I read the King James Version of Psalm 23, "The Lord is my shepherd..." We placed the urn with Carol's ashes in the grave, and I quietly remembered happy days in Yuma and Campbell playing with my beautiful sister.

An important, positive development for me during this time period was the invitation I received to join the Board of Directors for the John Muir Physician Network, the component of the John Muir Health System, headquartered in Walnut Creek, that was responsible for recruiting needed physicians to the community and making sure the physicians associated with John Muir Hospitals were contracted to care for patients covered by managed care health plans. I was eager to serve on this Board, thinking I could provide our community with some worthwhile service and learn a great deal about the practical aspects of running a health system. I served on the Board from 1999-2009, and as Board Chair from 2001-2004. This was the beginning of a long-term relationship. I would eventually serve on John Muir Health Boards for twenty years.

2000-2009

In 2000 Owen graduated from Colorado State University with a major in economics and a minor in history. Shortly after graduation he accepted a job in the Sales and Marketing Department of the Hilton Hotel in San Francisco, where he had worked as a summer intern while in college. This was the start of his long, successful career in the hotel business. Owen has worked for several of the top hotel chains in the world, and he is now the Director of Sales and Marketing for the prestigious Omni Hotel in San Francisco.

Jane and I also had something special to celebrate in 2000. May 24 was our 25th wedding anniversary. We decided to go to the Silverado Resort in Napa Valley to celebrate the occasion. We were having a great time, enjoying the beautiful scenery, food, and wine. I went to play golf at the Silverado Golf Course while Jane was supposedly taking the morning to relax. Little did I know. When I returned from playing golf, I was going to put my golf clubs away in my car, but I couldn't find my Ford Explorer. I went to our room to see if Jane had moved it. Jane said she wanted to walk me to my car. As we walked in the parking lot, I didn't see my Explorer anywhere. Then Jane stopped in front of a brand new silver BMW and said, "Here's your car." I was stupefied. My response was, "You mean for the day?" I thought she had rented it. Jane assured me that this amazing car was the replacement for my old Explorer and that she bought it for me for an anniversary present. She had someone from the BMW dealership drive the new car to Silverado and drive the Explorer as the "trade in" vehicle back to the dealership. She arranged all of this in advance without giving me any hint about what she was up to. I have never been so surprised by anything in my life. I didn't think to buy Jane a car for our anniversary, but she didn't seem to mind. Jane's married women friends were not too happy with her, claiming she raised the bar too high. That BMW was my favorite car of all time. I kept it 12 years, and I wish I still had it.

My work life continued to flourish. I especially enjoyed working with Steve Shortell on research and School development projects. When Steve joined the Division of Health Policy and Management, his stature and the ongoing research he brought with him greatly enhanced our Division's reputation and national standing. We certainly had a strong group of faculty before Steve arrived. In addition to myself, the Division's tenured faculty included James Robinson, Joan Bloom, Helen Halpin, Leonard Duhl, Henrik Blum, Richard Scheffler, and Teh-wei Hu (two other great colleagues, Ann Keller and Will Dow, would join our department in a few years). Then, in 1998, Steve joined us. By 2000 I think we were all performing at the top of our games, and our Division of Health Policy and Management was probably the best of its kind in the U.S., perhaps the best in the world.

Then, family tragedy struck again. My sister, Cathy, was diagnosed with cancer. Yet another Rundall/Serbousek female diagnosed with cancer, going back at least as far as my grandmother Edna Rundall and my grandmother Alice Serbousek. I think Cathy's primary site was her breast. She admitted to having noticed a lump in her breast months before her diagnosis but was too afraid to see a doctor about it. It was overwhelming for me to hear about Cathy's diagnosis, but I'm sure what I was going through was nothing compared to what my sister was enduring. Cathy was married to Mark Merrill, and they had a young son, Patrick. Cathy also had a daughter, Carla, with her first husband, Craig Goodell. She had everything to live for. Cathy fiercely fought the disease. She went through months of treatments, including brain surgery to remove cancerous tissue from her brain. What courage she showed. But she slowly succumbed to the disease, and died on May 29, 2001. At the end she was so sick. I wanted to roll the years back to see my beautiful sister happy and healthy again. Mark said Cathy loved to go fishing with him on a boat off the coast of Monterey and he suggested that Cathy be cremated and that we spread her ashes over the ocean in their favorite spot. A few days later, the family gathered on a boat and we let Cathy go. Not long after our ceremony on the water for Cathy, the children of my three deceased sisters - Carla, Patrick, Debbie, Julie, and Ron – arranged to have a new headstone made for the gravesite at Oakhill Memorial Park where Sandy and Carol were buried. The new headstone included Cathy's name. My three sisters would always be thought of together.

My family members were still grieving the loss of Cathy when another, more far reaching tragedy struck: four coordinated terrorist attacks by the Islamic terrorist group Al-Qaeda against the United States on the morning of Tuesday, September 11, 2001. Nineteen terrorists hijacked four commercial airliners and were intending to use the planes to carry out suicide attacks against the World Trade Center, the Pentagon, and the U.S. Capitol. Two of the planes were flown into the twin towers of the World Trade Center, causing them to collapse. One of the planes also hit the Pentagon just outside Washington, D.C. The planned attack against the U.S. Capitol was prevented. The plane crashed into a field in Somerset County, Pennsylvania during a heroic attempt by the passengers and crew to regain control of the plane. Almost 3,000 people were killed during the 9/11 attacks, which triggered Operation Enduring Freedom, an American-led international effort to remove the Taliban regime in Afghanistan and destroy Osama Bin Laden's terrorist network based there. This military effort succeeded in removing the Taliban from operational power, but the war continued for many years against the Taliban insurgency campaign in Afghanistan and neighboring Pakistan. In the U.S., security fears led to the creation of the Department of Homeland Security and many other initiatives designed to prevent terrorist attacks, including strengthening border security and increasing surveillance of suspected terrorists. The 9/11 attacks and the U.S. government's response defined the presidency of George W. Bush. Americans settled into a "new normal" way of life with heightened concern for terrorist attacks that has persisted to this day.

I continued to do research and to teach classes in health policy and management, and my work was making a positive difference in the field and in the School. In 2001, I was awarded the Henry J. Kaiser Endowed Chair in Organized Health Systems. The School organized a celebration in my honor at the Faculty Club. All of my family came and many faculty colleagues were there as well. The endowed chair was formally bestowed upon me, and I gave a thank you speech expressing my gratitude to the organization that provided the funds for the chair, Kaiser Permanente. I also took that opportunity to publicly thank Jane for being so understanding about the many times I had to work during the evenings and weekends. When I first got to know Jane, she made it clear to me that she valued what academics do, and she was proud that I chose to become a university professor. I was, and am, deeply grateful to Jane for her support, and I said so at the celebration at the Faculty Club. Being awarded the endowed chair was a great honor for me, and provided me with not only the prestige of holding an endowed chair, but about $30,000 per year to spend on research expenses that were not covered by research grants.

Perhaps in 2002 the universe was attempting to balance things out when I was asked to serve in two other administrative positions, Division Chair (2001-2002) and Director of the Center for Health Research (2002-2005). I also continued to teach courses in evidence-based health services management and policy evaluation. My work in developing innovative courses and the articles I published about the importance of training health services managers in evidence-based management were acknowledged when I was awarded the 2005 Filerman Prize for Innovation in Health Administration Education by the Association of University Programs in Health Administration.

Off To A Good Start

In 2005, I started working with a post-doctoral scholar Katharina Janus, PhD, MBA, who was a German citizen and received her MBA degree from a program run by the Sorbonne in Paris and the University of Hamburg. Katharina went on to earn her doctoral degree in health policy and management from the Helmut-Schmidt-University in Hamburg. She had traveled extensively in the U.S., and knew a great deal about our health care systems. We worked on two research projects together: a study of job satisfaction among physicians in academic medical centers in the U.S. and Germany, published in 2008 in the *Journal of Health Politics, Policy and Law*; and a study of California hospitals with a challenging payer mix that managed to remain consistently profitable. On the latter study, Shelley Oberlin joined our research team, and the three of us made site visits to five hospitals in California to interview managers about the ways they managed their hospital to achieve profitability. The three of us made a great team, and became life-long friends. In 2012 we published a very useful article about what we learned in the *Journal of Healthcare Management*. Although we live far apart, Jane and I stay in contact with Shelley, and now with her husband Jeffrey Poffenbarger and son Ryan. We have also remained great friends with Katharina, and we have become friends with her aunt, Barbara Hyland, who lives in San Francisco. Over the next fifteen years I continued to work with Katharina on the founding and development of her Center for Healthcare Management at Columbia University and her educational center in Paris. I've enjoyed many trips to Europe to attend the Center's Annual Forum, and Jane and I look forward to Katharina's regular visits to the Bay Area.

Also in 2005, after 15 years working at ISMRM and 13 years as the society's Executive Director, Jane decided to retire. She had accomplished an enormous amount over that period of time. ISMRM was the premier professional society for clinicians and scientists who used magnetic resonance imaging in their work. Every year, the scientific program at the annual meeting grew in size and featured many presentations on advanced, path-breaking research. Through her astute business management, Jane had also accumulated a large financial reserve for the society. The Society's Board of Directors tried to keep Jane from retiring, but she knew it was time. At the annual meeting that year in Miami, Jane was given the heartfelt appreciation of the Board, and after her farewell speech at the meeting the entire membership of several thousand people gave her a standing ovation. It was very well deserved.

During the 2000s, my mom lived in an apartment in a senior housing complex in Gilroy, not far from my sister Sue's house. The arrangement worked well for Mom, although it placed a burden on Sue and her husband Mike to be first responders whenever Mom needed something. One day in 2003, Mom fell and injured herself, requiring a stay in St. Louise Hospital. Sue, Wayne, and I knew Mom should not continue living alone. We wanted her to move to an assisted living facility. But Mom was intent on returning to her apartment. She very reluctantly compromised and moved into a board and care facility with only five other elderly women living in the house. The staff of this facility took great care of mom. She regained her strength, and had a social network of women in similar circumstances. Mom was still close to Sue's house, and I drove to Gilroy once or twice a month to visit her. This arrangement worked very well, until one day in 2006 when Mom had another fall, this time suffering a crack in her pelvis, the same injury she suffered on our family's road trip to the Grand Canyon in the early 1950s. Mom was transported to St. Louise Hospital.

It is very dangerous for elderly people with congestive heart failure to lie down too much. They must get up and move about to increase circulation and reduce the accumulation of fluid in their lungs. Mom tried to get up from her hospital bed, but she couldn't do enough. Her heart began to fail, and in time her doctor advised Mom to be placed in hospice care, which would make her comfortable for as long as possible. Family members began to visit Mom to say their goodbyes, including her sisters, Rose Mary and LaVerne. Mom had not seen them in a long time, and I know it helped her to be able to be with her sisters once more. Mom died in the early morning hours of March 28, 2006. Sue stayed with mom continuously until she left us, and I will always be thankful for that. We did as Mom wished, and had her body cremated. Later that year all her remaining children and their families drove to Shelter Cove, where after his death Dad's ashes were spread over the Pacific waters. We hired a boat to take us out to a point near the cove and spread Mom's ashes over the water. As soon as we did this, two Orca whales, a couple, began swimming near our boat and slightly breeching as they swam away. How could this be? It was a beautiful, touching sight. The boat captain said he had never seen Orcas swim so close to a boat. We didn't understand what had just happened, but we all agreed we felt some closure. Mom and Dad were happy to be together again.

Even before mom's passing, it became clear to me that Sue was the glue that held our family together. She regularly talked with all of us: my brother, nieces, nephews, cousins, and, of course, her husband, Mike, and her own children. Sue has the kind of warm, sincere personality that allows people to trust her and tell her what is going on in their life: the good and the bad. We all value her thoughts and suggestions about how to deal with issues. She is a friend, a counselor, and a great sister. Sue and Mike have hosted our family's Christmas party, a much-loved gathering, nearly every year for the last 30 years.

Throughout the 2000s, my administrative, research, teaching, and service work was in full flight. In 2006, I accepted an invitation to serve on the Board of Directors of On Lok, an internationally recognized Program of All-inclusive Care for the Elderly (PACE program). On Lok is an integrated health care delivery system for frail seniors. The organization provides a comprehensive array of benefits, including delivered meals and transportation services; ambulatory healthcare services, including dental and primary care; and in-hospital care when needed. It also includes social and recreational centers at On Lok facilities that members can visit to meet with friends and enjoy playing various recreational games, such a mahjong and Nintendo's Wii video game. The goal is to keep frail seniors out of nursing homes and living in their own homes as long as possible. On Lok is remarkably good at doing this. One of Jane's friends from her undergraduate days at Stanford, Bob Edmondson, was On Lok's Chief Executive Officer, and I enjoyed working with him. I strongly supported the On Lok approach to senior services, and I was proud to serve on On Lok's Board through 2016, and as Chair of the Board of one of the organization's key subsidiaries, the On Lok Senior Services Corporation, from 2013- 2016.

In 2009, my term of service on the board of the John Muir Physician Network ended, and I was asked to join the Board of Directors for the overall John Muir Health System. I served on the John Muir Health Board until 2019, with a term as Board Chair from 2015-2017. These were prestigious organizations that were already making substantial impacts on the health of the populations they served, and I was fortunate to help guide each of them through a somewhat tumultuous period of time.

When I joined the Board of Directors for John Muir Health, the system consisted of a 554-bed hospital in Walnut Creek, a 245-bed hospital in Concord, a 73-bed behavioral health center also in Concord, some urgent care clinics, and the Physician Network I had previously worked with. At that time, John Muir Health was primarily known for the quality of its hospitals. Ken Anderson had been the CEO of John Muir Health for 36 years. Ken and his leadership team had built John Muir Health in the image of other outstanding hospital-centric health systems of the day. The hospitals in Walnut Creek and Concord were superb inpatient facilities. In 2010, Ken Anderson announced he was going to retire. Before beginning the search for Ken's replacement, the John Muir Health Board of Directors discussed how patient care needs were likely to change in the coming years, and how John Muir Health would need to adapt to the new environment. Two obvious trends were the growing proportion of seniors in the U.S population, and the related growth in the prevalence of chronic conditions. These trends required health systems that had been primarily designed to care for patients with acute conditions, including John Muir Health, to develop different strategies and capabilities for caring for large numbers of patients with chronic illnesses. A strong ambulatory care system, timely information sharing across multiple providers and sites of care, and effective coordination of care across all caregivers were necessary for the health system to be successful in the future. The Board was ready to move John Muir Health in those directions. We initiated a search for Ken's replacement, and we hired Calvin Knight, from Swedish Health Services in Seattle.

Cal shared the Board's vision for transforming John Muir Health into a modern integrated delivery system, and he had a great deal of experience developing community-based clinics, urgent care

171

centers and partnering with physician practices, surgical centers, and other hospitals. Cal was exactly the transformational leader we needed. A high priority was terminating an agreement the health system had negotiated years before with the Muir Independent Practice Association (IPA), a group of physicians that had formed to enable them to contract with John Muir Health's Physician Network to provide services to patients covered by managed care plans. The agreement, interestingly called the "Treaty," gave the doctors veto power over many of the growth and development decisions that John Muir Health needed to make in order to become a better health system. The doctors felt they needed that veto power to protect their practices if John Muir Health's leaders decided, for example, to recruit new physicians to the community or expand John Muir Health's own ambulatory care clinics. The John Muir Health Board of Directors and senior management team offered physicians an alternative type of power: more active participation in health system decision making. The number of positions on the Board of Directors reserved for physicians was increased from four to six, and four additional non-voting board positions were also allocated to physicians. By participating in Board discussions and serving on Board-level committees, such as strategic planning, physicians could influence the ways in which John Muir Health developed its services. In time, most physicians accepted this new approach, and the "Treaty" agreement was allowed to expire. Cal Knight led the organization through the implementation of many developments that improved patient access to care and patient outcomes, including a comprehensive system-wide electronic health information system, new outpatient care centers and urgent care centers in several communities, a partnership with Stanford Health to develop a neo-natal intensive care unit at the Walnut Creek hospital, a partnership with the University California, San Francisco to develop a comprehensive ambulatory clinic in Berkeley and a cancer treatment program at the Walnut Creek hospital. Today, John Muir Health is a nationally recognized health care system, and its cardiac care, orthopedic surgery, and several other service lines are ranked among the best in the country. I was proud to be a part of such a transformational period in John Muir Health's history.

In 2007 my coauthors and I published a book, *Implementing an Electronic Medical Record System*, reporting the results of a qualitative study of the implementation of a new electronic medical record system in the Hawaii Region of Kaiser Permanente. Electronic medical record systems were just starting to be implemented by many health systems, and this was the first in-depth study of the successes and failures of a leading health system's effort. The book and the related article we published in the *BMJ* (formerly the *British Medical Journal*) got a lot of attention. This work got me interested in health information technology and its effects on patient care, a topic I would continue to study throughout the next ten years.

In 2002, Steve Shortell was appointed Dean of the School of Public Health. In 2007, Steve asked me to join him in the Dean's Office as Executive Associate Dean. I would be primarily responsible for the internal operations of the school, freeing up Steve to do more on external affairs and fundraising. With some reluctance, I agreed to serve, and I spent three years as the "internal" Dean of the School. I was reluctant because I had a full plate already with my service work, research, and teaching obligations, all of which I enjoyed. But, again the call of a unique learning experience and the chance to make a positive difference in the operations of the school encouraged me to accept Steve's offer. Some of my work as Executive Associate Dean involved changing the culture of the faculty, making faculty members more aware of the resource limits of the School and working with them to prioritize spending on teaching assistants, supplies, and other expenditures. I also implemented improvements to the financial reporting systems for School expenditures, and created Division and program budgets that helped control expenditures. I was also responsible for reviewing and commenting in writing on the performance of every faculty member who was eligible for a promotion or merit increase. In 2008, perhaps to recognize my efforts in performing these and other administrative tasks, I was awarded the School's Alfred Childs Outstanding Faculty Service Award.

My activities as Executive Associate Dean were made a little burdensome by a change in my health. In 2007, shortly after becoming the Executive Associate Dean, I was diagnosed with thyroid cancer. Of course, I immediately thought of my family's history with cancer. But it was papillary cancer, a malignant, slow growing cancer, which is the most treatable of the various types of thyroid cancer. My biopsy and other examinations showed that the cancer was localized to my thyroid, which was a great relief. In February of 2008 Dr. Deborah Kerlin performed my thyroidectomy at John Muir Hospital in Walnut Creek. She did a terrific job, cutting away the thyroid tissue close to my vocal chords, but not damaging the chords in any way. After several rounds of radioiodine treatment to kill off any remaining thyroid cells, and ten years of regular blood monitoring, my endocrinologist declared me cancer free! Nothing focuses one's mind on what they want to do with their life more than being diagnosed with malignant cancer. For the first time, I began to imagine my life after being a professor at U.C Berkeley. But for the next three years I continued to carry on with my academic and administrative responsibilities.

It was a little surprising to me that given my administrative responsibilities during the 2000s I was able to successfully partner with several colleagues on major research projects. In fact some of my most important work and most frequently cited publications came during that period of time. My research themes included physician organizations, performance improvement, doctor-manager relationships, health information systems, and evidence-based management. I co-authored articles with wonderful colleagues, including Kieran Walshe, Steve Shortell, James (Jamie) Robinson, John Hsu, Katharina Janus, Huw Davies, Anthony Kovner, Thomas Bodenheimer, Ilana Graetz, and Dorothy Hung, among others. My most frequently cited publication is Evidence-based Management: From Theory to Practice in Healthcare, published in 2008 in the *Milbank Quarterly* (708 citations in other articles). Other frequently cited articles include External Incentives, Information Technology, and Organized Processes to Improve Health Care Quality for Patients with Chronic Diseases, published in 2003 in the *Journal of the American Medical Association* (583 citations); Improving Patient Care by Linking Evidence-based Medicine and Evidence-based Management, published in 2007 in the *Journal of the American Medical Association* (302 citations); and As Good As It Gets? Chronic Care Management Practices in Nine Leading Physician Organizations in the United States, published in 2003 in the *BMJ*, formerly known as the *British Medical Journal* (213 citations).

During the decade of the 2000s, I was fortunate to be able to travel to give research presentations or for vacation to many countries, including Spain, Sweden, Australia (again!), New Zealand, England, Scotland, China, Singapore, Hong Kong, and Japan. It was an exhilarating time, seeing beautiful sites and learning about different cultures and national health systems. In 2009, Jane and I joined Ann and Nelson Shelton on a vacation to London. One day we went in search of an old water pump. In 1854, there was a severe outbreak of cholera in London that killed 616 people. Dr. John Snow established some of the methods of modern epidemiology by tracing the cause of the cholera outbreak to a particular pump on Broad Street. In spite of opposition from many people who did not believe his research findings, on September 8, 1854, Snow took bold action by removing the pump handle from the Broad Street pump. With the contaminated water no longer being drunk by people, the spread of the disease was stopped, and many lives were saved. The Broad Street pump is legendary in public health, an early example of how epidemiological research and environmental action can be used to solve a serious public health problem. We found the pump, still without its handle, and marveled at John Snow's scientific work and personal courage.

As the end of the decade approached, and I recovered from thyroid cancer treatments, Jane and I talked about where we wanted our lives to go in the future. Jane retired in 2005, so her time was completely flexible. We were both healthy (I beat my cancer). I wanted to be able to take advantage of the coming years to do more things with Jane, travel to places we still wanted to visit, and to have life move at a little slower pace. I decided I would retire from the regular faculty at the end of 2010 and become an emeritus professor.

During the 2009-2010 academic year I continued all of my regular Executive Associate Dean duties, but Steve and I also decided to try and convince our school's faculty, and the faculty on various relevant campus and system-wide committees, that it was time to implement an online MPH degree program. This was to be my final big contribution to the School. I studied online degree programs in other schools of public health, including Harvard, Johns Hopkins, and the University of Michigan. I wrote a proposal to implement an online MPH degree program in our school, and sent draft versions of the proposal to the School faculty and to several campus committees that would have to approve the idea. This was very controversial at U.C. Berkeley. The opinion of the faculty in general was that this was "beneath" U.C. Berkeley, and that an online degree program was inherently a second-rate education. Steve and I wrote responses to all the objections, including data and testimonials from other elite universities that had implemented such a program. One of the compelling arguments was that this was an opportunity for highly qualified people in low-income, minority communities who had no chance of being able to quit work and attend U.C. Berkeley as full-time, residential students to earn a University of California degree. With some reluctance, all the campus and system-wide committees approved our proposal. One of my colleagues, Napoleon (Nap) Hosang, MD was appointed Director of the Online, On Campus MPH degree program (called OOPMH for short), and he deserves great credit for successfully guiding the program through its first five years.

How attitudes change. In the spring of 2020, as our country and the world is fighting against the corona virus pandemic by implementing social distancing, all U.C. Berkeley courses are being taught online. University faculty and administrators express great pride in our ability to teach courses online, and argue that in no way is this educational experience inferior to taking courses on-campus. This makes me smile a little.

2010
My Final Class

During the spring of 2010 I taught my final class, Innovations in Health Care Delivery Systems. The class was a seminar with about 20 students who were interested in learning about the way innovations typically occur in any industry, and particularly learning about some of the important recent innovations in health care systems, such as patient-centered medical homes and accountable care organizations. The course gave me a chance to teach much of what I had learned in my research and from my service on the Boards of Directors of On Lok and John Muir Health. The students were a terrific bunch. Each of them brought their own work experiences to the class, and we had great discussions of the process of innovating and of specific innovations that improved the performance of healthcare delivery systems. The students were required to form teams and work with managers in a local health-related organization to assess a performance problem the organization was having. The students then worked together to create an innovation – typically a new work process – that would alleviate the problem. Each team gave a verbal report to the class. It was a fun course to teach, and I learned a lot from the students. The students knew this was the last course I was going to teach at U.C. Berkeley. At the end of our last class session, the students were very kind and applauded for some time. Each of them shook my hand and thanked me as they left. I liked all of the students in this class, but one student in particular stood out, Terese Otte-Trojel. Terese was an exchange student from Denmark. I was impressed with her intelligence, the energy she brought to class discussions, her contributions to her team's project, and her friendly, happy personality. I didn't know that before long I would be Terese's doctoral advisor, and she and I and our families would become life-long friends.

As the end of my time as a regular faculty member approached, I reflected on the students I mentored. There were a lot of them. Students I especially enjoyed working with who are now in research, teaching, and management positions in highly regarded organizations include:

- Herodia (Klatt) Allen, MPH, MBA, Executive Director, Regional Resource Stewardship, Utilization Management and Long Term Care, Kaiser Permanente Greater Los Angeles Area
- Terese Otte-Trojel Antonsen, PhD, Senior Consultant, Danish Regions' Center for Health Innovation
- James Bellows, PhD, Managing Director, the Care Management Institute, Kaiser Permanente
- Larry Casalino, MD, PhD, Livingston Farrand Professor in the Department of Healthcare Policy and Research, Weill Cornel Medical College
- Janet Coffman, PhD, Professor of Health Policy, Phillip R. Lee Institute for Health Policy Studies, University of California, San Francisco

- Daniel Gentry, PhD, President and Chief Executive Officer, the Association of University Programs in Health Administration
- Ilana Graetz, PhD, Associate Professor of Health Policy and Management, Rollins School of Public Health, Emory University
- Dorothy Hung, PhD, MSA, MPH, Associate Scientist, Palo Alto Medical Foundation Research Institute
- Bruce Kieler, DrPH, Public Health Specialist, Nuclear Energy Institute
- Judy Li. DrPH, MBA, Co-Director, Joint Venture Health Program, University of California, Berkeley
- Peter Martelli, PhD, MSPH Associate Professor, Sawyer Business School, Suffolk University
- Jill Marsteller, PhD, MPP, Professor of Health Policy and Management, Bloomberg School of Public Health, Johns Hopkins University
- Sara McMenamin, PhD, Assistant Professor, Department of Family Medicine and Public Health, University of California, San Diego
- Barbara Norrish, PhD, RN, Director of Education and Research Kaiser Permanente
- Kathryn Phillips, PhD, Professor of Clinical Pharmacy, University of California, San Francisco
- Mary Reed, PhD, Research Scientist, Kaiser Permanente Northern California, Division of Research
- Rhonda Sarnoff, DrPH, Adjunct Professor, University of San Francisco
- Julie Schmittdiel, PhD, Research Scientist, Kaiser Permanente Northern California, Division of Research
- Jodi Simon, DrPH, Health Services Researcher, AllianceChicago
- Margaret Wang, PhD, MPH, Researcher, Kaiser Permanente Northern California
- Frances Wu, PhD, MS, Research Associate, THIS Institute, University of Cambridge

Each year in May, the School of Public Health holds its graduation ceremony. All the students are awarded their degrees. Special awards of various types are given to students and faculty who excelled in some way. At the 2010 graduation ceremony, I received a special award. Dean Steve Shortell asked me to join him at the front of the stage. Steve gave some heartfelt comments about my contributions to the School of Public Health and the University. Then Steve announced that on behalf of the Chancellor of the University of California, Berkeley, he was awarding me the Berkeley Citation. The Berkeley Citation is a very high honor and is only awarded to individuals whose achievements exceed the standards of excellence in their fields. The beautifully framed citation Steve handed me read:

> The University of California, Berkeley honors
>
> Tom Rundall
>
> for distinguished achievement and for
> notable service to the University

The citation is stamped with the official seal of the University of California and signed by University of California, Berkeley Chancellor Robert J. Birgeneau. I looked out to the audience and saw Jane crying. It was all I could do not to cry myself.

Off To A Good Start

Wheeler Hall and the Campanile, U.C. Berkeley

Owen in Orinda Baseball Uniform, circa, 1987

68 Ardilla Rd. after remodeling in 1991-92

Jane and Owen bottling wine, circa 1988

Ann, Nelson, Jane, and I on Vacation

Dad at his linotype machine at Stanford

Off To A Good Start

My thank you brick for Dad at Evelyn Lloyd Dees Plaza, Stanford

Carol, Wayne, Sandy, Sue, Cathy, and I, 1987

Owen's High School graduation with Jane, Robert, and Ruth Tiemann, 1995

Jane and I at Oxford University

Off To A Good Start

Jane and I in St. Mark's Square, Venice

Bob and Becky Ozaki, Honolulu

Jim Chiddix and Trudy Evard's wedding in Honolulu

Jennifer Alexander and I on a U.S. hospital study tour, circa 1998

Tiemann family celebrating Maggie and Jason's wedding
at The Great Wall, 2013

At the Swilken Bridge, St. Andrew's Old Course

Tiemann Family at Ruth Tiemann's Memorial Service

My colleague, Katharina Janus, in Germany

Mom and Dad, 1981

Mom with her two sisters, Rose Mary and LaVerne

Jane and I holding the Berkeley Citation, 2010

10

Owen, Mananya, and Genevieve

The Claremont Hotel is a historic hotel situated at the opening of Claremont Canyon at the base of the Berkeley Hills. The hotel building is entirely in Oakland, as are the spa, the gardens and parking area. However, a small portion of the property located just east of the Berkeley Tennis Club is within the city limits of Berkeley, and the resort uses the street address of this parcel as the hotel address, 41 Tunnel Road, Berkeley CA. After several false starts, including a halt in construction caused by the 1906 earthquake, the hotel was completed and opened in 1915 as the Claremont Hotel. When it was built, the Claremont was the largest hotel on the west coast, with 279 rooms on ten floors. While its current name is Claremont Club & Spa, A Fairmont Hotel, in the early 1980s we knew it simply as the Claremont. That is where Owen and Mananya met in 2003, when they were both working at the hotel, Owen in sales and Mananya in the spa.

I first met Mananya at Owen's apartment in Lafayette one Saturday afternoon in 2003. I went to his place to drop something off, and he and his roommate Ray Badock were having a few friends over to watch a football game. Mananya was one of their guests. She easily stood out in the crowd. Mananya was the dark-haired beautiful one with the great smile. We said hello. I only stayed a few minutes, then I started to leave. At the same time Mananya said she had to leave as well, and Owen said he would walk her to her car. The three of us walked together, and I said goodbye as they peeled off to go to Mananya's car. As I got into my car I saw Owen and Mananya give each other a hug goodbye. It was a friendship hug. But as I watched them hug I sensed sparks flying, and I thought to myself "this is the start of something big."

Owen and Mananya's first date was on New Year's Day 2004. As their relationship progressed, we started to hear a little bit more from Owen about Mananya. At some point in 2004 Owen asked if he could bring Mananya to our house for dinner. Of course we said yes, and we arranged a day and time. This was the first time Jane and I met Mananya as Owen's girlfriend. We were having a spell of great weather, so I thought barbequed pork ribs with lots of sauce, Brentwood corn on the cob, and a green salad would be the perfect menu. Years later, Mananya told me she was extremely nervous about eating the ribs and corn, afraid she would make a huge mess and fail the "first dinner" test. Of course, none of that occurred to me. I thought we had a great dinner together. Jane and I knew we liked Mananya. She was smart, well-educated, funny, family oriented, and ambitious about what she wanted from her life. She was everything we could hope to find in a woman Owen would call his girlfriend, and that would not have changed a bit if she had smeared barbeque sauce all over her dress.

Their journey together had some setbacks. In July 2005, Owen left the Claremont and accepted a position as Director of Sales at the Lafayette Park Hotel. It was a bad match. He was let go after 10 weeks. The hotel's General Manager delivered the news without warning on September 13, my birthday. Of course Owen was in shock when he showed up at the restaurant where we had planned to celebrate my birthday. As usual, in a time of distress Owen focused on what other people needed and insisted that we continue with our birthday dinner plan.

At the time this happened, Owen and Mananya were "on a break." But after my birthday dinner, Owen needed to talk to Mananya more than anyone else in the world. He drove to her apartment, and Mananya gave him emotional and psychological support then and for the months that followed as Owen looked for a new job. They have been together ever since.

In 2006, Owen accepted a job in the Sales Department of the Fairmont Princess Hotel in Scottsdale, Arizona. His first day on his new job was on his birthday, July 10. Part of the Rundall family was in Arizona again. This was a good job working for a good management team. Owen quickly became the highest producing sales person on the staff. Except for the blistering heat, he enjoyed working at the Princess, and he learned a lot.

Getting Engaged and Married

While Owen was working in Arizona, Mananya began the MBA Program at the University of California, Davis. They learned to maintain a long-distance relationship, alternating visits and logging many hours on the phone. During his visit to our house for Christmas in 2007, Owen said he wanted to propose to Mananya, and he would like to have engagement and wedding rings made that would have family heirloom diamonds in them. Jane remembered a broach that had belonged to her step grandmother, Erna Tiemann, which was stored in a safe deposit box. They recovered the broach from the box, and Jane urged Owen to use the diamonds for Mananya's rings. Owen took the broach to Morrison's Jewelers in Orinda, and asked them to use the diamonds to make engagement and wedding rings, styled after one of the rings sold by Tiffany and Co.

I had surgery to remove my thyroid scheduled for February 2008. Owen came home to be with me in the hospital on the day of my surgery. Jane, Owen, and my sister Sue waited for me to come out of the recovery room, and then they came to see how I was doing. Afterward, they told me that my biggest concern after my surgery was whether Owen had picked up the rings from Morrison's. He had not, but he did so right after leaving the hospital. Morrison's did a fantastic job on the rings. They were beautiful.

On March 22, 2008, Mananya was visiting Owen in Scottsdale. He cooked her breakfast in bed, and as part of the presentation he asked her to remove the domed plate cover. Mananya thought there was some sort of sweet surprise under the cover. In a way there was … an engagement ring! Mananya accepted, and they started making plans to be together.

Owen thought he could do his work for the Princess Hotel from a home office, with occasional trips to the hotel as needed. He pitched the idea to his boss that he not only work from a home office, but also that his home office be located in the East Bay. His boss agreed and in April Owen moved to Alamo, and he and Mananya began planning their wedding.

Off To A Good Start

Owen and Mananya were married on September 20, 2008, at the Claremont Hotel, where they first met. It was a beautiful, memorable wedding. The Claremont staff, with guidance from Owen and Mananya, turned the hotel's large ballroom into a charming, romantic room with a sense of intimacy. Mananya's very ill mother, Araya, made a great effort to attend in a wheelchair, accompanied by Mananya's stepfather, Dr. Thomas (Tom) Phuriphan. Mananya's father, Dr. Malut Chansanchai, and many other relatives came from Thailand. Her brother, Anute and his girlfriend LiChia, and her sister Athima, also came from out of town. Of course, the "O" Gang was there in full force, as were many other friends and Rundall and Tiemann family relatives. Athima, who everyone calls Tima, gave a particularly heartfelt and funny speech. I also gave a speech, welcoming everyone, saying what a fine man Owen was, how much Jane and I loved Mananya, and how happy we were that they were married. David Callaham, Owen's best friend, had arranged to be authorized to perform weddings in California and officiated the marriage ceremony. The ceremony was romantic, emotional, and at times funny. It was terrific. The reception and dinner afterward were filled with good cheer and friends' wishes for a lifetime of happiness for Owen and Mananya.

Araya

Sadly, Araya left this life in peace on October 22, 2008, only a little more than a month after the wedding. She was a remarkable woman in the midst of an amazing life that was cut short far too soon. Araya Suntharanund was born July 2, 1946 in Bangkok, Thailand. In 1966, she entered the Medical School at Siriaj Hospital, Mahidol University. In 1970 Araya married Dr. Malut Chansanchai, and in 1971 she was awarded her M.D. degree. Araya did additional training and residency in Philadelphia and New York, becoming board certified in internal medicine in 1977. She had three children with Malut - Athima, Anute, and Mananya - while also practicing medicine in Maryland, Mississippi, and Florida. In 1995, after she and Malut divorced, Araya and Mananya moved to the Bay Area. In 1996, she married her college classmate, Dr. Thomas Phuriphan, a Kaiser orthopedic surgeon, and they established their home in Alamo. Araya worked as a Kaiser hospital-based specialist in

Vallejo. She was diagnosed with breast cancer in 1997, which metastasized to her brain in 2003. Treatments held Araya's cancer in check for several years, but during 2008 it began to grow and she became incapacitated. She was very ill at the time of the wedding, but was determined to see her daughter get married. Of course, everyone was happy she was able to do that. In the weeks after their wedding Mananya and Owen spent as much time as they could with Araya. Since Owen was working from his home office, he regularly took his laptop computer to Araya's house and sat with her, chatting and making sure she did not feel alone. Jane and I attended a memorial service for Araya that was held in her home. Many people spoke about her life and what a superb physician, mother, and friend she was. Jane and I met Araya a few times when she was still well enough to go out to lunch and visit with people. She was a delightful, smart, beautiful woman. We liked her and Tom a lot. We were deeply sorry we did not have many years to be friends and share the joy of going through life with our married children. Mananya is filled with the spirit of her mom, and we think of Araya many times when we are together, especially when we get together with Tom P. for dinner.

Starting Life Together

During the next two years, Mananya completed her MBA degree at the University of California, Davis. She wanted to work in the energy sector, and specifically in a company that would make important contributions to increasing energy efficiency. She worked for a "start-up" firm in Davis for a while, but soon decided that the company that offered her the best chance to make a difference in energy efficiency was Pacific Gas and Electric (PG&E). In 2013 she accepted a position in their corporate office in San Francisco. Today, Mananya is Manager, Energy Efficiency Portfolio Strategy & Optimization at PG&E. Her work reduces the demand for electricity in Northern California and helps the environment by reducing the need for more power plants. During this time Owen was working in his home office for the Princess Hotel in Scottsdale. But eventually a new general manager at the hotel decided he wanted all his sales staff to be located on the hotel property, so Owen quickly moved on to work for Starwood Hotels and Resorts. In time he would also serve in the sales and marketing departments of other hotels, including the Hotel Nikko. Owen is now the Director of Sales and Marketing for the Omni Hotel, one of the best hotels in San Francisco.

On the fourth of July in 2010, a black and white puppy was born. He is a mixed breed, showing a lot of Labrador and Border Collie heritage. In October of 2010, Owen and Mananya drove to Modesto where the dog was being raised, and they fell in love with him. They adopted the puppy, which they named Jackson. Jackson has a black coat with white accents around his face and chest that make him look older than he is. He loves playing games. Jackson is very fetch-oriented. He will chase any ball or thrown toy, and he loves to run outdoors. He also loves being with his humans. Jackson's a great dog.

Only a month after getting Jackson, Owen and Mananya bought a house at 315 Denise Lane in Lafayette. It is a beautiful two-story house with four bedrooms and two and a half bathrooms on a cul-de-sac with a cluster of five other similar homes. When they purchased it, the house was just ten years old and needed only cosmetic improvements. Over the years, they have made some changes to the house to suit their style, and planted a vineyard of 105 zinfandel vines in their backyard. It is a lovely family home in a great community.

Our Trip to Thailand

Owen and Mananya had barely finished unpacking in their new house when the four of us took a trip to Thailand to visit Mananya's relatives in Bangkok and tour some of the other parts of the country. We had a wonderful trip. Our first stop was Bangkok, where we met Malut, his sisters, and several other Chansanchai relatives for the first time since the wedding. We also spent time with Araya's brothers, Phubest and Pishnu Suntharanund, and their families. Pishnu (everyone called him Tom) drove us to many scenic places, successfully navigating the densely packed, adventurous roads in and around Bangkok. We took a boat tour on one of the rivers near the city. Phubest (everyone called him Tui) took us to the Chatuchak Weekend Market, where he tried to sell American jeans he brought from Chicago. Unfortunately, he learned the market stalls were well supplied with Levis. The most surprising thing we learned about Bangkok was how they embrace Christmas, or at least the commercial aspects of Christmas. In spite of the heat and humidity, the stores were decorated with traditional scenes of falling snow, icicles, reindeer, Santa Claus, Christmas trees, and presents. There was no special recognition of Christmas Day, but the Christmas marketing season continued well into January.

After about five days in Bangkok, we flew to Krabi, a low-key resort town on the west coast of southern Thailand at the mouth of the Krabi River. We stayed in the Aonang Phu Petra Resort, which had small villas for sleeping, a lovely wood paneled dining room (with a Christmas tree), and a beautiful pool. We relaxed, walked through the small town, and took a boat ride some distance to a place where the ocean's water level was so shallow we could easily walk across a stretch of sandy ocean floor to an island. Krabi was beautiful. Since it was not a tourist destination resort town, such as Phuket, I felt we experienced a few vacation days that were similar to the type of vacation many Thai people would take. We returned to Bangkok for a couple of days. Malut hosted us for dinner one night at a Chinese restaurant where, among other delicacies, I got to taste chicken brains.

Although they were different in many ways, Bangkok and Krabi had one wonderful thing in common: the Thai culture. Outside of possibly Hawaii, I have never been in a place with a culture that values kindness as much as I experienced in Thailand. The people I met were invariably nice, sincere, and happy to talk with me. They were friendly and always polite, often greeting us with the traditional slight bow, with palms pressed together in a prayer-like fashion. Jane and I returned home with great appreciation for Thailand and its sweet people.

Genevieve

In early December of 2015 Mananya told us the happy news that she was pregnant. It was too soon to tell others, so at the annual Rundall family Christmas party at Sue's house, Mananya secretly filled her wine glass with pomegranate juice. But as the weeks went by and all was well, Mananya told everyone she was pregnant and that her baby was due in August. All of her family members and friends were over the moon about this news, especially Jane and I. As August approached we all got into nesting mode. Baby clothes and diapers were stockpiled. A crib and dresser were ordered and assembled in the nursery. A big, comfortable stuffed chair was also placed in the nursery, with plenty of room for a mom to nurse her baby. Infant car seats were purchased. Infant first aid and CPR classes were taken. When on August 12 Mananya started feeling contractions, Owen drove her to John Muir Hospital in Walnut Creek. I was serving as Chair of the John Muir Health Board of Directors at that time, and I was proud that Mananya was going to deliver her baby in "my" hospital. At 4:41 am on the morning of August 13, 2016, Mananya gave birth to a baby girl. At 4:45 am, Owen texted Jane and me to tell us we had a granddaughter. There really are no words to describe the feelings we had. We were excited, happy, deeply moved, and a little overwhelmed. I can only imagine how Mananya and Owen felt. We waited a few of hours to let Mananya rest, and then we drove to the hospital and saw her holding our granddaughter. Owen and Mananya told us that as soon as they saw her, they knew that one of the names on their list of "possible" names was the right one. They named her Genevieve Araya Rundall. Jane and I took turns holding Genevieve and assuring Mananya and Owen they had the most beautiful daughter in the world.

Mananya and Owen (and Jane and Tom) wanted to hire a nanny for Genevieve, rather than having to drop her off each workday morning at a child-care facility. But a good nanny's services are expensive, so Owen and Mananya looked for a family who also wanted a nanny for their child and were willing to share the cost. Through an online site called Nextdoor, Mananya became acquainted with Adrienne and Evan Tozier, and their daughter, Ellie, who was almost the same age as Genevieve. The two couples got along great (Evan also went to Colorado State), with very similar views on child rearing and what they wanted a nanny to do. After several months and a thorough search process, the two couples selected Tareksh Hagos, an experienced nanny with a heart of gold, to care for Genevieve and Ellie. Each workday morning Ellie and Tareksh come to Genevieve's house, and they spend the day together. Tareksh has been exactly what everyone hoped she would be, giving the girls the best of care and helping them learn and develop as they grow. Genevieve, Ellie, and Tareksh have been together for over three years now. It is clear Tareksh loves those girls, and they love her, too. The arrangement has been wonderful for all involved. Tareksh is like a second mom to the girls, and Genevieve and Ellie are as close as sisters.

Jane and I are, of course, besotted with Genevieve. She has a happy, joyful personality. Genevieve loves listening to music and watching animated videos. She also loves using her imagination: practicing to be a doctor, pretending to be the invisible girl, and being mommy to her baby dolls. Genevieve's current passions are riding her scooter and shooting baskets in her backyard. The hugs and kisses she gives us are everything. We are fortunate to live only nine miles away from the house where the clan we call OMG lives. We are together a lot, reading children's books, having meals at each other's house, going to the park, taking walks together, eating out at restaurants, spending Friday mornings at the Pleasant Hill library listening to Librarian Patrick play children's songs on his guitar, singing Beatles songs while watching Beat Bugs videos, going on day trips, and any other fun activities we can think of. Fortunately, OMG seem to enjoy our adventures together as much as we do. We are a very close family, and none if us would have it any other way.

It came as a little bit of a surprise to me that after 40 years of doing academic research, teaching university students, and serving on health system boards I learned the real reason I was put on this earth was to be a grandfather.

Owen, Mananya, Jane, and I in Thailand

Owen and Mananya on their wedding day with the Rundall family

Owen and Mananya on their wedding day at the Claremont Hotel, September 20, 2008

Owen, Mananya, Jane and I with newborn Genevieve, 2016

Newborn Genevieve with Mananya's family

Genevieve looking cute in her Santa's hat

Genevieve's big smile

Jane holding newborn Genevieve

Genevieve reading in the corner with her sippy cup

Mananya, Owen, Jane, and I at an A's game

Genevieve and Ellie riding a library toy, 2018

Off To A Good Start

Owen and Genevieve at A's game

Genevieve posing in front of Oahu waterfall, 2019

Jane and Genevieve talking on the lanai at Ko Olina, 2019

11

It's Not Retirement, It's My Next Phase

On July 1, 2010, after 34 years as a professor, I became an emeritus professor at U.C. Berkeley. This meant that I was retired and would now receive my pension benefits. But emeritus professors are allowed, and to some extent encouraged, to continue doing research and to teach classes. I still had an office on campus, and I intended to stay active at the university. One reason I decided to become emeritus was that I no longer wanted to be tied down to a teaching schedule. I wanted the freedom to travel and do other things without the obligation to be in a classroom on certain days and times. Although, I did not want to teach any classes, I still enjoyed research and I decided I would work on some interesting research projects, but leave most of my time uncommitted. What I wanted to experience was not retirement, but a "next phase" of my life, one that would be similar to my life as a professor, but had room in it for other things I wanted to do.

The Monday Morning Golf Group

In 2010 Nelson Shelton told me he had reconnected with two friends from his high school years, Jack Baldassari and Steve Dawkins. Nelson asked if I was interested in playing golf with the three of them. We all played together at the Franklin Canyon Golf Course, and we had a great time. We played golf at about the same level. But at that time in our lives, golf was mostly a social event for us, and we enjoyed talking about life experiences, politics, history, or anything else that came up. We laughed a lot and enjoyed our time together. We started playing regularly on Monday mornings. With the opportunity to play regularly, my golf game got better. I scored in the low 80s or high 70s most of the time. I lowered my scoring index to eight, meaning on average I would score about eight above par for 18 holes. Whenever I shot below 80, I took my family out to dinner. My golfing buddies and I had a lot of fun.

Our foursome played regularly together for about six years. Sadly, our Monday golf outings have ended. In 2016, Steve had a recurrence of lymphoma, which he had been fighting for years. He went through chemotherapy treatments that were very hard on his body. Steve died of a heart attack during one of his treatments. Nelson also had health problems, and had quadruple coronary artery bypass graft surgery. He has played very little since his surgery. Jack and I play together occasionally, but we miss Steve and Nelson. It isn't the same.

While I was on the Board of Directors of On Lok, the organization held an annual fund-raising golf tournament. On June 30, 2014, the tournament was held at Harding Park in San Francisco. Nelson played with me. On the 190-yard 8th hole, I hit my #4 hybrid club and watched the ball follow the perfect line and trajectory to the green. As the ball got near the green, I could no longer see it because the sun was in my eyes. I knew it was a good shot, and the ball was probably close to the hole. I didn't know how close until I walked to the green. My ball was nowhere to be found. But when I looked in the hole, there it was! My first, and so far only, hole in one.

Research with Frances Wu on Health Information Technology in ACOs

The first research project I worked on in my "next phase" was a study of the ways in which Accountable Care Organizations (ACOs) use health information technology to improve their patient outcomes. ACOs were a fairly new form of health care delivery organization in which physicians (and sometimes hospitals) voluntarily joined together to implement evidence-based care practices to improve their Medicare patients' outcomes while simultaneously reducing the cost of care. If an ACO is successful at improving outcomes and reducing the cost of care, it will receive a financial reward from the Medicare program. Of course, the use of information technology was an important part of most ACOs' strategy. On this project I worked with Steve Shortell and Frances Wu, a terrific doctoral student. We conducted semi-structured phone interviews with leaders of ACOs across the United States about their use of information technology. Frances did qualitative analyses of these interviews. As we suspected, information technology, such as electronic medical records, was believed to be essential for coordinating medical care provided in ACOs, especially for patients with multiple, complex illnesses. We identified the specific ways information technology was used by successful ACOs. We published several articles together with Frances as first author, including The Impact of Information Technology in Advancing Care Management and Coordination in Accountable Care Organizations in *Health Care Management Review*. Frances completed her dissertation on this topic and spent two years as a post-doctoral fellow at Stanford and the Veterans Administration Palo Alto Health Care System. Frances is doing very well in her career. Recently she and her husband moved to England, where she is a research associate at an organization called THIS Institute at the University of Cambridge. THIS Institute is a health services research organization working to improve care in England's National Health Service. Frances will be a great asset for them.

Mom Tiemann Passes

Beginning around 2010, Mom Tiemann's health started slowly deteriorating. Ruth had congestive heart failure, and in time she was not able to be very active. Her son Tom and daughter-in-law Eileen visited her frequently. She was well looked after by the staff of Galloway Ridge. She never felt alone, and she was comfortable in her room. Ruth died in her sleep on July 7, 2011 at the age of 92 years. The Tiemann family arranged for Ruth to be transported to St. Louis, and we all gathered there to watch her be buried next to her husband, Robert, in the family plot at St. Paul Churchyard. Ruth and Robert Tiemann were good people who lived full happy lives. They raised five wonderful children, and paid for each of them to attend a prestigious private college. They were loving parents who did their best to start each of their children on the way to their own interesting journey. They found comfort and support in their church and the community in which they lived, and they paid that forward by the support they gave to others. I think all of us hope to be able to say as much about our lives.

After Mom Tiemann died, her children decided that they wanted to find a way to regularly get together to stay connected as a family, and also for their children to have opportunities to build relationships with each other. The Tiemann family reunion is held every other year. So far, we have met at Deer Isle, Maine; San Juan Island near Seattle, Washington; and at the shore of Lake Michigan near Grand Rapids. We all love these gatherings and we look forward to the next one.

Research with Terese Otte-Trojel on Patient Portals

It was a pleasant surprise when in 2012 I received an email from Terese Otte-Trojel, a Danish exchange student who participated in the last course I taught in 2010 before becoming emeritus professor. Terese explained that she had been accepted as a doctoral student at Erasmus University in Rotterdam. Specifically, Terese was a doctoral student in the Health Services Management and Organization research group, and was working with Professors Joris van de Klundert and Antoinette de Bont. She explained that her research interest was in understanding how patient portals were being implemented in health organizations' health information systems, and assessing the effects of these portals on the care patients received. A patient portal is a secure online website that gives patients convenient, 24-hour access to personal health information from every care site or provider with an Internet connection. Using a secure username and password, patients can view health information such as doctor visit and hospital discharge summaries, medications, immunizations, and lab results. Some patient portals also allow patients to message their doctor, request prescription refills, schedule appointments, view educational materials, and perform other functions. Portals have become quite common now and are used by virtually all integrated delivery systems. But in 2012, portals were relatively new and many health systems and their patients were not sure how best to use them. Since a multi-year empirical study of the effects of patient portals on patients' objective health status was far too big and expensive an undertaking, Terese's research would involve systematic literature reviews of already published research studies and qualitative analysis of interviews with people involved with implementing portals. Since the Bay Area was one of the regions in the world where patient portals were widely used, Terese and her advisors agreed she should spend a lot of her time studying the patient portals at Kaiser Permanente and other Bay Area health systems. In light of my longstanding interest in health information technology, Terese asked if I was interested in becoming a co-supervisor of her dissertation work and working with her to complete the studies required by her research plan. I reviewed Terese's research proposal, which was very thoughtful. This was a doable dissertation that would provide the field with an excellent assessment of patient portals. Based on my experience with her in my 2010 class, I knew Terese was completely fluent in English, very smart, and took her work responsibilities seriously. She also had a wonderful sense of humor and was fun to work with. I agreed to join Terese's dissertation committee, and I helped arrange permission for her to return to U.C. Berkeley as an exchange doctoral student.

Terese was one of the best doctoral students I ever worked with. She was remarkably productive. In a typical meeting with her, I would ask her to review several published manuscripts, write a draft of a report on some phone interviews we conducted, and outline a manuscript we would write for publication. I expected her to take a couple of weeks to complete this work. I learned to change my expectations for Terese. Usually, she would meet with me again after three or four days, and all the work was completed. She would sometimes have also done additional work on her own initiative. Our work proceeded very well, and our research team started submitting articles for journal publication, with Terese as lead author.

Terese's Accident

In the early afternoon of Wednesday, June 11, 2014, Terese called me at my U.C. Berkeley office. She asked if we could meet that afternoon. I said, "of course," and she said she would come to the office shortly. I was working on a writing project for a while when I realized a couple of hours had passed. I thought something must have come up, and Terese could not come to the office as we planned. In retrospect, I was stupid. Terese would never leave me waiting so long. She would call if she were delayed for some reason. But I went home, not thinking too much about what happened to Terese. A couple of hours later, while Jane and I were driving somewhere, I got a call on my mobile phone from Terese's best friend, Kyra Harrington, who told me the awful news that while riding her bicycle to meet me Terese had been hit by a car. She had been knocked unconscious and badly injured. Terese was at Highland Hospital in Oakland. She had a fractured pelvis, a damaged eye socket, and a lot of bad bruising. My heart sank. Terese was one of the nicest people in the world, and we were becoming good friends. How could I not have worried about her? I was angry and embarrassed at my thoughtlessness.

Jane and I decided that I should immediately go to the hospital to see if there was anything I could do. At the hospital, I had to wait a while, chatting with Kyra and her husband, Dave, before I could see Terese. I learned that Kyra had called Terese's parents, Marie-Louise and Torben, and told them about the accident. I was sure they were devastated by the news. When I entered her room, Terese tried to smile. I could see that Terese was as Kyra described. One eye was swollen shut and her face was bruised. She was in pain and couldn't move much. Her pelvis was broken and would require surgery. I was barely able to say anything. In time, we did talk about what happened, and Terese described her injuries. I knew she was going to get better, but it was going to take time for healing, rehabilitation, and physical therapy to bring her back. I told Terese to think about coming to live with Jane and me for as long as she needed after she was discharged from the hospital. I said we had a guest bedroom, with a private bathroom and office on one side of our house, and I hoped she would be willing to stay there. I also said I knew she had a lot to think about right now, and there was no reason to make an immediate decision. The option was always available for her. I was very pleased when a few days later, Terese said she would like to spend some of her recovery time with us.

Marie-Louise arrived from Copenhagen to see Terese and stayed several days. We invited her to our house for dinner one night, and Jane and I showed her the guest room that Terese would use after she left the hospital. I saw Marie-Louise every day and we often visited Terese together. Marie-Louise's visit was very reassuring to her and to Terese as well. To thank Jane and me for helping Terese, Marie-Louise gave us some beautiful Royal Copenhagen Christmas china. We love it and use it every Christmas.

After her surgery, two weeks in Highland Hospital, another two weeks at a rehab facility, and a week in our guest room, Terese went back, still on crutches, to her rented apartment in Berkeley. Through all of this, my relationship with Terese changed. We went from being a professor and his student who liked each other, to being true friends. We have been so ever since. Through all of the difficulties of her injury and recovery, Jane and Terese also bonded, and we became friends with Marie-Louise and Torbin. We are Terese's American family.

Terese Defends Her Dissertation in Rotterdam

In time, Terese got back to work on her dissertation research. She made steady progress. As each research review or series of interviews was completed, Terese would take the lead on writing up a manuscript for publication. We published six articles that are the core of her dissertation work, including: How Outcomes are Achieved Through Patient Portals: A Realist Review, published in the *Journal of the American Medical Informatics Association*; The Organizational Dynamics Enabling Kaiser Permanente's Patient Portal's Impact Upon Operational Performance and Patient Health: A Qualitative Study, in *BMC Health Services Research*; and What Do We Know About Patient Portal Development? A Review of the Evidence, in the *Journal of the American Medical Informatics Association*.

In 2015, Terese completed her dissertation, *Patient Portals: Development and Outcomes in Integrated and Fragmented Health Systems*, and her public dissertation defense was scheduled for September 11, 2015 at Erasmus University in Rotterdam. I traveled to Rotterdam and served as one of her examiners. The examination was a formal event. The audience included students and faculty with an interest in the topic, and many of Terese's family members and friends. Terese stood at a podium at the center of a stage, and we examiners asked her questions, to which she gave thoughtful, professional responses. Of course, Terese passed the examination, and most of the people in attendance went to a reception held afterwards. I got to again meet Marie-Louise, and met for the first time Terese's father, Torbin, her brother, Detliv, and Detliv's wife Tine. Jane and I gave Terese a graduation present: a silver necklace with an artistically shaped " *T* " representing her first name. My trip to Rotterdam was memorable in every way. I was proud of Terese's performance, and I was very pleased to be able to meet the rest of her family. Joris gave me a tour of the windmills at Kinderijk, a world heritage site. Also I slipped in a trip to the Mauritshuis in The Hague to see Johannes Vermier's magnificent painting, Girl With a Pearl Earing.

Terese and Mikkel's Wedding

After returning to Copenhagen, Terese began working for a consulting firm doing projects in the information technology space. She soon met Mikkel Antonsen, and in time they fell in love with each other. From Terese's descriptions, I learned that Mikkel works in financial management, and is a modern Danish man who loves Terese very much and wants to have a family: just the kind of man the American family hoped for Terese. We were looking forward to meeting him. Fortunately, we were able to spend time with Terese and Mikkel in August of 2016, when they came to visit us and other friends in California. We enjoyed meeting and getting to know Mikkel. He is smart, thoughtful, and laughs easily. Jane and I liked him very much. We had dinner together, and they stayed the night in what we called Terese's room. Mikkel soon proposed to Terese, and we were delighted to be invited to their wedding. We traveled to Copenhagen for the marriage ceremony, which was held on June 16, 2018. The wedding was beautifully done in a traditional Danish way at a Lutheran Church, with Mikkel in a formal suit and Terese in a classically beautiful white wedding dress. At the reception and dinner we were seated at the "family table" with Terese and Mikkel and their parents. We learned that Danish wedding customs include a lot of singing by the guests, the newly married coupled kissing under the table and standing on chairs, and a special dance that brings the entire crowd of guests close around the couple to show their support. Jane and I were beyond happy for Terese. It was a wonderful day.

Jane's Accident

Two days later, we joined Terese, Mikkel, and their beautiful daughter, Ava, on a trip to Tivoli Gardens, an amusement park in central Copenhagen. We were enjoying the park and had just finished lunch when Jane stumbled on an entrance to a downstairs bathroom. The first step had a lip that stood slightly above the dirt path leading to it, and Jane's shoe toe caught the lip and she fell over. She hit her face on the handrail and was shaken up by her fall. In this unfortunate way, we got to learn about the remarkable Danish health system, which paid for a taxi for Jane and me to be driven to a hospital, and her examination by an ear, nose, and throat specialist. The doctor was very thorough in his examination. Jane's nose was fractured in three places, but no bones were displaced. The doctor provided Jane with a written summary of his findings in English. He recommended she visit another doctor in three days after returning home. The health system also paid for our taxi trip back to our hotel. Despite my repeated efforts to ask how we could pay for this care, we were told the Danish health care system could not accept money from us. We weren't even Danish citizens!

The Goose Girl

Terese took the taxi with us to make sure we got to the hotel without trouble. We told her that we were going to rearrange our future travel plans, cancel the trip to Paris we planned for the next week, and fly home as soon as possible. But first we wanted to come to their apartment later that day to say goodbye. Actually, our main reason for wanting to go to their apartment was to give them a wedding present we brought from the United States: a porcelain figurine of a Danish girl and her goose out on a walk. It is called the "Goose Girl" and was made by Royal Copenhagen in the 1950s. Apparently it was bought in the 1950s by an American visiting Copenhagen and brought back to the United States. I found it listed online by a gift store in Bryn Mawr, Pennsylvania. We were sure they would like the Goose Girl, but we learned from Terese that her grandmother worked at Royal Copenhagen at the time the figurine was made, which made it an even more special gift for her. Jane and I are very happy that Terese and Mikkel have a special place for the Goose Girl in their home.

The next day we returned to Orinda, and after several weeks Jane's nose healed. It is, however, one of our "special" memories of our trip to Copenhagen. Terese and Mikkel have since added to their family with the birth of another daughter, Emily. Terese now works as a Senior Consultant at an organization called the Danish Regions' Center for Health Innovation. We can't wait to go back and return to Tivoli, now with Ava and Emily and our expert knowledge about the dangerous first step to the downstairs bathroom.

A Cruise from Venice to Athens

In 2017, Tom and Eileen asked if we were interested in joining them on a Viking cruise from Venice, Italy to Athens, Greece. We had a wonderful time with them touring the Dalmatian Coast, including the beautiful town of Dubrovnik. In Athens, we went to the amazing Acropolis to see the ancient ruins of the Parthenon. We also tracked down the site, as yet not completely restored, of Aristotle's Lyceum, a school of philosophy founded in 334 BC. We could see the outlines of some buildings and an athletic field, where scholars took their physical exercise. This, along with Plato's earlier school, was an early model of the academic institutions that are so familiar to us today. It was exciting to see these sites and imagine what school life was like back then.

Establishing the Center for Lean Engagement and Research

In the late 1940s, the Toyota Motor Corporation began developing a new way of managing their automobile production that involved creating an organizational culture that empowered employees to improve the production process. Specifically, employees were encouraged to identify expenditures of time, effort, and material that do not generate value for customers, and to redesign their work processes to eliminate the waste. This management approach was eventually called the Toyota Production System (TPS). It has been adopted by manufacturing companies all over the world. A version of the TPS called Lean management has also been adopted in the service sector. In the United States about 60 percent of hospitals are using some version of Lean management.

In 2015, the leaders of Catalysis, an internationally recognized organization promoting Lean management in healthcare organizations, asked Steve Shortell if he would consider establishing a research center to increase the evidence base about the effects of

Lean management on healthcare organizations. Catalysis was willing to provide some financial support for such a research center, and they would use their connections to generate support from other organizations. Steve asked me to join him in this effort as co-director of the new research center at U.C. Berkeley, which we named The Center for Lean Engagement and Research in Healthcare (CLEAR). One of our first and best decisions was to hire Janet Blodgett as our Research Director and Program Manager. Janet has been an invaluable colleague, making important contributions to the management of CLEAR and to our research projects.

We have done important, path-breaking research on Lean management in hospitals. In 2017, we partnered with the American Hospital Association to conduct a national survey of hospitals in the United States, and we linked the Lean-related data for each hospital to federal data from 2011 - 2015 on financial performance, patient outcome, and patient satisfaction with their care. We have also developed an instrument to assess the extent of Lean implementation in health care organizations that have adopted Lean management, which is being used in hospitals in the U.S. and several other countries. Some of our publications include: Use of Lean and Related Transformational Performance Improvement Systems in Hospitals in the United States: Results from a National Survey, published in *The Joint Commission Journal on Quality and Safety*; Lean Management and U.S. Public Hospital Performance, in the *Journal of Healthcare Management*; and Adoption of Lean Management and Hospital Performance: Results from a National Survey, published in *Health Care Management Review*. Thus far, our research has shown beneficial relationships between Lean and many of the performance measures we have looked at. There is always a time lag between when these data are collected and when they become available for research purposes. In 2020, we are adding hospital performance measures for 2018, the year after our 2017 hospital Lean survey, which will give us a much stronger research design for testing hypotheses about the extent of Lean implementation and hospital performance. I can't wait for that! This has been a very enjoyable period of work. The issues are interesting and important, and I am working with a great team. We have been remarkably productive and added a good deal of knowledge to the field over a short period of time. We are

Off To A Good Start

continuing our research on Lean in healthcare organizations with Elina Reponen, MD, PhD from Finland, and with other colleagues in the U.S. and other countries.

Ending the Decade of the 2010s With Travel
Pasadena with Ann and Nelson

In May of 2019 Jane and I went on vacation with Ann and Nelson to Pasadena, the home of the Rose Bowl and the famous New Year's Day Parade. We stayed at the Langham Hotel, a great old-world looking but recently re-built hotel. We visited the Norton Simon Museum, the Huntington Library and Botanical Gardens, and Bungalow Heaven. We also took tours of the Gamble House and other historically important early 20th century estates. We were in awe of Pasadena's beautiful City Hall, with its early Renaissance architectural style. We ate in terrific restaurants that we wished were located near Orinda. We had a great time.

The Baseball Trip

In June of 2019, I was booked to attend two conferences only a week apart in the same hotel in Washington, D.C. Owen said the only reasonable thing to do was for him to fly to Washington, D.C. at the end of conference #1, and for us to take a week to attend baseball games in some of the eastern cities with especially interesting stadiums. We saw games in Washington, D.C., Pittsburgh, Philadelphia, and New York. We saw the Mets play with Owen's cousins, Anne and Erik Fahlgren, and after the game their daughter, Sydney, joined us for dinner. Just before the start of the Yankees game, it was called off because of rain, but we were able to visit the centerfield monuments to famous players and the Yankees' own Hall of Fame, which were going to be the best parts of going to Yankee Stadium anyway.

A Cruise up the Rhone River

We enjoyed our 2017 cruise with Tom and Eileen so much, that in July of 2019 we happily joined them and Jane's sister, Liz, and her husband, John, on another Viking cruise, this time up the Rhone River from Avignon to Lyon. We were on the river during a heat wave, with temperatures near or over 100 degrees each day. Still, we had a great time together. We visited Chateauneuf du Pape, nearby vineyards, and ancient towns, many of which were established by the Romans. We ended the cruise with a foodie tour of Lyon. We had a memorable trip, especially enjoying an extended period of time with Tom, Eileen, Liz, and John. They are wonderful people who live too far away from us.

The "Makeup" Trip to Paris

Only a month after we returned from our Rhone River cruise, Jane and I flew to Paris. I attended a conference for a day organized by Katharina Janus, but the main reason for this trip was to make up for the trip we had to cancel in 2018, when Jane injured herself during a visit to Tivoli Gardens in Copenhagen. We spent a week visiting sights and museums we especially like, seeing the fire-ravaged Cathedral of Notre Dame, going on a Hemingway tour in the Latin Quarter, and celebrating my birthday with dinner with Katharina and her friend, Barbara.

The Family Trip to Hawai`i

In September 2019, Jane, Owen, Mananya, Genevieve, and I went to Hawai`i together. We stayed a week in a condo at the Ko Olina resort, which is only a few miles from the Wai`anae Coast, where I worked as a VISTA volunteer from 1971-1972. We tried our best to see all the places that were important to my VISTA experience, and also to get in a lot of time on the beach. We ended our last day in Hawai`i having mai tais and milk from a sippy cup at the House Without a Key at the Halekulani Hotel on Waikiki Beach. All of us agree, Genevieve especially, that we have to go back to Hawai`i soon.

Aunt Rose Mary's 100th Birthday

In December, we flew to Phoenix to help celebrate my Aunt Rose Mary Smith's 100th birthday. This is my Teta Rose, who invited me to live with her family in Waterloo, Iowa for the first six months of 1958. I loved seeing Rose Mary looking and feeling so good at her birthday party, and visiting with Aunt LaVerne and the many relatives I have on the Smith/Serbousek side of my family. They always make us feel welcome and loved.

Two Unexpected Developments

The Election of Donald Trump

One thing I did not anticipate dealing with in my "next phase" was the 2016 election of Donald Trump as President of the United States. Early in the election campaign it was easy to dismiss Trump's candidacy. He was clearly a vain man, prone to lying and bullying others. But, as the campaign rolled on, it became apparent that there were very large numbers of voters who felt that past federal policies supporting globalization of manufacturing and the shift to a service economy in the U.S. reduced opportunities for skilled and unskilled workers and had cost them and their children jobs and financial security. In addition, immigration from Mexico and other countries generated a lot of racist opposition to people of color, with many white Americans seeking to blame Mexican-Americans and undocumented workers for their misfortune. There was a great deal of anger and resentment among many voters. They wanted someone to punch the federal government in the nose. Trump sensed all of this earlier than most people, and campaigned to "Make America Great Again" by promising to undo international trade treaties, restore jobs that had been lost to modernization and globalization, and build a wall across the U.S. – Mexico border. Trump lost the total vote count to Hilary Clinton, but won the majority of delegates in the Electoral College (which gives small, rural states more political weight in the Presidential election). I think to his own surprise, Donald Trump, became the 45th President of the United States.

From the beginning Trump was in way over his head. His speeches, tweets, and actions demonstrated that he much preferred basking in the adulation of his supporters at presidential campaign rallies and attacking his critics than actually doing the hard work of governing and uniting the country. He was impeached by the House of Representatives for abuse of power and obstruction of Congress. I believe that Trump is the worst President in the history of the United States. Sadly, it is not certain he will fail to be re-elected.

We are in the midst of the 2020 Presidential campaign. Although it has not been officially decided, the Democratic nominee probably will be Joseph (Joe) Biden, who served as the 47th vice president of the United States from 2009 to 2017. He performed well as vice president, but there are reasons for concern. Biden is 77 years old and has clearly lost a step. Also, a woman has recently alleged that Biden sexually assaulted her sometime in the spring of 1993 in a Capital Hill office building when she worked as a staff assistant in his Senate office. Biden has addressed the woman's claim and said, "It never happened." Former staff members who the women claims she told about the assault say they did not receive a complaint from her. Searches are underway for documents that were supposedly filed at the time to document her complaint. It is not at all clear how this accusation will ultimately affect Biden's campaign. It is certainly taking a lot of wind out of his sails, and the Democratic Party has been thrown into a state of confusion, all of which will help Trump's reelection prospects. I will vote for whoever is the Democratic nominee. In fact, I would vote for a brass doorknob against Trump.

The Coronavirus Pandemic

As I write this memoir, the world is in the midst of a pandemic. In December of 2019, a new strain of coronavirus named SARS-CoV-2 was reported from Wuhan, China. By June 1, 2020 confirmed cases of infection, called COVID-19, had been found in 219 countries. Worldwide, there are 5.95 million confirmed cases and 365,000 deaths from this disease. COVID-19 has hit Asia, Europe and America very hard, especially China, the United States, Spain, Italy, the United Kingdom, France, Germany, Russia, Turkey, and Brazil. The world has not seen anything like this since the 1918 influenza pandemic. A global health emergency has been declared.

In the U.S. there have been 1.79 million confirmed cases and 104,000 deaths. Those numbers are expected to increase daily for the foreseeable future. The Bay Area was one of the first regions in the United States to recognize the danger to public health that COVID-19 posed, and counties, followed quickly by the state government, announced that all non-essential businesses must close and other social distancing requirements were put in place. Jane and I, along with all others who are not working in essential businesses, such as grocery stores, or who are medical care providers or first responders, have been sheltering-in-place since early March, about nine weeks thus far. We only leave the house once a day to go on a 2.5-mile walk to downtown Orinda and back, taking care to avoid other people. Mananya and Owen do our shopping for us, allowing us to avoid exposure at grocery stores. We are extremely grateful to them. In parts of California, and in other states, some people have been protesting the enforcement of social-distancing, claiming it violates their constitutional right as Americans to do whatever they want regardless of the risk their behavior brings to other people. They are selfish idiots who have no understanding of their responsibility to protect fellow citizens from this virus. They only care about their own individual freedom. Fortunately, most people in the Bay Area are cooperating with the social distancing requirement. These efforts have been effective. The Bay Area has fewer cases and fewer deaths per capita than most other regions. The restrictions are starting to be slowly lifted so that infections do not suddenly spike. In order to have some sort of personal contact with Mananya, Owen and Genevieve, we have started having dinner together once a week, sitting on their driveway in Lafayette, at least six feet apart at all times. This has helped, but still the hardest part of our sheltering-in-place experience is not being able to hold Genevieve.

Jane and I have a lot of time to work on projects at home. Jane is using Ancestry.com to research her family genealogy and history and reading books. She is also crocheting a blanket for a niece, Dorothy Anne, born last week to Allison and Rob Howard, and joining their other two children, John David and Ivy. I have been working on CLEAR research and writing projects from home, meeting with my colleagues via Zoom video conferencing. I have taken the unexpected opportunity presented by sheltering-in-place to also write this memoir.

What Have I Learned From My Life Journey?

Preparing to write the first chapter of this book and Appendix 1, I learned a great deal about my Rundall and Serbousek families. I have a deep appreciation for those who came before me. The courage, strength, and perseverance shown by my ancestors who emigrated from England and the Czech Republic and their descendants make me humble and proud. The struggles my more recent ancestors went through in homesteading in South Dakota, working their farms in Iowa, fighting for survival during the Great Depression, and serving our country during World War II are inspiring, and also sad because those hard times took the lives of several dear relatives. I learned that I have an obligation to live a life worthy of the sacrifices others have made.

I was fortunate to grow up and come of age during a time when federal and California political leaders shared a belief in the concept of the commonwealth, enacting policies that provided for the common good. In the post-World War II era, a lot of public policy was designed to increase opportunities and provide incentives for people to attain higher education, buy a house, have a family, start a business, and work productively. I benefitted enormously from the policies of that era. I'm sad to see our nation's retreat from pursuing the common good, and the current favoritism for economic elites built into our country's taxation and economic policies. To some extent, Jane and I have tried to make the commonwealth concept work within our family by helping Owen, Mananya, and Genevieve pursue opportunities and achieve the goals they have for their lives as individuals and as a family.

Through my research on health care organizations and my experiences on the boards of directors of two health systems, I came to realize that our hospitals and healthcare systems needed to go through transformational change to provide timely, high quality care at an affordable price. That journey is now well under way for many healthcare organizations. Along the way, I developed profound respect for the doctors, nurses, support staff, and managers who organize and provide care to patients. Like most other people, medical providers are skeptical of change, and like doing things in their own way. But when they are provided with good evidence that a new way of organizing and delivering care improves patient outcomes, they are very willing to accept change. Their concern for their patients, and their commitment to doing all they can to help them recover, are qualities that set them apart from most other professionals. The sacrifices made by tens of thousands of medical care personnel, and the personal risk they accepted to care for patients during the COVID-19 pandemic, did not surprise me at all. Throughout my career, I took great pride in working with people in the fields of public health and medicine.

I enjoyed going to college so much I never left. Stanford University changed my life and gave me the opportunity to join the faculties of Cornell University and the University of California at Berkeley. I saw the transformative power of education in my own life, and I was committed to making such transformation possible for my students. Many of my former students have seized their opportunities and are working to build better healthcare systems in the U.S. and in many other countries. The greatest possible legacy for a university professor is to have former students in successful careers and making beneficial contributions to their community and country. I am profoundly pleased that so many of my former students are doing exactly that.

Mom and Dad started their married lives together with no financial resources. Dad learned to be a linotypist, a skilled trade but one that never paid him a high salary. As a child, I was always aware that we did not have much discretionary money. Still, my parents provided a good home for their six children, making many personal sacrifices for our benefit. We established strong family bonds. Of course, I was heartbroken when each of my parents died. But the early deaths of so many of my family members took an especially heavy toll. My sisters died at young ages: Sandy at 43 years, Carol when she was 53, and Cathy at 47 years of age. Even though Dad lived 68 years, I expected him to live much longer. I learned to treasure the time I have with family members and close friends. That means staying connected to them, spending quality time with them whenever possible, and never taking them for granted. I hope and plan for the future, but I try to live in the present.

I have always been thankful for the life lessons I learned playing competitive sports: being passionate about whatever you do; having a positive, can-do attitude; being a good team member; understanding fair play; being prepared; having perseverance; showing leadership by example; setting goals and working hard to achieve them. Successful athletes, even the most talented ones, know that there is no substitute for hard work, and that it is their responsibility to put in that work. Following these lessons does not guarantee victory or success, but it will increase your chances. You will do the best you are able to do, and you will sleep well knowing you did all you could to meet the challenge before you. I have found these lessons to work well for me in other areas of my life, including academic research, classroom teaching, and organizational leadership.

My travel throughout the United States and to other countries has enriched my life in many ways. Being exposed to different languages, art, music, cuisines, beliefs, traditions and customs has broadened my horizons. Travel enabled me to learn a great deal of history and to understand important events in especially meaningful ways. For example, standing next to the Berlin Wall, walking the beaches of Normandy, and visiting the USS Arizona in Pearl Harbor gave me a deep appreciation for the sacrifices my family and millions of others made during World War II. Travel to other countries allowed me to see the diverse ways the physical and social aspects of life can be organized and made to work. Not everyone drives on the right side of the road. Without doubt, my travels around the world have made me a better person.

At the age of sixteen, I envisioned a future life in which I had a career as a professional in some field that was interesting to me and also provided some social benefit. I wanted to be considered one of the top professionals in my field. I wanted a career that provided financial security. I wanted a career and lifestyle that would allow me to travel, not only around the United States but to other countries as well. Looking back, I can say that I have more than met those goals. Along the way, however, I learned how incomplete that vision was. At sixteen years of age I was too young and inexperienced to know that my connection to members of my family and friends would be necessary to make all of my accomplishments meaningful. The career success, professional standing, financial security, and wisdom gained from experiencing a remarkable life, are important now only to the extent they help insure that my family members and close friends are well, and that they continue to inspire the joy and love I have in my life.

Finally, I've learned that it is important to me to live a purposeful life, to have it make some difference that I have lived. For most of my 71 years I have been happily busy making contributions to the field of health services research, teaching thousands of students, providing leadership to my university, building better health systems in my community, enjoying travel and leisure activities with friends, and sharing a rewarding family life with my parents and siblings, and with Jane, Owen, Mananya, and Genevieve. I'm off to a good start.

The 40th year reunion of the Hawaii VISTA Volunteers and their spouses, 2012

Bob Ozaki and I playing golf, 2010

Jane and Eileen McGrath in Dubrovnik, 2017

Terese and Mikkel Antonsen's Wedding, Copenhagen, June 2018

Jane, Ann, Nelson, and I in Charleston, South Carolina, 2011

The CLEAR Team in 2018 included me, Steve Shortell, Christie Ahn, Janet Blodgett, and Noah Forougi

Owen and I playing golf at Pebble Beach, November 2014

My family at the Halekulani Hotel in Honolulu, September 2019

Appendix 1

Genealogy of the Rundall and Serbousek Families in America

The Rundall and Serbousek families have been in America for many generations. This is especially true of the Rundall family.

Rundall Family in America

George Ardel Rundall (born October 22, 1924, died 2008), my cousin once removed, spent much of his adult life researching the Rundall family genealogy. He published much of what he learned in a book co-authored with Pauline C. Austin, E. Jean McKinzie Brownhill, Edward V. Randall, Jr., and Robert Emerson Parker. Over the centuries, ancestors have spelled our family name in many different ways, which made George's task especially hard. For the title of his book, George recognized the different spellings he encountered in his research, by calling it The Rundle, Rundel, Randle, Randol, Randall, Rundall, Rundell, Runnell Ancestry of Long Island and Greenwich, 1667-1992. Much of what I know about my Rundall ancestors beyond my parents and grandparents comes from George's research. Much more information about the Rundall ancestry than I can offer here can be found in cousin George's book.

William Rundle, Sr. was the first Rundle (Rundall) in America, emigrating from England about 1665-1667. I am in the ninth generation of William Rundle's descendants in America, making my son, Owen, tenth generation, and my granddaughter, Genevieve, the eleventh generation of the Rundall (Rundle) family in this country.

Below I present an annotated genealogy of these eleven generations.

William Rundle, Sr. (first generation in America)

William Rundle Sr. was probably born in 1646-1647, possibly in Tonbridge, Kent, England. His parents probably were John Randoll and Ann Goldstone. As a young man, William emigrated from

Off To A Good Start

England to America, probably about 1665-1667. No record has been found to establish the date of William's arrival in America. The earliest documentation of William's presence in America is a land grant from the town of Greenwich, CT to William Rundle dated Dec. 23, 1667. He also received a grant of land December 30, 1670 for part of the uppermost meadows lying south of the Westchester Path, and on March 1, 1671 8 acres of land to be laid out by the Mianus River. He was one of 27 landowners in Greenwich in 1672. William died in October or November 1714, and was buried in Greenwich, CT, probably in an unmarked grave in one of the pioneer cemeteries. Given the belongings recorded at the time of his death, he may have been a weaver. But, as indicated by the property he owned, he also was a farmer and landowner. He was a Puritan. During his lifetime, William married three women: Hannah Edwards, Abigail Mills, and Abigail Tyler. With those three wives, William had fourteen children. My specific line of ancestors is derived from one of Abigail Mills' children, Samuel Rundle (second generation).

> Born: probably sometime in 1646 -1647, possibly Tonbridge, Kent, England
>
> Baptized: April 2, 1647, Tonbridge, Kent, England
>
> Religion: Puritan
>
> Immigrated to America: In the 1660s, probably 1665-1667
>
> Died: after October 22, 1714 (his will was executed on November 26, 1714), Horse Neck, now part of Greenwich, Fairfield County, Connecticut
>
> Buried: probably in an unmarked grave in one of the pioneer cemeteries ay Greenwich, Connecticut
>
> Married 1: Hannah Edwards, about 1670
>
> Born: unknown
>
> Died: October or November 1674
>
> Children: John
>
> Married 2: Abigail Mills, about 1675
>
> Born: about 1658
>
> Died: about 1689
>
> Children: Sarah, Mary, Abigail, Deborah, Samuel, Patience

Married 3: Abigail Tyler, about 1689
Born: about 1664
Died: before 1722
Children: Hannah, Abraham, Elizabeth, Issac, Jacob, Joseph

Samuel Rundle (second generation)

Samuel Rundle was a farmer and carpenter. About 1720, Samuel built his family home in Greenwich. It is listed in the Historical Register of Homes of the Greenwich Historical Society: an excellent example of early architecture of the colonial homes in Greenwich. The address is 951 Lake Avenue, North Greenwich, CT.

Born: November of 1685, Horse Neck (Greenwich), Connecticut
Died: July 6, 1761
Buried: Pioneer Cemetery, Greenwich, Connecticut
Married: Hannah Hardy
Born: probably July 6, 1693
Died: December 1768
Buried: Pioneer Cemetery, Greenwich, Connecticut)
Religion: Episcopal and Congregational Church of Greenwich
Children: Hannah, Rebecca, Samuel, Ezra, Nathaniel 1 (died in infancy), Nathaniel 2, Amy, Rachel, Reuben, and Ann

Reuben Rundle (third generation)

Reuben was a farmer and landowner. On November 11, 1776, at the age of 41, he enlisted in the Revolutionary War as a Sargent In the Company of Joseph Hobby under the command of Colonel John Mead. He was discharged as a Lieutenant on January 11, 1777. He was a trusted member of his community. At a special Greenwich town meeting in December, 1777 Reuben was elected to serve on a committee to insure that soldiers' families were supplied with clothing, food, and other necessities of life. A year later, at the annual town meeting in December, 1778, Reuben was elected to membership of the Committee of Safety and Inspection, which was charged with insuring that the "'vile wretches' that have gone over to and

Off To A Good Start

joined the common enemy of the United States of America shall not remain in Greenwich, nor return to it, or ever be capable of obtaining any settlement in it." (Ye Historie of Ye Town of Greenwich by Spencer P. Mead) Reuben is my only direct ancestor who was of an age to allow him to fight in the Revolutionary War (April 19, 1775 – September 3, 1783).

> Born: July 14, 1735, Greenwich, Fairfield County, Connecticut
>
> Died: February 11, 1815, Greenwich, Fairfield County, Connecticut
>
> Buried: Possibly in the old Tomac Cemetery, Greenwich
>
> Married: Amy Hobby
>
> Born: about 1737
>
> Died: December 25, 1829)
>
> Buried: Possibly in the old Tomac Cemetery, Greenwich
>
> Children: Reuben, Jr., Amy, Hardy, Deborah, Samuel, Hannah, Jonathan, Shadrack

Shadrack Rundle (fourth generation)

Shadrack and his sons were enterprising manufacturers and land developers. They used the trees on his land to manufacture rails, briquettes, shingles, lumber, and other materials needed by the early pioneers; he then sold the cleared land parcels to farmers. Shadrack and his first wife Phebe, the mother of all his children, were married 40 years, and he was married to his second wife, Abashaba, 30 years.

> Born: June 5, 1780, Greenwich, Fairfield County, Connecticut
>
> Died: January 14 or 15, 1873, Kent, New York
>
> Buried: Baxter Cemetery, Putnum Valley, Putnam County, near Wiccopee Road
>
> Married 1: Phebe Brown
>
> Born: March 21, 1778, Greenwich, Connecticut
>
> Died: June 29, 1840, Putnam Valley, New York
>
> Buried: Baxter Cemetery, Putnam County, New York
>
> Children: Reuben John, Gilbert P., Shadrack, John, Benjamin, Margaret, Betsy, Robert, Solomon, Fanny

Married 2: Abashaba (Bashaba/Bersheba) Shaw
Born: May 19, 1797
Died: November 19, 1870
Buried: Baxter Cemetery, Putnam County, New York
Children: none

John Rundall, Sr. (fifth generation)

John Rundall, Sr. was the first of my ancestors to spell his name Rundall. He also was the first to move west, with records indicating he lived first in Ohio and later in Iowa, then traveling to Butler County, Kansas to join the wagon trains heading west. John Sr.'s family (with Elizabeth Hall) is the first of my direct ancestors identified as residing in Linn County, Iowa. John married five times. His first three wives died (as was also the case with one child, Cephus), leaving him by 1848 with eight sons. These deaths, and others among family and friends were caused by the "great epidemic" that swept the countryside. The epidemic was probably typhus, although cholera also swept through the central states a various points in time. He had three more children with his fourth wife, Sarah Ann, including my great grandfather, George Washington Rundall. John, Sr. died while traveling on the Oregon Trail, and was buried in a coffin made from their wagon box. John had travel lust and was an adventurer, leaving many children and little wealth behind.

Born: April 16, 1806, Peekskill Valley, New York

Died: October 1867, on the Oregon Trail

Buried: on the Oregon Trail in a coffin made from their wagon box

Married 1: Zillah Adams

Born: 1801

Died: August 8, 1832, 17 days after giving birth to William Henry

Children: Cephus (Seith), William Henry

Married 2: Loretta (last name unknown)

Born: unknown

Died: about March 30, 1836)

Children: George Raymond, Steve Clarence

Married 3: Elizabeth Hall

Born: about 1820,

Died: about 1847/48 of an epidemic disease, probably typhus or cholera.

Children: Shadrack Spartan, John Wesley, James Monroe, Oscar, Robert Brown

Married 4: Sarah Ann (Herron) Storm, widow of Joseph Storm

Born: about 1824

Died: after 1893

Children: Ammi Jasper, George Washington, Zillah Ann

Divorced: September 11, 1850

Married 5: Lydia Gregg (b. ?, d. ?)

Children: None

George Washington (Wash) Rundall (sixth generation)

Wash married Kate Sherwood on December 13, 1874. Kate was only 17! After Wash married Kate, she inherited a farm in Linn County, Iowa from her mother, and she, Wash, and their children ran the farm together. She deeded the farm to Wash upon her death in 1897. Wash and his family continued to live on their farm until he sold it in 1909. He and sons, Clyde, Earl, and George Wesley moved to Haakon County, South Dakota, residing near the town of Philip. They were homesteading, seeking to take ownership of the allowed one hundred and sixty acre parcel of land by building a sod house and living there for five years. They earned rights to their properties. Wash died March 24, 1915.

Born: February 12, 1851, Brown Township, Linn County, Iowa

Died: March 24, 1915, Hartley, Haakon County, South Dakota

Buried: both George and Sarah are buried in Springfield Cemetery, Springfield, Linn County, Iowa

Married: Sarah Catherine (Kate; Katie) Sherwood; the wedding was December 13, 1874.

Born: July 15, 1857, Viola, Linn County, Iowa

Died: July 21, 1897, Viola

Religion: Methodist Episcopal Church

Children: William Leon, Clyde Enoch, Lena Maude, Earl Sherwood, and George Wesley.

Earl Sherwood Rundall (seventh generation)

Early in his life my grandfather, Earl, was a farmer. He worked on his family farm in Linn County Iowa. In 1909, his father sold the farm and Earl moved with his father and two brothers to Haakon County in South Dakota, near the town of Philip and the Rosebud Indian Reservation. They were homesteaders trying to take ownership of uncultivated land, one hundred and sixty acres of promise, as permitted by the Homestead Act of 1862. They lived in a sod house, a dwelling of at least 12x14 feet as required by the Act. After five years of residence, they owned the land. In 1912, Earl married Edna Hoag in Pierre, South Dakota. They had three children, Wilma, Richard, and Wayne. Their earliest playmates were children of the Sioux Tribe. The Rosebud Reservation is not far from Little Bighorn in southern Montana, and Earl knew some of the Sioux Indians who as young men served as scouts for General George Custer during his 1876 trip to that fateful battlefield. Earl's father, George Washington, died March 24, 1915. In 1928, Earl sold his property, and the family moved to Cedar Rapids, Iowa. Their house was at 1626 N Street, S.W. In Cedar Rapids, Earl worked at Penick and Ford, a plant that made molasses and other food additives. In 1949 he and Edna moved to Yuma, Arizona as part of a Rundall family plan that included Wilma Rundall Zavoral and her husband Lee, and Richard Rundall, his wife, Georgiena and their three children moving to Yuma. In Yuma Earl owned a house and property that included a small walnut tree farm. In about 1956, he and Edna moved to Anaheim, California. Edna died in 1958, and several years later Earl moved to San Francisco to live with his daughter, Wilma, in an apartment at 2306 Union Street #2.

Born: January 18, 1886, Woodbine, Harrison County, Iowa

Died: January 21, 1971, San Francisco, California

Married: Edna Minnie Hoag

Born: August 27, 1890, Bristol, Minnesota

Died: November 11, 1958, Anaheim, California

Buried: both Earl and Edna are buried at the Melrose Abbey Memorial Park and Mortuary, Paradise Garden Lawn, lot 374, graves 3&4, Anaheim, California

Children: Wilma Sarah born February 28, 1915; Richard Earl, born June 21, 1918; Wayne Calvin, born June 15, 1920.

All were born near Philip, South Dakota.

Richard Earl Rundall (eighth generation)

My father, Richard, was born on June 21, 1918, on his father's ranch near Philip, South Dakota. In 1928, Earl and Edna Rundall sold the ranch and moved the family to Cedar Rapids, Iowa. Dad worked as a laborer at Penick and Ford, the same plant in which his father, Earl, worked. On January 18, 1941, Dad married Georgiena Serbousek in St. Ludmila Catholic Church. On November 26, 1942 he joined the U.S. Navy. Dad served as an Aviation Ordnanceman, 2nd Class aboard the USS Kadashan Bay (CVE-76), an escort aircraft carrier. He was discharged from the Navy on September 9, 1945. Dad's brother Wayne enlisted in the Navy within a month of the bombing of Pearl Harbor. Wayne was killed on November 13, 1942, when his ship, the USS Laffey (DD-459), was sunk during the Battle of Guadalcanal. After the war, Dad returned to Cedar Rapids and went back to work at the Penick and Ford plant. Richard, Georgiena, and their children, Jovette (called Sandy), Carol, and Tom, lived at 1002 2nd Street, S.W. In 1949, largely to avoid continuing problems with pneumonia he experienced in Cedar Rapids, Richard and Georgiena moved with their three children to Yuma, Arizona. Richard got a job as a linotypist (a new skill he had to learn) at Southwest Printers (later known as Cactus Press), which was managed by his brother-in-law, Lee Zavoral. After ten years in Yuma (where two more children were born: Catherine Sarah and Susanne Marie), the family moved to Campbell California, where Dad worked as a linotypist at the Los Gatos Times newspaper, and later at the Stanford University Press. Their sixth child, Wayne Michael was born while they lived in Campbell. In 1977, Dad and Mom retired to Lucerne, California, on the shores of Clear Lake. Their home was at 6146 2nd Ave., Lucerne, CA. Dad experienced cardiovascular disease late in life. After heart surgery and a long hospitalization, Dad died on December 22, 1986. His ashes were spread over the water at Shelter Cove, California.

    Born: June 21, 1918, Phillip, Haakon County, South Dakota

    Died: December 22, 1986, Lucerne (Clear Lake), California, ashes spread over water at Shelter Cove, Humboldt County, California

    Married: Georgiena Alice Serbousek

    Born: February 17, 1922, Fairfax, Linn County, Iowa

    Died: March 28, 2006, ashes spread over water at Shelter Cove, Humboldt County, California

    Children: Jovette Sherwood, Carol Anne, Thomas Gene, Catherine Sarah, Susanne Marie, and Wayne Michael

Thomas Gene Rundall (ninth generation)

Although I was born in Cedar Rapids Iowa, my family moved to Yuma, Arizona during the winter of 1949 when I was about six months old. My family lived in Yuma until the late summer of 1959, when we moved to Campbell, California, where I lived until I attended Stanford University. Jane Tiemann and I were married in 1975. In 1976, after completing my undergraduate and doctoral education at Stanford, I joined the faculty at Cornell University in Ithaca, New York. Jane also worked at Cornell as a lecturer teaching professional writing classes. In 1980, longing to return to the Bay Area, I accepted a faculty appointment at the University of California, Berkeley, and we moved to Orinda, California, near the Berkeley campus. I served as a professor at U.C. Berkeley for 30 years, becoming an emeritus professor in 2010.

    Born: September 13, 1948, Mercy Hospital, Cedar Rapids, Iowa

    Married: Jane Ellen Tiemann

    Born: March 17, 1945, Columbus, Ohio

    Children: Owen Tiemann

    Born: July 10, 1977, Ithaca, New York

Owen Tiemann Rundall (tenth generation)

Owen was born in Ithaca, New York when Jane and I served on the faculty of Cornell University. When Owen was three years old, I accepted a faculty position at U.C. Berkeley, and our family moved to Orinda, California. Owen attended Miramonte High School and Colorado State University, where he majored in economics with a minor in history. On September 20, 2008 Owen married Mananya Chansanchai at the Claremont Hotel, where they first met when both worked there. They have one daughter, Genevieve Araya Rundall. Owen is in the hotel business, currently the Director of Sales and Marketing for the Omni Hotel in San Francisco. Mananya works at Pacific Gas and Electric as manager of a department working to increase energy efficiency in Northern California. Owen and his family live in Lafayette, California at 315 Denise Lane.

Born: July 10, 1977, Ithaca, New York

Married: Mananya Chansanchai,

Born: July 3, 1979, Baltimore, Maryland

Children: Genevieve Araya

Born: August 13, 2016, Walnut Creek, California

Genevieve Araya Rundall (eleventh generation)

Owen and his wife, Mananya Chansanchai, have a daughter, Genevieve.

Born: August 13, 2016, John Muir Hospital, Walnut Creek, California

Serbousek Family in America

I know much less about my mom's Serbousek family. Including my mother Georgiena's generation, I have some information about four generations of Serbouseks in America. I begin with my great, great grandparents, Ignac Enos Serbousek and his wife, Jozefa (Josephine) Kopetska Serbousek, who emigrated from Bohemia to the United States in the mid-nineteenth century.

Ignac Enos Serbousek (first generation)

Based on Ignac's and Jozefa's birth years and the birth year of their first born child, William Michael Serbousek (born in 1860 in Johnson County, Iowa), it is likely Ignac and Jozefa immigrated to the United

States between 1835 and 1858, probably in 1848, when Czech "Forty Eighters" fled to the United States to escape political persecution by the Austrian Habsburgs.

Born: 1816, Javornice, East Bohemia in the Czech Republic

Died: unknown

Married: Jozefa Kopetska Serbousek

Born: 1819, Bohemia

Died: unknown

Immigrated to the United States: probably 1848

Children: William Michael, Marie, Joseph, and four other children whose names are unknown

William Michael Serbousek (second generation)

Born: 1860, Johnson County, Iowa

Died: 1939

Married: Anna Skala Serbousck

Born: 1868

Died: 1941

Children: William H., Tillie, Anna, Josef, Ben, Frank, Wesley, Charles

Buried: Anderson Cemetery, Swisher, Iowa

Josef Serbousek (third generation)

Josef married Alice Housar in 1916. Alice was only 19 years old! Alice's parents, Joseph and Magdaline Jindrich Housar were born in the Czech Republic. Joseph on March 19, 1844 in Roupov, East Bohemia; Magdaline on June 12, 1856 in Vojtesice, East Bohemia. Alice had eleven siblings. Josef, his wife Alice, and their daughters last lived together at 1406 M St. S.W. in Cedar Rapids.

Born: May 27, 1891

Died: May 15, 1943

Married: Alice Housar (Houser) Serbousek in 1916.

Born: November 16, 1895

Died: July 14, 1943

Children: Agnes, Rose Mary, Georgiena, La Verne

Buried: Czech National Cemetery, Cedar Rapids, Iowa

Georgiena Alice Serbousek (fourth generation)

Mom was born in Fairfax, Linn County, Iowa. She married Richard Rundall on January 18, 1941 at St. Ludmila Church in Cedar Rapids. Mom and Dad lived most of their lives in Yuma, Arizona and Campbell and Lucerne in California. After Dad died in 1986, Mom moved from Lucerne to Gilroy. She died of congestive heart failure on March 28, 2006.

Born: February 17, 1922

Died: March 28, 2006, Gilroy, California; ashes were spread over water at Shelter Cove, Humboldt County, California

Married: Richard Earl Rundall, January 18, 1941

Children: Jovette Sherwood, Carol Anne, Thomas Gene, Catherine Sarah, Susanne Marie, and Wayne Michael

Appendix 2

My Curriculum Vitae

THOMAS G. RUNDALL, Ph.D.
Henry J. Kaiser Professor of Organized Health Systems, Emeritus
University of California, Berkeley
School of Public Health

EDUCATION

Stanford University, Ph.D. in Sociology, conferred 1976.
Stanford University, B.A. in Sociology, conferred 1970.
West Valley Community College, A.A. Degree, conferred 1968

UNIVERSITY POSITIONS

2007 – 2010 Executive Associate Dean, School of Public Health

2001 – 2010 Henry J. Kaiser Professor of Organized Health Systems

2000 – 2003 Director, Center for Health Management Research, School of Public Health, University of California, Berkeley

2002 – 2005 Director, Center for Health Research, University of California, Berkeley

2000 – 2001 Acting Director, Program in Health and Public Policy, School of Public Health and Goldman School of Public Policy, University of California, Berkeley.

1996 – 1999 Founding Director, Center for Health Management Studies, School of Public Health, University of California, Berkeley.

1994 – 1999, 2002 – 2003 Director, Graduate Program in Health Management, Haas School of Business and School of Public Health, University of California, Berkeley.

1994 – 1995, 2001 – 2002 Head, Division of Health Policy and Management, School of Public Health, University of California, Berkeley.

1989 - 2010 Professor of Health Policy and Administration (Management), School of Public Health, University of California, Berkeley.

1987 – 1990 Chair, Department of Social and Administrative Health Sciences, School of Public Health, University of California, Berkeley.

1984 – 1989 Associate Professor of Social and Administrative Health Sciences, Department of Social and Administrative Health Sciences, School of Public Health, University of California, Berkeley.

1980 – 1983 Assistant Professor of Social and Administrative Health Sciences, Department of Social and Administrative Health Sciences, School of Public Health, University of California, Berkeley.

1976 - 1980 Assistant Professor of Medical Care Organization, Sloan Program in Hospital and Health Services Administration, Cornell University.

RESEARCH GRANTS AND CONTRACTS (since 1995)

Principal Investigator, Success Under Duress, funded by the California HealthCare Foundation, 2009 – 2010, $125,000.

Principal Investigator, Improving Diabetes Efforts Across Language and Literacy (IDEALL), funded by the Agency for Healthcare Research and Quality via University of California San Francisco, 2004-2007, $21,061.

Principal Investigator, Impact of Information Technology on Clinical Care: An Evaluation of the Technology on Safety, Quality, and Efficiency of Chronic Disease Care (IMPACT), funded by the Agency for Healthcare Research and Quality via Kaiser Permanente Division of Research, 2004-2007, $1,500,000.

Principal Investigator, Methods for Developing Actionable Evidence for Consumers of Health Services Research (MATCH), Agency for Healthcare Research and Quality via Kaiser Permanente Division of Research, 2004-2006, $300,000.

Principal Investigator, Baseline Survey of Primary Care Practices in the Prescription for Health Program, funded by the Robert Wood Johnson Foundation via the University of Medicine and Dentistry of New Jersey, 2003-2004, $55,000.

Principal Investigator, Center for Health Management Studies, A National Science Foundation funded Industry/University Collaborative Research Center, 2001-2006, $150,000.

Co-investigator, National Study of Physician Organizations and the Management of Chronic Illness, funded by the Robert Wood Johnson Foundation, 2000-2002, $2,378,959.

Principal Investigator, Hospital – Physician Relationships, funded by the Center for Health Management Studies' Research Partner Program, 1999-2000, $15,000.

Principal Investigator, Evaluation of the First Things First Initiative, funded by the California HealthCare Foundation, 1998-2000, $290,729.

Principal Investigator, Evaluation of the Strengthening Hospital Nursing Program, funded by the Robert Wood Johnson Foundation (co-funded with the PEW Charitable Trusts), 1994-1997, $190,000.

PUBLICATIONS

Books

1. Battistella, Roger and Thomas G. Rundall (eds.). Health Care Policy in a Changing Environment. Berkeley: McCutchan Press, 1978.

2. Rundall, Thomas G., David B. Starkweather, and Barbara R. Norrish. After Restructuring: Empowerment Strategies at Work in America's Hospitals. San Francisco: Jossey - Bass Publishers, 1998.

3. Scott J. Tim, Thomas G. Rundall, Thomas M. Vogt, and John Hsu. Implementing an Electronic Medical Record System: Successes, Failures, Lessons. Oxford: Radcliffe Publishing, 2007.

4. Northridge, Mary, Donna Shelley, Thomas G. Rundall, Ross C. Brownson (eds.). eBook: Methods and Applications in Implementation Science. Lausanne, Switzerland: Frontiers in Public Health, 2019.

Refereed Articles in Journals

1. Tichenor, Carol Chinn and Thomas G. Rundall. Attitudes of Physical Therapists Toward Cancer. Journal of the American Physical Therapy Association, 1977, Vol. 57, No. 2, pp. 160-165.

2. Rundall, Thomas G. Life Change and Recovery from Surgery. Journal of Health and Social Behavior, 1978, Vol. 19, No. 4, pp. 418-427.

3. Rundall, Thomas G. and John R.C. Wheeler. Factors Associated with Utilization of the Swine Flu Vaccination Program Among Senior Citizens in Tompkins County. Medical Care, 1979, Vol. 16, No. 2, pp. 191-200.

4. Rundall, Thomas G. and John R.C. Wheeler. The Effect of Income on Use of Preventive Care: An Evaluation of Alternative Explanations. Journal of Health and Social Behavior, 1979, Vol. 20 (December), pp. 397-406.

5. Wheeler, John R.C. and Thomas G. Rundall. Secondary Preventive Health Behavior. Health Education Quarterly, 1980, Vol. 7, No. 4, pp. 243-262.

6. Rundall, Thomas G. A Suggestion for Improving the Behavioral Model of Physician Utilization. Journal of Health and Social Behavior, 1981, Vol. 22 (March), pp. 103-104.

7. Rundall, Thomas G. and John O. McClain. Environmental Selection and Physician Supply. American Journal of Sociology, 1982, Vol. 87, No. 5, pp. 1090-1112.

8. Rundall, Thomas G. and Connie Evashwick. Social Networks and Help-Seeking Among the Elderly. Research in Aging, 1982, Vol. 4, No. 2, pp. 205-226.

9. Rundall, Thomas G. Commentary on "Effectiveness in Professional Organizations." Health Services Research, 1983, Vol. 18, No. 1, pp. 7-12.

10. Rundall, Thomas G. Hospital Contract Management: Organizational and Public Policy Issues. Health Services Research, 1984, Vol. 19, No. 4, pp. 455-459.

11. Rundall, Thomas G. and Wendy K. Lambert. The Private Management of Public Hospitals. Health Services Research, 1984, Vol. 19, No. 4, pp. 519-544.

12. Alexander, Jeffrey A., Connie Evashwick, and Thomas G. Rundall. Hospitals and the Provision of Care to the Aged: A Cluster Analysis. Inquiry, 1984, Vol. 21, No. 4 (Winter), pp. 303-314..

13. Alexander, Jeffrey A. and Thomas G. Rundall. Public Hospitals Under Contract Management. Medical Care, 1985, Vol. 23, No. 3, pp. 209-219.

14. Evashwick, Connie, Thomas G. Rundall, and Betty Goldiamond. Hospital-based Services for Older Adults, The Gerontologist, 1985, Vol. 25, No. 6, pp. 631-637.

15. Rundall, Thomas G. The Organization of Medical Practice: A Population Ecology Perspective. Medical Care Review, 1987, Vol. 44, No. 2, pp. 375-405.

16. Bruvold, William H. and Thomas G. Rundall. A Meta-analysis and Theoretical Review of School Based Tobacco and Alcohol Intervention Programs. Psychology and Health: An International Journal, 1988, Vol. 2, pp. 53-78.

17. Rundall, Thomas G. and William H. Bruvold. A Meta-analysis of School-based Smoking and Alcohol Use Prevention Programs. Health Education Quarterly, 1988, Vol. 15, No. 3, pp. 317-334.

18. Sofaer, Shoshanna, Thomas G. Rundall, and Wendy Lambert Zellers. Restrictive Reimbursement and Uncompensated Care in California Hospitals, 1981 to 1986. Hospital and Health Services Administration, 1990, Vol. 35, No. 2, pp. 189-206.

19. Rundall, Thomas G. and Kathryn Phillips. Informing and Educating the Electorate About AIDS. Medical Care Review. 1990, Vol. 47, No. 1, pp. 3-13.

20. Rundall, Thomas G. La Asistencia Sanitaria Para Una Sociedad Que Envejece (Health Care for an Aging Society). Anthropos, 1991, No. 118-119 (March-April), pp. 64-70.

21. Rundall, Thomas G. Health Services for an Aging Society. Medical Care Review, 1992, Vol. 49, No. 1, pp. 3-18.

22. Feldman, Sanford E., and Thomas G. Rundall. The Health Care Quality Improvement Initiative: Insights from Fifty Cases of Serious Medical Mistakes. Medical Care Review, 1993, Vol. 50, No. 2 (Summer), pp. 123-151.

23. Rundall, Thomas G. The Integration of Public Health and Medicine. Frontiers of Health Services Management,1994,Vol. 10, No. 4 (Summer), pp. 3-24.

24. Marconi, Katherine, Thomas G. Rundall, Daniel Gentry, Jennafer Kwait, David Celentano, and Paul Stolley. The Organization and Availability of HIV-related Services in Baltimore, MD and Oakland, CA. AIDS and Public Policy, 1994, Vol. 9. No. 4, pp. 173-181.

25. Gentry, Daniel, and Thomas G. Rundall. Staffing in AIDS Service Organizations: The Volunteer Contribution. Journal of Health and Human Resources Administration, 1995, Vol. 18, No. 2, pp. 190-204.

26. Kieler, Bruce, Thomas G. Rundall, and Ishak Saporta. The Oakland HIV/AIDS Planning Council: Its Organizational Form and Environment. International Journal of Public Administration, 1996, Vol. 19, No.2, pp. 1203-1219.

27. Rundall, Thomas G. Conducting and Writing Research Reviews. Medical Care Research and Review, 1996, Vol. 53 (supplement March), pp. s132-s145.

28. Kieler, Bruce W., Thomas G. Rundall, Ishak Saporta, Rusty Keilch, Patricia Carson Sussman, Laura Barney, Barry

Brinkley, Susan Black, and Nancy Warren. Challenges Faced by the HIV Health Services Planning Council in Oakland, California, 1991-1994. American Journal of Preventive Medicine, 1996, Vol. 12, No. 4 (supplement), pp. 26-32.

29. Rundall, Thomas G., and Helen H. Schauffler. Integration of Health Promotion and Disease Prevention and the Role of Market Forces. American Journal of Preventive Medicine, 1997, Vol. 13, No. 4, pp. 244-250.

30. Gordon, Nancy P., Thomas G. Rundall, and Laurence Parker. Type of Health Care Coverage and the Likelihood of Being Screened for Cancer. Medical Care, 1998, Vol. 36, No. 5, pp. 636-645.

31. Sarnoff, Rhonda and Thomas G. Rundall. Meta-Analysis of Effectiveness of Interventions to Increase Influenza Immunization Rates Among High-Risk Population Groups. Medical Care Research and Review, 1998, Vol. 55, No. 4, pp. 432-456.

32. Rundall, Thomas G. Managed Care and the Transformation of the American Health Care System. Keio Business Forum, 1999, Vol. 17, No. 2, pp. 3-18.

33. Rundall, Thomas G., Jennafer Kwait, Katherine Marconi, Stephanie Bender-Kitz, and David Celentano. Impact of the Ryan White CARE Act on the Availability of HIV/AIDS Services. Policy Studies Journal, 1999, Vol. 27, No. 4, pp. 826-839.

34. Kwait, Jennafer, Katherine Marconi, Deborah Helitzer, Matthew Rodieck, Thomas Rundall, and David Celantano. Ryan White CARE Act Title I Funding Priorities and Unmet Needs in Baltimore, Maryland. Policy Studies Journal, 1999, Vol. 27, No. 4, pp. 855-871.

35. Davies, Huw Talfryn Oakley and Thomas G. Rundall. Managing Trust in Managed Care. Milbank Quarterly, 2000, Vol. 78, No.2, pp. 1-29.

36. Norrish, Barbara and Thomas G. Rundall. Hospital Restructuring and the Work of Registered Nurses. Milbank Quarterly, 2001, Vol. 79, No. 1, pp. 55-79.

37. Walshe, Kieran and Thomas G. Rundall. Evidence-based Management: From Theory to Practice in Healthcare. Milbank Quarterly, 2001, Vol. 79, No. 3, pp. 429-457. Reprinted in Ann Mahon (Editor), A Reader in Health Policy and Management, Maidenhead, England: Open University Press, 2008.

38. Rundall, Thomas G. Stephen M. Shortell, Margaret C. Wang, Lawrence Casalino, Thomas Bodenheimer, Robin R. Gillies, Julie A. Schmittdiel, Nancy Oswald, and James Robinson. As Good As It Gets? Chronic Care Management Practices in Nine Leading Physician Organizations in the United States. BMJ: British Medical Journal, 2002, Vol. 325, No. 7370 (October 26), pp. 958-961.

39. Casalino, Lawrence, Robin R. Gillies, Stephen M. Shortell, Julie Schmittdiel, Thomas Bodenheimer, James C. Robinson, Thomas Rundall, Nancy Oswald, Helen Schauffler, and Margaret C. Wang. External Incentives, Information Technology, and Organized Processes to Improve Health Care Quality for Patients with Chronic Diseases. JAMA: Journal of the American Medical Association, 2003, Vol. 289, No. 4, pp. 434-41.

40. Davies, Huw T. O., Claire-Louise Hodges, and Thomas G. Rundall. Views of Doctors and Managers on the Doctor-Manager Relationship in the NHS. BMJ: British Medical Journal, 2003, Vol. 326, March 22, pp. 626-628.

41. Davies, Huw T.O., Claire-Louise Hodges, and Thomas G. Rundall. Consensus and Contention: Doctors' and Managers' Perceptions of the Doctor-Manager Relationship. British Journal of Health Care Management, 2003, Vol. 9, No. 6, pp. 170-176.

42. Castaneda, Xochitl, Zoe Cardoza Clayson, Tom Rundall, Liane Dong, and Margo Sercaz. Promising Outreach Practices: Enrolling Low-Income Children in Health Insurance

Programs in California. Health Promotion Practice, 2003, Vol. 4, No.4, pp. 430-438.

43. McMenamin, Sara B., Helen Halpin Schauffler, Stephen M. Shortell, Thomas G. Rundall, and Robin R. Gillies. Support for Smoking Cessation Interventions in Physician Organizations: Results from a National Study. Medical Care, 2003, Vol. 41, No. 12, pp. 1396-1406.

44. Gillies, Robin R., Stephen M. Shortell, Lawrence Casalino, James C. Robinson, and Thomas Rundall. How Different is California? A Comparison of U.S. Physician Organizations. Health Affairs, October 15, 2003 Web Exclusive (http://www.healthaffairs.org/WebExclusives/Gillies_Web_Excl_101503.htm).

45. Rundall, Thomas G. Refocusing Future Faculty on Evidence-based Health Services Management Research. Journal of Health Administration Education, 2003, Vol. 20, No. 4, pp. 1-12.

46. Rundall, Thomas G., Huw T.O. Davies, Claire-Louise Hodges. Doctor-Manager Relationships in the United States and the United Kingdom. Journal of Healthcare Management, 2004, Vol. 49, No. 2, pp. 251-270.

47. McMenamin, Sara B., Julie Schmittdiel, Helen Ann Halpin, Robin Gillies Thomas G. Rundall, Stephen M. Shortell. Health Promotion in Physician Organizations: Results from a National Survey. American Journal of Preventive Medicine, 2004, Vol. 26, No. 4, pp. 259-264.

48. Robinson, James C., Stephen M. Shortell, Rui Li, Lawrence P. Casalino, Thomas Rundall. The Alignment and Blending of Payment Incentives within Physician Organizations. Health Services Research, 2004, Vol. 39, No. 5, pp. 1589-1606.

49. Rundall, Thomas G., Jeffrey Alexander, and Stephen M. Shortell. A Theory of Physician-Hospital Integration: Contending Institutional and Market Logics in the Health Care Field. Journal of Health and Social Behavior, 2004, Vol. 45 (extra issue), pp. 102-117.

50. Bodenheimer, Thomas, Margaret C. Wang, Thomas G. Rundall, Stephen M. Shortell, Robin R. Gillies, Nancy Oswald, Lawrence Casalino, and James C. Robinson. What are the Facilitators and Barriers in Physician Organization's Use of Care Management Processes? Joint Commission Journal on Quality and Safety, 2004, Vol. 30, No. 9, pp. 505-514.

51. Schmittdiel, Julie, Sara B. McMenamin, Helen Ann Halpin, Robin R. Gillies, Thomas Bodenheimer, Stephen M. Shortell, Thomas Rundall, Larry Casalino. The Use of Patient and Physician Reminders for Preventive Services: Results from a National Study of Physician Organizations. Preventive Medicine, 2004, Vol. 39, Issue 5 (November), pp. 1000-1006.

52. Shortell, Stephen M., Julie Schmittdiel, Margaret C. Wang, Rui Li, Robin Gillies, Lawrence Casalino, James C. Robinson, and Thomas G. Rundall. An Empirical Assessment of High Performing Medical Groups: Results from a National Study. Medical Care Research and Review, 2005, Vol. 62, No. 4, (August), pp. 407-434.

53. Coffman, Janet M. and Thomas G. Rundall. The Impact of Hospitalists on the Cost and Quality of Inpatient Care in the United States: A Research Synthesis. Medical Care Research and Review, 2005, Vol. 62, No. 4 (August), pp. 379-406.

54. Halpin, Helen Ann, Sara B. McMenamin, Julie Schmittdiel, Robin R. Gillies, Stephen M. Shortell, Thomas G. Rundall, Larry Casalino. The Routine Use of Health Risk Appraisals: Results from a National Study of Physicians. American Journal of Health Promotion, 2005, Vol. 20, No. 1, pp. 34-38.

55. Simon, Jodi S., Thomas G. Rundall, Stephen M. Shortell. Drivers of Electronic Medical Record Adoption Among Medical Groups. Joint Commission Journal on Quality and Patient Safety, 2005, Vol. 31, No. 11, pp. 631-639.

56. Scott, J. Tim, Thomas G. Rundall., Thomas M. Vogt, and John Hsu. Kaiser Permanente's Experience of Implementing an Electronic Medical Record: A Qualitative Study. BMJ, doi:10.1136/bmj.38638.497477.68 (published 3 November

2005). Also published in paper copy of the BMJ, 2005, Vol. 331, December 3, pp. 1313-1316.

57. Schmittdiel, Julie, Stephen M. Shortell, Thomas Rundall, Thomas Bodenheimer, and Joe V. Selby. The Effect of Primary Health Care Orientation on Chronic Illness Care Management. Annals of Family Medicine, 2006, Vol. 4, No. 2, pp. 117-123.

58. Kovner, Anthony, and Thomas G. Rundall. Evidence-based Management Reconsidered. Frontiers of Health Services Management, 2006, Vol. 22, No. 3, pp. 3-22. Translated into German and published as Aktuelle Uberlegungen zum Evidenzbasierten Management im Gesundheitswesen in (Sabine Bohnet-Joschko, editor) Wissensmanagement in Krankenhaus (Knowledge Management in Hospitals). Wiesbaden: Deutscher Universitats-Verlag, 2007. Republished in A. Kovner, R. D'Aquilla and D. Fine (Eds.) The Practice of Evidence-based Management. Chicago: Health Administration Press, 2009, and in A. Kovner, A.S. McAlearny, and D. Neuhauser (Eds.) Health Services Management: Cases, Reading and Commentary. Chicago: Health Administration Press, 2009.

59. Kovner, Anthony, and Thomas G. Rundall. Response from the Feature Authors. Frontiers of Health Services Management, 2006, Vol. 22, No. 3, pp. 41-44.

60. Hung, Dorothy Y., Thomas G. Rundall, Benjamin F. Grabtree, Alfred F. Tallia, Deborah J. Cohen, Helen A. Halpin. Influence of Practice and Provider Attributes on Preventive Service Delivery. American Journal of Preventive Medicine, 2006, Vol. 30, No. 5 (May), pp. 413-22.

61. Hung, Dorothy Y., Thomas G. Rundall, Deborah J. Cohen, Alfred F. Tallia, and Benjamin F. Crabtree. Productivity and Turnover in Primary Care Practices: The Role of Staff Participation in Decision Making. Medical Care, 2006, Vol. 44, No. 10, pp. 946-51.

62. Hung, Dorothy Y., Thomas G. Rundall, Benjamin F. Crabtree, Alfred F. Tallia, Deborah J. Cohen, Helen A. Halpin. Rethinking

Prevention in Primary Care: Using the Chronic Care Model to Improve Health Risk Behaviors. Milbank Quarterly, 2007, Vol. 85, No. 1, pp. 69-91.

63. Simon, Jodi S., Thomas G. Rundall, and Stephen M. Shortell. Adoption of Order Entry with Decision Support for Chronic Care by Physician Organizations. Journal of the American Medical Informatics Association, 2007, Vol. 14, No. 4 pp. 432-439.

64. Goldman, Lauren Elizabeth, Margaret Handley, Thomas G. Rundall, Dean Shillinger. Current and Future Directions in MediCal Chronic Disease Care Management: A View From the Top. American Journal of Managed Care, 2007, Vol. 13, No. 5, pp. 263-68.

65. Shortell, Stephen M., Thomas G. Rundall, and John Hsu. Improving Patient Care by Linking Evidence-based Medicine and Evidence-based Management. Journal of the American Medical Association, 2007, Vol. 298, No. 6 (August 8), pp. 673-676.

66. Rundall, Thomas G., Peter F. Martelli, Laura Arroyo, Rodney McCurdy, Ilana Graetz, Estee Neuwirth, Pam Curtis, Julia Schmittdiel, Mark Gibson, and John Hsu. The Informed Decisions Toolbox: Tools for Knowledge Transfer and Performance Improvement. Journal of Healthcare Management, 2007, Vol. 52, No. 5, pp. 325-41.

67. Overtveit, John, Tim Scott, Thomas G. Rundall, Stephen M. Shortell, Mats Brommels. Improving Quality Through Effective Implementation of Information Technology in Healthcare. International Journal for Quality in Health Care, 2007, Vol. 19, No. 5, pp. 259-266; doi:10.1093/intqhc/mzm031.

68. Rundall, Thomas G. Evidence-Based Management. Hospitals and Health Networks, 2007, Vol. 81, No. 2, pp. 72.

69. Overtveit, John, Tim Scott, Thomas G. Rundall, Stephen M. Shortell, Mats Brommels. Implementation of Electronic Medical Records in Hospitals: Two Case Studies. Health Policy, 2007, Vol. 84, pp. 181-190. doi:10.1016/j.healthpol.2007.05.013.

70. Overtveit, John, Robin Gillies, Thomas G. Rundall, Stephen M. Shortell, and Mats Brommels. Quality of Care for Chronic Illnesses. International Journal of Health Care Quality Assurance, 2008, Vol. 21, Number 2, pp. 190-201.

71. Janus, Katharina, Volker E. Amelung, Laurence C. Baker, Michael Gaitanides, and Thomas G. Rundall. Job Satisfaction and Motivation Among Physicians in Academic Medical Centers: Insights from a Cross-National Study. Journal of Health Politics, Policy and Law, 2008, Vol.33, No. 6, pp. 1133-1168.

72. Janus, Katharina, Volker E. Amelung, Laurence C. Baker, Michael Gaitanides, Thomas G. Rundall, Friedrich W. Schwartz. Warum sind amerikanische Arzte zufriedener? Ergebnisse einer internationalen Studie unter Klinikarzten [Are America Physicians more Satisfied? – Results from an International Study of Physicians in University Hospitals]. Gesundheitswesen, 2009, March 13. Reprinted in Arbeitsbedingungen und Befinden von Arztinnen und Artzen: Befunde und Interventionen. Koln: Deutscher Artze-Verlag GmbH, 2010, pp. 219-234.

73. Evashwick, Connie and Thomas Rundall. No Better Time: The Effects of the Recession Make Evidence-based Management All the More Compelling for Health Care Leaders. Health Progress, 2010, January - February, pp. 37-41.

74. Kim, Yeuen, Maryann Situ, Margaret Handley, Ivonne McLean, Thomas Rundall, Dean Shillinger. Ecology Matters: Contextualizing Safety-Net Patients' Experiences with Diabetes Self-Management Support Strategies. Asia-Pacific Journal of General Practice, 2009, July, pp. 1-14.

75. Graetz, Ilana, Mary Reed, Thomas Rundall, James Bellows, Richard Brand, and John Hsu. Care Coordination and Electronic Health Records: Connecting Clinicians. AMIA Annual Symposium Proceedings, 2009, November 14, pp. 208-12.

76. Strandberg-Larsen, Martin, Michaela L. Schiotz, Jeremy D. Silver, Anne Frolich, John S. Andersen, Ilana Graetz, Mary Reed, Jim Bellows, Allan Krasnik, Thomas Rundall, John Hsu. Is the Kaiser Permanente Model Superior in Terms of Clinical Integration? A Comparative Study of Kaiser Permanente, Northern California and the Danish Healthcare System. BMC Health Services Research, 2010, April, pp. 10-91. doi: 10.1186/1472-6963-10-91. Article URL: http://www.biomedcentral.com/1472-6963/10/91.

77. Ratanawongsa, Neda, Vijay K. Bhandari, Margaret Handley, Thomas Rundall, Hali Hammer, Dean Schillinger. Primary Care Provider Perceptions of the Effectiveness of Two Self-Management Support Programs for Vulnerable Patients with Diabetes. Journal of Diabetes Science and Technology, 2012, Vol. 6, No. 1 (January 1), pp. 116-124.

78. Rundall, Thomas, Katharina Janus, Shelley Oberlin, Brian Thygesen. Success Under Duress: Policies and Practices Managers View as Keys to Profitability in Five California Hospitals with Challenging Payer Mix. Journal of Healthcare Management, 2012, March/April, pp. 94-111.

79. Otte Trojel, Terese, Antoinette de Bont, Thomas Rundall, and Joris van de Klundert. How Outcomes are Achieved Through Patient Portals: A Realist Review. Journal of the American Medical Informatics Association, 2014, Vol. 21, No. 4, pp. 751-757. Published on-line first: February 6, 2014. doi:10.1136/amiajnl-2013-002501.

80. Graetz I, Mary Reed, Stephen M. Shortell, Thomas G. Rundall, James Bellows, and John Hsu. The Association Between EHRs and Care Coordination Varies by Team Cohesion. Health Services Research, 2014, February, Vol. 49, No.1 (Pt 2, February), pp. 438-52. doi: 10.1111/1475-6773.12136. Epub 2013 Dec 21.

81. Otte-Trojel, Terese, Antoinette de Bont, Joris van de Klundert, Thomas G. Rundall. Characteristics of Patient Portals Developed in the Context of Health Information Exchanges:

Early Policy Effects of Incentives in the Meaningful Use Program in the United States. Journal of Medical Internet Research, published online November 21, 2014, Vol. 16, No.11, e258. doi: 10.2196/jmir.3698.

82. Graetz, Ilana, Mary Reed, Stephen M. Shortell, Thomas G. Rundall, James Bellows, John Hsu. The Next Step Towards Making Use Meaningful: Electronic Information Exchange and Care Coordination Across Clinicians and Delivery Sites. Medical Care, 2014, Vol. 52, No. 12 (December), pp. 1037-41. doi: 10.1097/MLR.0000000000000245.

83. Rundall, Thomas, Frances M. Wu, Valerie A. Lewis, Karen E. Schoenherr, Stephen M. Shortell. Contributions of Relational Coordination to Care Management in ACOs: Views of Managerial and Clinical Leaders. Health Care Management Review, 2016, Vol. 41, No. 2, pp. 88-100. doi: 10.1097/HMR.00000000000064

84. Graetz, Ilana, Jie Huang, Richard Brand, Stephen M. Shortell, Thomas Rundall, Jim Belows, John Hsu, Marc Jaffe, Mary Reed. The Impact of Electronic Health Records and Teamwork on Diabetes Care Quality. American Journal of Managed Care, 2015, Vol. 21, No. 12 (December), pp. 878-84.

85. Otte-Trojel, Terese, Antoinette de Bont, Joris van de Klundert, and Thomas Rundall. Developing Patient Portals in a Fragmented Healthcare System. International Journal of Medical Informatics, 2015, Vol. 8, No. 10, pp. 835-846.

86. Otte-Trojel, Terese, Antoinette de Bont, Joris van de Klundert, Thomas Rundall, and Mary Reed. The Organizational Dynamics Enabling Kaiser Permanente's Patient Portal's Impact Upon Operational Performance and Patient Health: A Qualitative Study. Published online, December 16, 2015, BMC Health Services Research, doi: 10.1186/s12913-015-1208-2.

87. Wu, Frances, Stephen Shortell, Joan Bloom, and Thomas Rundall. The Impact of Health Information Technology in Advancing Care Management and Coordination in Accountable Care Organizations. Health Care Management

Review, 2017 Vol. 42, No. 4 (Oct/Dec), pp. 282-291. doi: 10.1097/HMR0000000000000123.

88. Wu, Frances, Stephen Shortell, Thomas Rundall, Joan Bloom. Using Health Information Technology to Manage a Patient Population in Accountable Care Organizations. Journal of Health Organization and Management, 2016, Vol. 30, No. 4, pp. 581-596.

89. Otte-Trojel, Terese, Antoinette de Bont, Joris van de Klundert, and Thomas Rundall. What Do We Know About Patient Portal Development? A Review of the Evidence. Journal of the American Medical Informatics Association, 2016, Vol. 23, No. e1 (April), pp. e162-e168.

90. Otte-Trojel, Terese, Thomas Rundall, Antoinette de Bont, and Joris van de Klundert. Can Relational Coordination Help Interorganizational Networks Overcome Challenges to Delivering Patient Portals? International Journal of Healthcare Management, 2015 Vol. 10, No. 2, pp. 75-83.

91. Otte-Trojel, Terese, Thomas Rundall, Antoinette de Bont, and Joris van de Klundert. Response to Randell, et al. Using Realist Reviews to Understand How Health IT works, for Whom, and In What Circumstances. Journal of the American Medical Informatics Association, 2015, Vol. 22, No. e1, pp. e218.

92. Shortell, Stephen M., Janet C. Blodgett, Thomas G. Rundall, Peter Kralovec. Use of Lean and Related Transformational Performance Improvement Systems in Hospitals 9in the United States: Results from a National Survey. Joint Commission Journal on Quality and Patient Safety. 2018, Vol. 44, No. 10 (Oct.), pp. 574-582. doi: 10.1016/j.jcjq.2018.03.002.

93. Shortell, Stephen M., Thomas G. Rundall, Janet C. Blodgett. Assessing the Relationship of the Human Resource, Finance, and Information Technology Functions on Reported Performance in Hospitals Using the Lean Management System. Health Care Management Review. 2019, June 6. doi: 1097/HMR.0000000000000253.

94. Po, Justine, Thomas G. Rundall, Stephen M. Shortell, Janet C. Blodgett. Lean Management and U.S. Public Hospital Performance. Journal of Healthcare Management. 2019, Vol. 64, Vol. 6, 363-379. doi:10.1097/JHM-D-18-00163

95. Rundall, Thomas G., Stephen M. Shortell, Janet C. Blodgett, Rachel Moser Henke, Dave Foster. Lean Management and Hospital Performance: Results from a National Survey. Health Care Management Review, forthcoming.

96. Northridge, Mary E., Donna Shelley, Thomas G. Rundall, Ross C. Brownson. Editorial: Methods and Applications in Implementation Science. Frontiers in Public Health. 2019, Vol. 7, No. 213 (July 31). doi: 10.3389/fpubh.2019.00213.

Refereed Chapters in Books

1. Battistella, Roger M. and Thomas G. Rundall. The Future of Primary Care Services. In Roger M. Battistella and Thomas G. Rundall (eds.) Health Care Policy in a Changing Environment. Berkeley: McCutchan Press, 1978, pp. 294-318.

2. Heatherington, Robert W. and Thomas G. Rundall. The Social Structure of Work Groups. Chapter Five in S.W. Shortell and A.D. Kaluzny (eds.), Health Care Management: A Text in Organizational Theory and Behavior. New York: John Wiley and Sons, Inc., 1983, pp. 167-202.

3. Rundall, Thomas G. Evaluation of Health Services Programs. In John Last (ed.), Maxcy-Rosenau Public Health and Preventive Medicine, 13th Ed. New York: Appleton-Century-Crofts, 1986, pp. 1831-1847.

4. Rundall, Thomas G. and Robert W. Hetherington. The Social Structure of Work Groups. Chapter five in S.M. Shortell, A.D. Kaluzny and Associates, Health Care Management: A Text in Organizational Theory and Behavior, 2nd Edition. New York: John Wiley, 1987, pp. 187-212.

5. Rundall, Thomas G., Shoshanna Sofaer, and Wendy K. Lambert. Uncompensated Hospital Care in California: Private and Public Hospital Responses to Competitive Market Forces. In R.M. Scheffler and L.F. Rossiter (eds.) Advances in Health Economics and Health Services Research, Volume 9. Greenwich, Conn: JAI Press, 1988, pp. 113-133.

6. Rundall, Thomas G. Health Program Planning and Evaluation. In John Last (ed.), Maxcy-Rosenau Public Health and Preventive Medicine, 14th Edition. New York: Appleton-Century-Crofts, 1991, pp. 1079-1094.

7. Rundall, Thomas G. and Laura Gardner. Evaluation and Quality Assurance in Mental Health Care. In National Perspectives on Quality Assurance in Mental Health Care. Geneva: World Health Organization, Division of Mental Health, 1991, pp. 31-44.

8. Estes, Carroll and Thomas G. Rundall. Social Characteristics, Social Structure, and Health In the Aging Population. In M.G. Ory and R.P. Abeles (eds.) Aging, Health and Behavior. Newbury Park, CA: Sage Publications, 1992, pp. 299-327.

9. Fried, Bruce J. and Thomas G. Rundall. Groups and Teams in Health Services Organizations. Chapter 6 in S.M. Shortell, A.D. Kaluzny and Associates, Health Care Management: A Text in Organizational Theory and Behavior, Third Edition. Delmar Publishers, 1994, 137-163.

10. Fried, Bruce J. and Thomas G. Rundall. Managing Groups and Teams. Chapter 6 in S.M. Shortell and A.D. Kaluzny (eds.) Essentials of Health Care Management. Albany, New York: Delmar Publishers, 1997, pp. 163-197.

11. Evashwick, Connie and Thomas G. Rundall. Organizing the Continuum of Long-Term Care. Chapter 10 in C. Evashwick (ed.) The Continuum of Long-Term Care: An Integrated Systems Approach. Albany, New York: Delmar Publishers, 1995.

12. Morris, Anne and Thomas Rundall. The HIV Services Partnership: A Community-Based Collaboration Addressing the Psychosocial Needs of People with HIV/AIDS in San Francisco. Chapter 23 in C. Evashwick (ed.) The Continuum of Long-Term Care: An Integrated Systems Approach. Albany, New York: Delmar Publishers, 1995.

13. Rundall, Thomas G. Public Health Management Tools: Evaluation. In Robert B. Wallace (ed.) Public Health and Preventive Medicine, 14th Edition. Stamford, Connecticut: Appleton& Lange, 1998, pp. 1165-1168.

14. Rundall, Thomas G., David B. Starkweather, and Barbara R. Norrish. Evaluation of the Strengthening Hospital Nursing Program. Chapter six in Stephen L. Issacs and James R. Knickman (eds.) To Improve Health and Health Care. San Francisco: Jossey - Bass Publishers, 1998, pp. 101-128.

15. Fried , Bruce J., Sharon Topping, and Thomas G. Rundall. Groups and Teams in Health Services Organizations. Chapter 6 in S.M. Shortell, A.D. Kaluzny and Associates, Health Care Management: A Text in Organizational Theory and Behavior, Fourth Edition. Albany, New York: Delmar Publishers, 2000, pp. 154-190.

16. Rundall, Thomas G. and Connie Evashwick. Organizing the Continuum of Long-Term Care. Chapter 10 in C. Evashwick (ed.) The Continuum of Long-Term Care: An Integrated Systems Approach, 2nd. edition. Albany, New York: Delmar Publishers, 2001, pp.155-167.

17. Rundall, Thomas G. The Sisyphean Challenge: Health Services Integration. In H.T.O. Davies, M. Tavakoli, and M. Malek (eds.) Quality in Health Care: Strategic Issues in Health Care Management. Alderstot, U.K.: Ashgate Publishers, 2001,pp. 4-16.

18. Shortell, Stephen M. and Thomas G. Rundall. Physician-Organization Relationships: Social Networks and Strategic Intent. In Stephen S. Mick and Mindy Wyttenbach (eds.)

Advances in Health Care Organization Theory. San Francisco: Jossey-Bass Publishers, 2003, pp. 141-173.

19. Rundall, Thomas G. Hospital-Physician Relationships: Comparing Administrators' and Physicians' Perceptions. In H.T.O. Davies, M. Tavakoli (eds.) Policy, Finance, and Performance in Health Care. Alderstot, U.K.: Ashgate Publishers, 2004, pp. 47-79.

20. Rundall, Thomas G., John Hsu, Jennifer Elston Lafata, Vicky Fung, Kathryn A. Paez, Jan Simpkins, Steven R. Simon, Scott B. Robinson, Connie Uratsu, Margaret J. Gunter, Stephen B. Soumerai. Prescribing Safety in Ambulatory Care: Physician Perspectives. In Kerm Henriksen, James B. Battles, Eric Marks, and David I. Lewin (Eds.) Advances in Patient Safety: From Research to Implementation. Vol. 1, Research Findings. Rockville, MD.: Agency for Healthcare Research and Quality, 2005, pp. 161-172.

21. Rundall, Thomas G. and Connie J. Evashwick. Organizing the Continuum of Long-Term Care. Chapter 10 in C. Evashwick (ed.) The Continuum of Long-Term Care: An Integrated Systems Approach, 3rd edition. Albany, New York: Delmar Publishers, 2005, pp. 187-199.

22. Alexander, Jeffrey A., Thomas G. Rundall, and Timothy Hoff. Power and Politics in Health Services Organizations. Chapter 9 in S.M. Shortell, A.D. Kaluzny and Associates, Health Care Management: A Text in Organizational Theory and Behavior, Fifth Edition. Albany, New York: Delmar Publishers, 2006, pp. 276-310.

23. Rundall, Thomas G. Public Health Management Tools: Evaluation. Chapter 79 in Robert B. Wallace (ed.) Maxcy-Rosenau-Last Public Health and Preventive Medicine, 15th Edition. Stamford, Connecticut: Appleton & Lange, 2007, pp. 14-18.

24. Rundall, Thomas G., Peter Martelli, Rodney McCurdy, Ilana Graetz, Laura Arroyo, Estee Neuwirth, Pam Curtis, Julie Schmittdiel, Mark Gibson, John Hsu. Using Research

Evidence When Making Decisions: Views of Health Services Managers and Policy Makers. In A. Kovner, R. D'Aquilla and D. Fine (Eds.) The Practice of Evidence-based Management. Chicago: Health Administration Press, 2009.

25. Rundall, Thomas G. Evidence-based Management: Implications for Funding Health Services Research. In A. Kovner, R. D'Aquilla and D. Fine (Eds.) The Practice of Evidence-based Management (instructor resources). Chicago: Health Administration Press, 2009.

26. Rundall, Thomas G. and Anthony R. Kovner. Evidence-Based Management Reconsidered: 18 Months Later. In A. Kovner, R. D'Aquilla and D. Fine (Eds.) The Practice of Evidence-based Management. Chicago: Health Administration Press, 2009.

27. Hsu, John, Laura Arroyo, Ilana Graetz, Esther B. Neuwirth, Julia Schmittdiel, Thomas G. Rundall, Peter F. Martelli, Rodney McCurdy, Mark Gibson and Pam Curtis. Methods for Developing Actionable Evidence for Consumers of Health Services Research. In A. Kovner, R. D'Aquilla and D. Fine (Eds.) The Practice of Evidence-based Management. Chicago: Health Administration Press, 2009.

28. Rundall, Thomas and Terese Otte-Trojel. Research Opportunities and Examples. Chapter 7 in Evidence-Based Management in Healthcare, 2nd Edition. Edited by Anthony Kovner and Thomas D'Aunno. Ann Arbor, MI: Health Administration Press, 2016.

Other Published Work

1. Rundall, Thomas G. Review of Organizational Research in Hospitals by S.M. Shortell and M. Brown. Program Notes (The Journal of the Association of University Programs in Health Administration), No. 77, 1977, pp. 1-2.

2. Rundall, Thomas G. Health at the Top: Review of Executive Health by P. Goldberg. Executive, March 1979, p. 12.

3. Rundall, Thomas G. Review of The Unkindest Cut by Marcia Millman. Administrative Science Quarterly, December 1979, pp. 692-694.

4. Rundall, Thomas G. Medical Students and Medical Education: Review of Physicians in the Making by Davis Johnson. Review of Education Research, Vol. 10, No. 2, 1984, pp. 156-157.

5. Feighery-Ross, Ellen, Thomas G. Rundall, Frank Capell, and Patrick Mitchell. Health Risks in the North Bay: Their Prevalence and Implications. Petaluma, CA: North Bay Health Resources Center, 1987.

6. Rundall, Thomas G. Commentary on health care governance. The Journal of Health Administration Education, Vol. 9, No. 4, 1991, pp. 460-462.

7. Kieler, Bruce and Thomas G. Rundall. The Oakland Title I HIV/AIDS Planning Council: A Minimalist Organization Functioning in a Turbulent Environment. Intitute of Industrial Relations, University of California, Berkeley, Working Paper No. 57, October 1993.

8. Rundall, Thomas G. and Bruce Kieler. The Use of Organizational Consortia to Coordinate Community Services for Persons with HIV/AIDS Disease. Proceedings of the Academy of Business Administration, June 1994.

9. Rundall, Thomas G., David B. Starkweather, and Barbara Norrish. All Politics is Local. Case study put on the website of the Electronic Hallway.

10. Rundall, Thomas G., David B. Starkweather, and Barbara Norrish. If It Ain't Broke, Fix It! Case study put on the website of the Electronic Hallway.

11. Rundall, Thomas G., David B. Starkweather, and Barbara Norrish. Maintaining Mission Through Organizational Change. Case study put on the website of the Electronic Hallway.

12. Rundall, Thomas G., Kelly J. Devers, and Shoshanna Sofaer. Introduction: Overview of the Special Issue on Qualitative Research Methods. Health Services Research, 1999, Vol. 34, No. 5, Part II, pp. 1091-1099.

13. Rundall, Thomas G. Commentary on Institutional Theory and Hospital Research. Medical Care Research and Review, Vol. 58, No.2, 2001, pp. 229-233.

14. Rundall, Thomas G. Introduction: Measuring Population Health. In Stephen L. Isaacs (editor), Improving Population Health: The California Wellness Foundation's Health Improvement Initiative, 2002, pp. 183-186.

15. Graetz, Ilana, Mary Reed, Thomas Rundall, James Bellows, Richard Brand, and John Hsu. Care Coordination and Electronic Health records: Connecting Clinicians. American Medical Informatics Association Annual Symposium Proceedings, Nov. 14, 2009, pp. 208-212.

Public Policy Reports

1. Bruvold, William and Thomas G. Rundall. A Meta-Evaluation of California School Based Adolescent Smoking and Alcohol Use Reduction Programs. Final Report to the State of California Department of Health Services, June 1984.

2. Rundall, Thomas G., Wendy K. Lambert and Shoshanna Churgin. Hospital Deductions from Revenue in California. Final Report to the Office of Health Facilities, Health Resources and Services Administration, August 1985.

3. Wallack, Lawrence, S. Leonard Syme, Thomas G. Rundall and Joyce G. Lashof. An Environmental Approach to Promoting Health. Final report to the Kaiser Family Foundation, September 1985.

4. Rundall, Thomas G., Charlotte Kent, Kathryn Phillips, and Daniel Shostak. The Public Health Impact of Proposition 102, The Reporting Exposure to AIDS Virus Initiative, October 1988.

5. Chang, Sophia, Mary Pittman-Lindeman, and Thomas G. Rundall. The Working Uninsured. Who They Are and Why They Don't Have Health Insurance: A Case Study at San Francisco General Hospital, January 1989.

6. Rundall, Thomas G. and Michael Gorman. Participatory Community Planning for HIV Service Delivery. Final Report to the State of California Office of AIDS, March 1991.

7. Rundall, Thomas G. and Karen Pertschuck. Evaluation of California Project LEAN, Final Report to the Kaiser Family Foundation, December 1991

8. Rundall, Thomas G. Community Health Assessment: Measuring the Impact of Health Promotion. A Report to the Western Consortium for Public Health, March 1989.

9. Gordon, Nancy P., Laurence Parker, Thomas G. Rundall, and Carin Perkins. The Proportion of the California Adult Working Population Reporting a Highly Restrictive Smoking Policy at Their Worksite. A Report to the Northern California Cancer Center and the California Department of Health Services, August 1991.

10. Rundall, Thomas G. CDC/UC Public Health Leadership Institute: End-of-year Evaluation Report, 1992-1993. A Report to the Public Health Leadership Institute, January 1994.

11. Rundall, Thomas G., David Celentano, Deborah Helitzer-Allen, Amanda Houston-Hamilton, Stephanie Bender-Kitz, Roger Doughty Daniel Gentry, Jae Kennedy, Bruce Kieler, Jennafer Kwait, Joan Griffen, Karen Heckert, Matthew Roderick, Kavoos Basseri, Althea Henry, Lois Lee Thompson. Implementation of Title I of the Ryan White CARE Act of 1990. A Report to the Kaiser Family Foundation, September 1994.

12. Starkweather, David, Mary Harris, Thomas Rundall, Ross Harris. External Evaluation of the National Program of Management Development for Australian Clinicians. A Report to the Royal Australian College of Medical Administrators, February 1995.

13. Rundall, Thomas G. and Helen Schauffler. Incorporating Health Promotion and Disease Prevention into Integrated Delivery Systems. A Report to the Center for Health Management Research, May 1995.

14. Rundall, Thomas G., Barbara Norrish, and David Starkweather. Evaluation of the National Strengthening Hospital Nursing Program. A Report to the Robert Wood Johnson Foundation and the Pew Charitable Trusts, December 1997.

15. Rundall, Thomas G., Liane Wong, Margo Sercarz, Xochitl Castaneda, and Zoe Clayson. Lessons Learned About Outreach: Findings From Ten First Things First Community Coalitions Created to Enroll Eligible Children in Medi-Cal. A Report to the California HealthCare Foundation, May 1999.

16. Rundall, Thomas G. and Sherilyn Tye. Hospital-Physician Relationships. A Report to the Center for Health Management Studies, University of California, Berkeley, July 2000.

17. Scott, Tim, John Hsu, Thomas G. Rundall, James Kinsman, Tom Vogt, and Judy Li. Catching a Wave: Implementing a Clinical Information System in Kaiser Permanente Hawaii. A Report to Kaiser Permanente Medical Care, May 2004.

18. Hsu, John, Thomas G. Rundall, Peter F. Martelli, Laura Arroyo, Rodney McCurdy, Ilana Graetz, Estee Neuwirth, Pam Curtis, Julia Schmittdiel, Mark Gibson. Evidence-based Management. Report to the Agency for Healthcare Research and Quality, January 2007.

UNIVERSITY AND PUBLIC SERVICE (since 1995)

Member, Board of Directors, John Muir Health, 2009 – 2019 (Chair 2015 - 2017)

Member, Board of Directors, On Lok, Inc., 2006 – 2016 (Chair Senior Health Services Corporation 2013 - 2016)

Executive Associate Dean, School of Public Health, 2007 – 2010

Chair, Graham (formerly Baxter) International Prize Selection Committee, 2005 – 2008

Co-director, Health Research and Educational Trust ACTION Program, 2005 - 2008

Member, Board of Directors, John Muir Physician Network, 2000 – 2009 (Chair 2001-2004)

Co-director, Center for Health Management Research, 2001 - 2006

Member, Advisory Committee, Sutter Health Institute for Research and Education,

2005 – 2009

Chair, AcademyHealth Annual Meeting Planning Committee, 2004-2005

Member, Advisory Board, Institute for Business and Economic Research 2004-2005

Co-chair, Annual Meeting of the Association of University Programs in Health Administration, 2004

Co-chair, Bay Area Health Care Quality and Outcomes Conference, 2002 - 2008

Director, Center for Health Research, 2002 – 2005

Member, Board of Directors, Association of University Programs in Health Administration, 2002 - 2005

Chair, Division of Health Policy and Management, 2001 –2002

Acting Director, Program in Health and Public Policy, 2000-2001

Elected Member, School of Public Health Faculty Council, 1996 – 1997, 1998 – 1999,

2000 - 2002

Acting Director, Program in Health and Public Policy, 2000-2001

Director, Center for Health Management Studies, 1996 -1999

Director, Graduate Program in Health Services Management, 1994 - 1999

Member, Board of Directors, New Century Health Care Institute, 1995 - 1998

Member, Board of Directors, Health Executives of Northern California, 1996 - 1999

Head, Division of Health Policy and Administration, 1994-1995.

Member Advisory Board, Kaiser Permanente International, 1996 - 1999

Member, Advisory Board, Center for Healthcare Innovation, 1995 - 1999

Member, Board of Directors, The Network for Health Care Management, 1994 - 1998

Member Board of Directors, Hospital Council Foundation, 1994 - 1997

Member Board of Directors, Health Services Research Foundation, 1994 - 1997

Member Executive Committee, Robert Wood Johnson Foundation Health Policy Scholars Program at U.C. Berkeley, 1993 - 1999

HONORS, FELLOWSHIPS, AND VISITING APPOINTMENTS

UC Berkeley Graduate Program in Health Management Distinguished Leadership Award, 2011

Berkeley Citation for Distinguished Achievement and Notable Service to the University, 2010

Alfred Childs Outstanding Faculty Service Award, School of Public Health, 2008,

Filerman Prize for Innovation in Health Administration Education, 2005

Henry J. Kaiser Endowed Chair in Organized Health Systems, 2001

Visiting Scholar, University of Sydney, 1999

Outstanding Teaching and Mentoring Award, UCB School of Public Health, 1997

Elected Fellow, Association for Health Services Research, 1996

Visiting Scholar, University of Woolongong, 1996

Visiting Scholar, University of Auckland, 1994

Visiting Scholar, Kings Fund College, London, 1994

Visiting Scholar, University of Barcelona, 1993

Visiting Scholar, Stanford Center for Organizations Research 1991-92

Robert Wood Johnson Foundation Health Policy Fellow, 1985-86
  Served as health policy advisor to Senator Dave Durenberger, United States Senate

State of California, Department of Health Services, Certificate of Recognition for Contributions to the Health of California's Population, 1985

Kaiser-Weissman Award for Outstanding Health Policy Paper, 1981

PROFESSIONAL ACTIVITIES

Professional Memberships

Center for Evidence-Based Management

Center for Healthcare Management

Academy of Management

American Public Health Association.

AcademyHealth (formerly Association for Health Services Research and Policy)

American Evaluation Association

Editing and Reviewing

Editorial Board, Journal of Management and Marketing in Healthcare, 2007 –

Editorial Board, Health Services Research, 1998 – 2005.

Special Issue Co-editor, Health Services Research, issue on qualitative research methods in health services research, 1999.

Editorial Board, Medical Care Research and Review, 1994-1997.

Editor, Medical Care Research and Review, 1987- 1994.

Editorial Board, Managing Senior Care, 1991- 1996.

Editorial Board, U.C. Berkeley Wellness Letter, 1983-1986.

Editorial Board, The Western Edition: The Journal of the Association of Western Hospitals, 1984-1986.

Associate Editor of Journal of Health and Social Behavior, 1980-84.

Editorial Board, Administrative Science Quarterly, 1978-82.

Guest Editor of Special Issue of Health Services Research on hospital contract management, October 1984.

Reviewer for Health Services Research, Medical Care Research and Review,

American Journal of Public Health, Administrative Science Quarterly,

Milbank Quarterly, Medical Care, Health Affairs

SELECTED RESEARCH PRESENTATIONS (since 2000)

"Evidence-Based Management," Association of University Programs in Health Administration, Monterey, California, June 2013.

"Evidence-Based Management in Healthcare," American College of Healthcare Executives, Chicago, August 2010.

"Success Under Duress," Hospital Council of Northern and Central California, Heavenly Valley, California, October 2010.

"Generating Research that Matters," Academy of Management, Philadelphia, August 2007.

"Accountable Care Organizations," AcademyHealth, Orlando, June 2007.

"Getting Beyond Money: What Else Drives Physician Performance?"

National Pay For Performance Summit, Los Angeles, February 2007.

"Evidence-based Health Management and Policy," U.C. Berkeley Advanced Health Leadership Forum, Berkeley, January 2007.

"Evidence and Organizational Decision Making: Never the Twain Shall Meet?" AcademyHealth Annual Research Meeting, Seattle, June 2006.

"IT in Health Care," CITRIS in Europe Meeting, Helsinki, June 2006.

"Evidence-based Decision Management in Healthcare," CITRIS in Europe Meeting, Helsinki, June 2006.

"Experiences and Results From Kaiser Permanente Health Connect," Healthcare Technology Seminar, FinnWell and TEKES (Finnish Funding Agency for Technology and Innovation), Helsinki, June 2006.

"Impact of Information Technology on Clinical Care: An Evaluation of Technology and the Quality, Safety, and Efficiency of Chronic Disease Care," Meeting of the Team for Research in Ubiquitous Secure Technology (TRUST) sponsored by the UC Berkeley Center for Information Technology Research in the Interest of Society," U.C. Berkeley, April 2006.

"Six Challenges Facing Hospitals in the United States," National Academy of Engineering Regional Meeting, U.C. Berkeley, April 2006.

"Evidence-based Management," SutterHealth Clinical and Management Excellence Program, Lafayette, California, February 2006.

"A Workshop on Decision Effectiveness: The Evaluation of Policies and Programs, Pre and Post Implementation. Advanced Health Leadership Program, San Francisco, January 2006.

"Impact of HealthConnect on Kaiser Permanente," Kaiser-Permanente Department of Quality and Operations Support, Oakland, December 2005.

"Opportunities for Greater Quality and Lower Cost: Building Integrated Delivery Systems," Singapore, The National Healthcare Group, September 2005.

"Use of Evidence-based Practices in Chronic Disease Care," United Kingdom, National Health Service Clinical Excellence Program, U.C. Berkeley, June 2005.

"Drivers of Electronic Medical Record Adoption Among Physician Organizations," Center for Information Technology Research in the Interest of Society, U.C. Berkeley, April 2005.

"Improving Evidence-based Decision Making: Challenges and Opportunities for Evaluation Researchers, Oregon State University, February 2005.

"Six Challenges Facing the U.S. Health Care System," presented to The Japan Society of Northern California, San Francisco, March 2005.

"Evidence-based Management," presented to the Sutter Health Managing Clinical Excellence Program, Lafayette, California, March 2005.

"Drivers of Electronic Medical Record Adoption Among Physician Organizations," presented to the School of Public Health Research Symposium, Berkeley, October 2004.

"Pay-for-Performance Programs in the United States," opening keynote address at the Annual Congress of the Australian Private Hospital Association, Brisbane, Australia, October 2004.

"An Overview of the US Healthcare System – Key Issues and Trends" Australian Private Hospital Association National Congress, Brisbane, Australia, October 2004.

"The US Health Care System: Key Developments and Future Directions," The Australian Health Insurance Commission, Canberra, Australia, October 2004.

"Pay-for-Performance Programs: the US Experience. Australian Department of Veteran's Affairs, Canberra, Australia, October 2004.

"Factors Affecting the Care of Patients with Chronic Disease in Physician Organizations: Results from a National Study," presented to Joint Research Symposium of the U.C. Berkeley Center for Health Research and the Karolinska Institute Medical Management Center, Stockholm, June 2004.

"The U.S. Health Care System: Current Trends and Themes," presented to the Seventh Annual U.S. Study Tour, Berkeley, June 2004.

Social Network Analysis in Health Services Research, Theory, Methods, and Examples," presented to the Annual Research Meeting of AcademyHealth, San Diego, June 2004.

"Evidence-Based Management in Health Care Organizations," presented to the Association of University Programs in Health Administration, San Diego, June 2004.

"Management Research and Organizational Performance," presented to Montefiore Hospital, New York City, June 2003.

"The National Study of Physician Organizations and the Management of Chronic Illness," presented to The Commonwealth Fund, New York City, September 2002.

"The U.S. Health Care System: Current Trends and Issues," presented to the U.S. Study Tour for New Zealand and Australian Health Executives, Berkeley, July 2002.

"Hospital-Physician Relationships," presented to the Blue Cross of California Hospital Relations Council, San Francisco, August 2002.

"Managed Care: Changing Course or at a Dead End?" Presented to the board of directors of the Fremont-Rideout Health System, Half Moon Bay, California, April 2002.

"Hospital-Physician Relationships: Comparing Administrator's and Physician's Perceptions," presented to the Fifth International Conference on Strategic Issues in Health Care Management, University of St. Andrews, St. Andrews, Scotland, April, 2002.

"Improving Quality of Care for Patients with Chronic Illness: Evidence from Emerging Research," chair of session at the 2002 Annual Meeting of the Academy of Health Services Research and Health Policy, Washington, D.C., June 2002.

"International Perspectives on Evidence-based Health Management and Policy Making," chair of session at the 2002 Annual Meeting of the Academy of Health Services Research and Health Policy, Washington, D.C., June 2002.

"Building Change Capability: Cultural Change," presented to the Healthcare Change Institute, Norwalk, Connecticut, June 2002.

"Successful Organizational Change Among Provider Organizations," presented at the Annual Meeting of the Academy for Health Services Research and Health Policy, Atlanta, Georgia, June 2001.

"Does Hospital Restructuring Really Work?" presented to the OD Partnerships, London, April 2000.

"The Sisyphean Challenge: The Integration of Health Care Services," presented at St. Andrews University, St. Andrews, Scotland, March 2000.

"The Evolution of the United States' Health Care System," presented at the University of Barcelona, Barcelona, Spain, March 2000.

SELECTED INVITATIONAL SPEECHES (since 2000)

Invited Speaker, Center for HealthCare Management, Hamburg, Germany, June 2011 and November 2013.

Invited Speaker, Ulm University, Ulm, Germany, 2010.

Invited Speaker, CITRIS in Europe Annual Meeting, Helsinki, 2006.

Invited Speaker, FinnWell/Tekes (Finnish Funding Agency for Technology and Innovation), Helsinki, 2006.

Invited Speaker, National Academy of Engineering Regional Meeting, U.C. Berkeley, 2006.

Invited Speaker, Kaiser Permanente, Oakland 2005.

Invited Speaker, Association of University Programs in Health Administration, 2005.

Invited Speaker, The National Healthcare Group, Singapore, 2005.

Invited Speaker, Advanced Health Leadership Forum, U.C. Berkeley, 2005.

Invited Speaker, Oregon State University, 2005.

Keynote Speaker, Japan Society of Northern California, San Francisco, 2005.

Opening Keynote Speaker, Annual Congress of the Australian Private Hospital Association, Brisbane, Australia, 2004.

Invited Speaker, Australian Commonwealth Department of Health and Aging, Canberra, Australia, 2004.

Invited Speaker, Australian Health Insurance Commission, Canberra, Australia, 2004.

Invited Speaker, Australian Commonwealth Department of Veterans' Affairs, Canberra, Australia, 2004.

Invited Speaker, Sutter Health, Management and Clinical Excellence Program, Lafayette, California, 2003, 2004

Invited Speaker, Montefiore Hospital, New York, 2004.

Invited Speaker, The Commonwealth Fund, New York, 2002.

Invited Speaker, Blue Cross of California Hospital Relations Council, San Francisco, 2002.

Invited Speaker, The California HealthCare Foundation, Oakland, California, 2002.

Invited Speaker, Adaptive Business Leaders, San Francisco, 2002.

Invited Speaker, HealthCare Change Institute, Norwalk, Connecticut, 2002.

Keynote Speaker, Fremont-Rideout Health System Retreat, Half Moon Bay, California, 2002.

Keynote Speaker, Conference on Strategic Issues in Health Care; St. Andrews University, St. Andrews, Scotland, 2000.

RESEARCH INTERESTS

Health care management, organizational theory, and evaluation research. Recent specific projects include studies of: Health Information Technology in the Management of Patients with Chronic Disease; Physician Organizations and the Management of Chronic Disease; Physician Job Satisfaction, Patient Portals in Fragmented and Integrated Health Systems, Use of Information Technology in Accountable Care Organizations, Lean Management and Hospital Performance.

COURSES TAUGHT

Foundations of Health Policy and Management

Cases in Health Management

Advanced Program and Policy Evaluation

Applied Public Health: Putting Theory into Practice

Health Services and Policy Analysis Doctoral Seminar

Introduction to the U.S. Health Care System

Hospitals, Health Systems, and Managed Care

Health Organizations and Behavior

Health Management MBA/MPH Seminar

CONSULTATIONS

Consulting Services have been provided to numerous health care organizations, foundations, associations and agencies, including the California HealthCare Foundation, Kaiser Permanente, Sutter Health, TEKES (the Finnish Funding Agency for Technology and Innovation), Montefiore Hospital, the Queen's Health System, the Agency for Health Care Policy and Research, Health Resources and Services Administration, Royal Australian College of Medical Administrators, World Health Organization, State of California Office of AIDS, Kaiser Family Foundation, California Wellness Foundation, The Archstone Foundation, American Hospital Association, California State Department of Health Services, and numerous hospitals, county health departments, and community-based health organizations.

www.ingramcontent.com/pod-product-compliance
Lightning Source LLC
Chambersburg PA
CBHW042145160426
43202CB00022B/2984